International Encyclopedia of
Unified Science

Volumes I and II: Foundations of the Unity
of Science

Volume II · Number 9

The Development of Logical Empiricism

Joergen Joergensen

The University of Chicago Press, Chicago, Illinois

Reprinted with the permission of Mr. Joergen Joergensen

JOHNSON REPRINT CORPORATION   JOHNSON REPRINT COMPANY LTD.
111 Fifth Avenue, New York, N.Y. 10003   Berkeley Square House, London, W1X6BA

International Encyclopedia of Unified Science

Editor-in-chief   Otto Neurath†
Associate Editors   Rudolf Carnap   Charles Morris

Foundations of the Unity of Science

(Volumes I-II of the Encyclopedia)

Committee of Organization

RUDOLF CARNAP
PHILIPP FRANK
JOERGEN JOERGENSEN

CHARLES MORRIS
OTTO NEURATH†
LOUIS ROUGIER

Advisory Committee

NIELS BOHR
EGON BRUNSWIK
J. CLAY
JOHN DEWEY
FEDERIGO ENRIQUES
HERBERT FEIGL
CLARK L. HULL
WALDEMAR KAEMPFFERT
VICTOR F. LENZEN
JAN LUKASIEWICZ
WILLIAM M. MALISOFF†

R. VON MISES
G. MANNOURY
ERNEST NAGEL
ARNE NESS
HANS REICHENBACH
ABEL REY
BERTRAND RUSSELL
L. SUSAN STEBBING†
ALFRED TARSKI
EDWARD C. TOLMAN
JOSEPH H. WOODGER

Copyright 1951. Copyright under the International Copyright Union by The University of Chicago. All rights reserved. Published 1951

First reprinting 1970, Johnson Reprint Corporation

Printed in the United States of America

International Encyclopedia of Unified Science
Volume II · Number 9
The Development of Logical Empiricism

Joergen Joergensen

Contents:

	PAGE
I. THE VIENNA CIRCLE: ITS PROGRAM AND PRESUPPOSITIONS	1
1. Introductory Remarks	1
2. The Vienna Circle	2
3. The Program	3
4. Predecessors	6
5. The Positivism of Ernst Mach	7
6. The Logical Positivism of Bertrand Russell	11
7. Ludwig Wittgenstein's Logical-philosophical Treatise	17
8. Rudolf Carnap's Theory of the Constitution of Concepts	28
II. LOGICAL EMPIRICISM: ITS EXPANSION AND ELABORATION	40
1. Publications, Congresses, and International Connections	40
2. The Berlin Group	48
3. The Lwow-Warsaw Group	54
4. Pragmatists and Operationalists	55
5. The Uppsala School	58
6. The Münster Group	58
7. Individuals	59
8. The Question of the Nature of Philosophy	61
9. Carnap's Logical Syntax of Language	62
10. Protocol-Sentences and Substantiations ("Konstatierungen")	68
11. Verifiability and Testability	71
12. Unity of Science and Physicalism	76
13. Present Tendencies and Tasks	83
NOTES AND BIBLIOGRAPHY	87
POSTSCRIPT. By *Norman M. Martin*	91

The Development of Logical Empiricism
Joergen Joergensen

I. The Vienna Circle: Its Program and Presuppositions

1. Introductory Remarks

In Volume II, No. 8, of this *Encyclopedia* Edgar Zilsel outlined the evolution of empiricism in its broad sense up to the beginning of this century. The present article will continue this history, sketching the development until 1940[1] of the recent form of empiricism generally called "logical empiricism."

It is characteristic of this movement, which may presumably be said to have been the leading movement within the philosophy of the last two or three decades, that it is an expression of a need for clarification of the foundations and meaning of knowledge rather than of a need for justification of a preconceived view; that it attempts to make philosophy scientifically tenable through critical analysis of details rather than to make it universal by vague generalizations and dogmatic construction of systems; and that it is more interested in co-operation among philosophers and between philosophers and investigators in the special sciences than in the advancement of more or less striking individual opinions. What unites its members is, therefore, not so much definite views or dogmas as definite tendencies and endeavors. An evidence of this is the often considerable divergence and lively discussion between its members and the amendments in the fundamental views that have occurred several times in the course of its development. On the other hand, the constant exchange of opinion has led to an increasing convergence toward certain basic principles that have gradually taken shape and that now form the common basis for the further discussion of still unsettled questions. The nature of these fundamental principles will be clarified in the following exposition.

The Vienna Circle: Its Program and Presuppositions

2. The Vienna Circle

The nucleus from which logical empiricism developed was the so-called "Vienna Circle," the origin of which is described by Herbert Feigl, one of its younger members, as follows:

"The Vienna Circle evolved in 1923 out of a seminar led by Professor Moritz Schlick and attended, among other students, by F. Waismann and H. Feigl. Schlick's teaching period in Vienna had begun in 1922, and by 1925 out of this nucleus a Thursday evening discussion group was formed. It is interesting to note that many of the participants were not professional philosophers. Even if some of them taught philosophy, their original fields of study lay in other disciplines. Schlick, for example, had specialized in physics, and his doctor's thesis, written under the guidance of Max Planck in Berlin, concerned a problem in theoretical optics. Among the other active members we may mention: Hans Hahn, mathematician; Otto Neurath, sociologist; Victor Kraft, historian; Felix Kaufmann, lawyer; Kurt Reidemeister, mathematician. An occasional but a most contributive visitor was the Prague physicist, Philipp Frank (now at Harvard). In 1927 and again in 1932 the brilliant Finnish psychologist and philosopher, E. Kaila, was present as an active and critical member of the group. Another visitor from Scandinavia was Å. Petzaell (Göteborg). Among the younger participants were K. Goedel (now at Princeton), T. Radakovic, G. Bergmann, M. Natkin, J. Schaechter, W. Hollitscher, and Rose Rand; and, among the visitors, C. G. Hempel, Berlin; A. E. Blumberg, Baltimore; and A. J. Ayer, Oxford. Among those more loosely affiliated with the group were K. Menger, E. Zilsel, K. Popper, H. Kelsen, L. v. Bertalanffy, Heinrich Gomperz, B. von Juhos.

"The most decisive and rapid development of ideas began in 1926 when Carnap was called to the University of Vienna. His contributions to axiomatics and particularly his theory of the constitution of empirical concepts (as published in *Der logische Aufbau der Welt*) proved a very stimulating source of discussions. In the same year also, Ludwig Wittgenstein's *Tractatus Logico-Philosophicus* was studied by the Circle. The philosophical position of Logical Positivism in its original form was the outcome of these profoundly incisive influences. Though many of the basic ideas had already been enunciated in a general manner by Schlick, they were formulated more precisely, stated more fully and radically, by Carnap and Wittgenstein, quite independently. These two men exerted an enormous influence upon Schlick, who was about ten years their senior.

"In contrast to Carnap, who became a regular and most influential participant in the group, Wittgenstein, then preoccupied with architecture, associated only occasionally with some of the members of the Circle. Even thus, more light was obtained on some of the rather obscurely written passages of his extremely condensed and profound *Tractatus*. A few years later Wittgenstein returned to his philosophical studies and was called to Cambridge, England, where he later became successor to G. E. Moore. Schlick, as a visiting Professor, went to California in 1929 and 1932. Carnap was called to Prague in 1930 (later, in 1936, to Chicago) and Feigl to the United States in 1930. Hans Hahn, who was an expert in *Principia Mathematica* and in general an enthusiastic follower of Russell, died prematurely in 1934. The Circle discussions, however, continued, with Schlick and Waismann leading, until Schlick's tragic death in 1936. A former student, for years under observation by psychiatrists and diagnosed as insane, assassinated Schlick. The passing of this kindly, truly great and noble man, was bitterly lamented by his many friends.

"The discussions of the Circle centered about the foundations of logic and mathematics, the logic of empirical knowledge, and only occasional excursions into the philosophy of the social sciences and ethics. Despite the many differences of opinion, there was a remarkable spirit of friendly cooperation in the Circle. The procedure was definitely that of a joint search for clarity."[2]

3. The Program

A more detailed exposition of the work of the Vienna Circle was given in 1929 in a publication entitled *Wissenschaftliche Weltauffassung: Der Wiener Kreis*, which marked the appear-

The Vienna Circle: Its Program and Presuppositions

ance of the Circle before the public as an organization with a scientific as well as an educational purpose. The publication was sent out by the Verein Ernst Mach, which was founded in November, 1928, with Schlick as a president, and had for its object to "further and propagate a scientific world view," as conceived by the members of the Circle, through public lectures and writings. According to this pamphlet, the main lines of their program may be described as follows:

The aim is to form an *Einheitswissenschaft*, i.e., a unified science comprising all knowedge of reality accessible to man without dividing it into separate, unconnected special disciplines, such as physics and psychology, natural science and letters, philosophy and the special sciences. The way to attain this is by the use of the *logical method of analysis*, worked out by Peano, Frege, Whitehead, and Russell, which serves to eliminate metaphysical problems and assertions as meaningless as well as to clarify the meaning of concepts and sentences of empirical science by showing their immediately observable content—"das Gegebene." In both respects the Vienna Circle continues the endeavors initiated by Ernst Mach; but, by the application of logical analysis, which is a distinctive feature of the new empiricism, and of positivism, as compared to the older forms of these movements, it obtains a hitherto unattained completeness and precision. The culmination so far has been reached in the "constitution theory" advanced by Rudolf Carnap in *Der logische Aufbau der Welt* (Berlin, 1928), according to which any tenable concept of real objects is constituted by being reduced to characteristics of that which is immediately given, and any meaningful statement is constituted by being reduced to a statement of the given. Thus a framework is created for the work of the Vienna Circle; its negative task is an expurgation of metaphysical-speculative statements as meaningless, while its positive task is to define ever more precisely and fully the meaning of scientifically tenable statements. "If anyone asserts: 'There is a God,' 'The first cause of the world is the Unconscious,' 'There is an entelechy which is the leading principle in living beings,' we do not say 'What you say is false'; rather,

The Program

we ask him, 'What do you mean by your statements?' It then appears that there is a sharp division between two types of statements. One of the types includes statements as they are made in empirical science; their meaning can be determined by logical analysis, or, more precisely, by reduction to simple sentences about the empirically given. The other statements, including those mentioned above, show themselves to be completely meaningless, if we take them as the metaphysician intends them. Of course, we can frequently reinterpret them as empirical statements. They then, however, lose the emotional content which is the very thing which is essential to the metaphysician. The metaphysicians and theologians, misinterpreting their own sentences, believe that their sentences assert something, represent some state of affairs. Nevertheless, analysis shows that these sentences do not say anything, being instead only an expression of some emotional attitude. To express this may certainly be a significant task. However, the adequate means for its expression is art, for example, lyric poetry or music. If, instead of these, the linguistic dress of a theory is chosen, a danger arises: a theoretical content, which does not exist, is feigned. If a metaphysician or theologian wishes to retain the usual form in language, he should understand thoroughly and explain clearly that it is not representation but expression; not theory, information, or cognition, but rather poetry or myth. If a mystic asserts that he has experiences that transcend all concepts, he cannot be challenged. But he cannot speak about it, since speaking means grasping concepts and reducing to facts which can be incorporated into science."[3]

The view of the Vienna Circle as to how such incorporation should be undertaken is particularly evident in the above-mentioned theory of constitution, which will be more explicitly dealt with presently. First, however, it would be expedient to look at the development of the opinions and points of view forming the background of the Circle's conception of philosophy and knowledge generally.

The Vienna Circle: Its Program and Presuppositions

4. Predecessors

The forerunners of logical empiricism are, in the opinion of the members of the movement themselves, all those philosophers and scientists who show a clear antimetaphysical or antispeculative, realistic or materialistic, critical or skeptical, tendency—as well as everyone who has contributed essentially to the development of their most important methodological instrument: symbolic logic. In antiquity the Sophists and the Epicureans are mentioned; in the Middle Ages the nominalists; and in modern times, Neurath[4] gives the following three lists of names, indicating the lines of development in England, France, and Germany that may be said to lead in the direction of logical empiricism: Bacon, Hobbes, Locke, Hume, Bentham, J. S. Mill, Spencer; Descartes, Bayle, D'Alembert, Saint-Simon, Comte, Poincaré; Leibniz, Bolzano, Mach. In their programs similar lines of development are noticed, only here the grouping has been made according to subject and not according to nationality:

1. Positivism and empiricism: Hume, the philosophers of the Enlightenment, Comte, Mill, Avenarius, Mach.
2. The basis, aims, and methods (hypotheses in physics, geometry, etc.) of the empirical sciences: Helmholtz, Riemann, Mach, Poincaré, Enriques, Duhem, Boltzmann, Einstein.
3. Logistics and its application to reality: Leibniz, Peano, Frege, Schröder, Russell, Whitehead, Wittgenstein.
4. Axiomatics: Pasch, Peano, Vailati, Pieri, Hilbert.
5. Eudaemonism and positivistic sociology: Epicurus, Hume, Bentham, Mill, Comte, Feuerbach, Marx, Spencer, Müller-Lyer, Popper-Lynkeus, Carl Menger (the economist).

The predecessors and teachers here mentioned were the ones especially studied and discussed by the Vienna Circle. Not until later did the Circle discover the American pragmatists, instrumentalists, and operationalists to whom they are closely related in several respects and with whom they have since co-operated, as well as with certain other affiliated groups. I shall return to this point in the following chapter, having mentioned here only

The Positivism of Ernst Mach

the authors whose works have actually played an important part in the development of the views of the Circle. There are, however, three of these philosophers whose influence has been so significant that they must be more explicitly dealt with: Ernst Mach, Bertrand Russell, and Ludwig Wittgenstein.

5. The Positivism of Ernst Mach

Mach (1838–1916), who started his scientific career as a professor of mathematics and later of physics, in 1895 received a professorship in philosophy, especially the history and theory of the inductive sciences, at the University of Vienna. Owing to bad health, however, he had to retire in 1901; he was succeeded by the well-known physicist, L. Boltzmann. From his youth Mach had been vividly interested in philosophical and epistemological questions as well as in the historical development of the natural sciences. This appears clearly from his main works, *Die Mechanik in ihrer Entwicklung, historisch-kritisch dargestellt* (1883) (English trans., *The Science of Mechanics* [Chicago, 1893]), *Die Analyse der Empfindungen und das Verhältnis des Physischen zum Psychischen* (1886) (English trans., *The Analysis of Sensations* [Chicago, 1914]), *Die Prinzipien der Wärmelehre, historisch-kritisch entwickelt* (1896), *Populär-wissenschaftliche Vorlesungen* (1896) (English trans., *Popular Scientific Lectures* [Chicago, 1895]), *Erkenntnis und Irrtum: Skizzen zur Psychologie der Forschung* (1905), and *Die Prinzipien der physikalischen Optik, historisch und erkenntnispsychologisch entwickelt* (finished 1913, published 1921) (English trans., *Principles of Physical Optics* [New York, 1926]).

In these books Mach advanced his positivistic theory of knowledge, according to which human knowledge from its most primitive forms to the heights of science is a biological phenomenon, part of the history of man. Influenced by Darwin's theory of evolution, he conceived knowledge as a never ending process of adjustment of thoughts to reality and to each other. A priori and eternal truths do not exist, nor is there any difference in principle between axioms and deduced sentences. All statements concerning the world, particular as well as general rules, natural laws, theories, and principles, are subject to continuous control and modification by experience. Even geometrical sentences are, in so far as they are statements about reality, empirical sentences whose validity depends simply on immemorial observations of regularities in the spatial conditions and movements of things; so considered, geometry is a part of natural science of the same kind as mechanics or the theory of heat or the theory of electricity. Accordingly, we are not bound to follow any definite kind of geometry but may choose the one that appears to attain most expediently the most thought-saving description of experiences of the spatial relations of things. Space itself is merely the totality of the spatial relations of things, and not—as believed by Newton and Kant—an empty container in which things have been located in "absolute" places or in which they perform "absolute" movements.

On a closer examination, things, too, appear to be merely relatively constant complexes of so-called "qualities," which Mach identified with our sensations and called "elements." A "thing-in-itself" existing behind these elements is a metaphysical illusion, presumably due to the fact that the same names are used to designate things, even though these change, so that we are led to believe that the "same" thing persists throughout the changes. What we do observe is actually never any such hidden things but simply qualities of their mutual relations. Natural laws should therefore be formulated as functional relations between the elements, i.e., between sensations such as green, hot, hard, extended, continuous, etc. These sensations are not in themselves illusory or deceptive, but, on the contrary, they are all that we know of reality. What we call "deception of the senses" is merely certain unusual complexes of elements deceiving us because they resemble familiar complexes and so raise expectations that are not fulfilled. If they are correctly conceived, there is nothing deceptive about them. The point is to distinguish between the various contexts in which any given element may occur. These contexts are all equally real; but, if they are confused with one another, contradictions arise which we attempt to avoid by declaring one of their terms il-

The Positivism of Ernst Mach

lusory. To a person measuring the site for a house, the surface of the earth is a plane, but to the person undertaking an exact measurement of the total surface of the globe, it is a spheroid. There is no contradiction in this, if only it is realized that the observations are made under different conditions and in different ways and that the words describing them take on different meanings when we pass from one standpoint to another. 'Up' and 'down', for instance, are everyday terms which have an easily understood sense in the world of our everyday life but which lose this sense when we proceed to describe the universe astronomically. And similarly the words 'red', 'yellow', and 'blue' are names designating sensations, and as such are well suited to describe the phenomena of our daily life; however, they must be replaced by words like 'wave movements' or 'corpuscle rays' if we want to describe the more subtle phenomena and contexts of phenomena observed by the physicist in his investigations of color. One kind of observation is not truer or more faithful to reality than is the other, but the contexts in which they occur differ and must be described by different words. Every scientific statement is a statement about complexes of sensations, and beyond or behind these there are no realities to be looked for, because the word 'reality' itself is merely a name for the sum total of the complexes of observable sensations.

What has been said here of physical things, according to Mach, also applies to the so-called "mental substances" of egos: they are merely special complexes of elements, even complexes with fluctuating boundaries, now expanding and now narrowing, but continuously changing in the course of life, disappearing in a dreamless sleep and altering completely in case of a mental disease or other abnormality. Although of great practical importance in our daily life, the word 'ego' does not signify any unchangeable or eternal object of a specific "mental" character; indeed, the difference between physical and psychical phenomena does not depend on the nature of the phenomena but solely on the context in which they occur: if a sensation is conceived as a link in a physical natural law, it is called a

The Vienna Circle: Its Program and Presuppositions

"physical phenomenon" or a quality of a physical thing, but if it is conceived as a link in a psychological law–directed regularity, i.e., as dependent according to natural law upon the condition of the observer, it is called a "psychical phenomenon." Physical and psychical phenomena are not essentially different, and all statements concerning them are of exactly equal rank, since they can all be reduced to statements about complexes of sensations which are all that is given or immediately observable.

In this the positivism of Mach differs from that of Comte. In Comte—who created the word 'positivism'—'positive', 'supposed', or 'given' signifies, in the first place, observable physical objects as opposed to fictive, speculatively constructed metaphysical entities; and in his system he found no room for psychology itself but classed it, without giving a detailed explanation, under biology. Further, the system of sciences assumed in Comte a hierarchic character, the six basic sciences—mathematics, astronomy, physics, chemistry, biology, and sociology, each presupposing the preceding ones without being capable of being deduced from them; this, expressed differently, means that the "higher" phenomena cannot be reduced to the lower; accordingly, the idea of a unity of science is incompatible with Comte's conception of the hierarchy of the sciences, whereas this idea was anticipated by Mach in his theory that all scientific statements should be reduced to statements of sensations. In this respect Comte's positivism is nearer to the dialectical materialism of Marx and the modern theory of emergent evolution than is the positivism of Mach—a fact which finds expression in Lenin's keen criticism of "Machism" in his *Materialismus und Empiriokriticismus* (1909) (English trans., *Materialism and Empirio-Criticism*, in *Collected Works of Lenin*, Vol. XIII [New York, 1927]). Although logical empiricists reject this criticism as being partially due to misunderstanding and consider themselves in accord with materialism[5] in all essentials, it cannot be denied that the positivism of the Vienna Circle is more closely related to the English empiricists than to the French materialists, with whom, from an epistemological point of view, it has, strictly speaking, in common only a strong aversion to speculative thinking. Among its great teachers we do not find the French encyclopedists or Comte, but Bertrand Russell;[6] Russell, the greatest living representative of English empiricism, may not unjustly be called the "father" of logical positivism, since in him is found for the first time the conscious and extensive application of logical analysis to the problems of epistemological empiricism,[7] a position which was reached by neither Comte nor Mach but which is characteristic of logical empiricism.[8]

6. The Logical Positivism of Bertrand Russell

Bertrand Russell (born 1872) is one of the great pioneers of modern logistics. In his *The Principles of Mathematics* (1903) and in *Principia mathematica*, Volumes I–III (1910–13), which he wrote in collaboration with Alfred North Whitehead (1861–1947), Russell made a more critical and comprehensive attempt than had yet been made to develop a symbolic logic and to show that all pure mathematics may be reduced to formal logic. This reduction he attempted to carry through by (*a*) trying to define all the main concepts of mathematics (such as the concepts of natural numbers and of the various kinds of numbers, the basic concepts of the theory of manifolds, and concepts like continuity and derivative) by means of half-a-dozen basic logical concepts and (*b*) by trying to prove all the axioms of mathematics by means of half-a-dozen logical axioms. In other words, the arithmetization of mathematical analysis, already carried through to a large extent by various mathematicians, Russell attempted to carry on by logicizing all mathematics, the concept of a natural number being, for instance, defined as "a class of similar classes." It is true that the attempt was not altogether successful; but its disadvantages as well as its advantages, and the wealth of ideas it contained, made it a unique source of inspiration to logicians, to investigators of the foundations of mathematics, and to philosophers. From among its many new features we shall mention here only three which came to play a special part in the formation of logical positivism.

The Vienna Circle: Its Program and Presuppositions

The study of logical paradoxes and of paradoxes within the theory of sets led Russell to set forth the theory of logical types, according to which, for instance, every class is of a higher type than are its members and every statement about another statement is of a higher type than the one about which it is made. If the types are kept apart, paradoxes can be avoided, whereas there is a risk of such paradoxes if the types are confused. Russell maintained that statements containing confusions of types are meaningless, even if, according to the usual linguistic syntax, they are correctly constructed; and so he replaced the current logical division of statements into true and false by the tripartition: true, false, and meaningless.

Another important partition of statements introduced in connection with the theory of types was the division into (1) elementary statements, i.e., statements whose truth or falsity may be realized without any knowledge of individual objects or qualities or relations other than the ones whose names occur in the statement in question, and (2) generalized statements, i.e., statements presupposing classes of individuals, qualities, or relations (which must be divided into a hierarchy of ascending types). The elementary statements are subdivided into (*a*) atomic statements, i.e., statements containing no other statements as constituents, and (*b*) molecular statements, i.e., statements containing other statements as constituents. An especially important group of the latter are the so-called "truth-functions," i.e., molecular statements, the truth or falsity of which does not depend upon the meaning of the statements forming part of them but solely upon their truth-values, i.e., their truth or falsity, such as, for instance, negations, disjunctions, conjunctions, conditionals, and biconditionals of elementary statements.

Further, Russell and Whitehead introduced the so-called "principle of abstraction," that may equally well be called "the principle which dispenses with abstraction": "When a group of objects have that kind of similarity which we are inclined to attribute to possession of a common quality, the principle in question shows that membership of the group will serve all the purposes of the supposed common quality, and that therefore, unless some common quality is actually known, the group or class of similar objects may be used to replace the common quality which need not be assumed to exist."[9] Any statement of the common quality may be replaced by a statement saying that something is a member of the class. 'Red', for instance, may be defined by our pointing at a red object and saying that everything of the same color as that object is red, making it unnecessary to analyze this quality further; and, similarly, the cardinal number three may be defined as the class of all classes having the same number of members as, for instance, the class of Paris, London, and Berlin, making it unnecessary to assume that all these triads possess a common quality.

In *Principia mathematica* formal logic was generalized, systematized, and made precise to such an extent, and couched in such expedient symbolic language, that we understand the great expectations of Russell when he said: "The old logic put thought in fetters, while the new logic gives it wings. It has, in my opinion, introduced the same kind of advance into philosophy as Galileo introduced into physics, making it possible at last to see what kinds of problems may be capable of solution, and what kinds must be abandoned as beyond human powers. And where a solution appears possible, the new logic provides a method which enables us to obtain results that do not merely embody personal idiosyncrasies, but must command the assent of all who are competent to form an opinion."[10]

This statement is found in the lectures on our knowledge of the external world which Russell delivered in Boston in 1914 and in which for the first time he used his new logical-analytical method for the solution of epistemological problems. The leading principle was here a form of Occam's razor or law of parsimony: "Entia non sunt multiplicanda praeter necessitatem." Russell later stated this principle in this form: "Wherever possible, substitute constructions out of known entities for inferences to unknown entities";[11] in the lectures here referred to he formulates it in the following way: "In other words, in dealing with any subject-matter, find out what entities are undeniably involved, and state everything in terms of these entities. Very often the resulting statement is more complicated and difficult than one which, like common sense and most philosophy, assumes hypothetical entities whose existence there is no good reason to believe in. We find it easier to imagine a wall-paper with changing colours than to think merely of the series of colours, but it is a mistake to suppose that what is easy and natural in thought is what is most free from unwarrantable assumptions, as the case of 'things' very aptly illustrates."[12]

The example to which he here refers is the analysis of things given in his lectures. Briefly expressed, it says that what we call a "thing" is not a permanent substance different from its changing qualities or appearances but may be defined as "a certain series of appearances, connected with each other by continuity and by certain causal laws."[13] To this view he was led by the following reasoning: every philosophical investigation starts from certain data which we must assume as being, on the whole and in a certain sense, pragmatically true. The data resisting the influence of critical reflection Russell calls "hard data" and thinks they are of two sorts: "the particular facts of sense, and the general truths of logic,"[14] to which must be added certain facts of memory and some introspective facts. By "facts of sense" he means "facts of *our own* sense-data" and maintains that "*in so far* as physics or common sense is verifiable, it must be capable of interpretation in terms of actual sense-data alone. The reason for this is simple. Verification consists always in the occurrence of an expected sense-datum. . . . Now if an expected sense-datum constitutes a verification, what was asserted must have been about sense-data; or, at any rate, if part of what was asserted was not about sense-data, then only the other part has been verified."[15] In order to be verifiable, statements of the external world must accordingly be about our own sense-data. Or, in other words, verifiable statements of the external world must be capable of definition or construction in terms of our own sense-data.

"For instance, a thing may be defined as 'a certain series of appearances, connected with each other by continuity and by certain causal laws.' In the case of slowly changing things, this is easily seen. Consider, say, a wall-paper which fades in the course of years. It is an effort not to conceive of it as one thing whose colour is slightly different at one time from what it is at another. But what do we really *know* about it? We know that under suitable circumstances—i.e. when we are, as is said, 'in the room'—we perceive certain colours in a certain pattern: not always precisely the same colours, but sufficiently similar to feel familiar. If we can state the laws according to which the colour varies, we can state all that is empirically verifiable; the assumption that there is a constant entity, the wall-paper, which has these various colours at various times, is a piece of gratuitous metaphysics. We may, if we like, *define* the wall-paper as the series of its aspects. These are collected together by the same motives which led us to regard the wall-paper as one thing, namely a combination of sensible continuity and causal connection. More generally, a thing will be defined as a certain series of aspects, namely those which would commonly be said to be *of* the thing. To say that a certain aspect is an aspect *of* a certain thing will merely mean that it is one of those which, taken serially, *are* the thing. Everything will then proceed as before: whatever was verifiable is unchanged, but our language is so interpreted as to avoid an unnecessary metaphysical assumption of permanence."[16]

As will be seen, this theory is in accordance with that of Mach, only a little more cautiously and precisely expressed; just as natural numbers are analyzed or constructed or defined as classes of classes, so the things of the external world are analyzed, constructed, or defined as combinations of sense-data. Similar conditions apply to various other entities which Russell defines in terms of sense-data alone, so that statements about them are reduced to statements about sense-data; later on he extended and modified these analyses in his *Analysis of Mind* (1921), in *The Analysis of Matter* (1927), as well as in *An Outline of Philosophy* (1927), without, however, changing his basic views in principle.

In a similar way, Whitehead analyzed in *The Organization of*

The Vienna Circle: Its Program and Presuppositions

Thought (1917), in *An Enquiry concerning the Principles of Natural Knowledge* (1919), and in *The Concept of Nature* (1920), various physical concepts, the only difference being that he did not reduce them to sense-data but to so-called "events." Altogether, philosophical analysis of objects and statements became a main preoccupation of the Cambridge analysts. As a leader of this group along with Russell, and perhaps before him, G. E. Moore (born 1873) should be mentioned. Moore is the author of the modern analytical method which he endeavored to formulate with increasing precision and subtlety without, however, drawing any positivistic conclusions from it; in the Preface to his *Principia ethica* (1903) he clearly indicated his method in the following words: "It appears to me that in ethics, as in all other philosophical studies, the difficulties and disagreements, of which its history is full, are mainly due to a very simple cause: namely, to the attempt to answer questions without first discovering precisely *what* question it is which you desire to answer. I do not know how far this source of error would be done away with if philosophers would *try* to discover what question they were asking before they set about to answer it; for the work of analysis and distinction is often very difficult: we may often fail to make the necessary discovery, even though we make a definite attempt to do so. But I am inclined to think that in many cases a resolute attempt would be sufficient to ensure success; so that, if only this attempt were made, many of the most glaring difficulties and disagreements in philosophy would disappear. At all events, philosophers seem, in general, not to make the attempt; and, whether in consequence of this omission or not, they are constantly endeavouring to prove that 'Yes' or 'No' will answer questions, to which *neither* answer is correct, owing to the fact that what they have before their minds is not one question, but several, to some of which the true answer is 'No,' to others 'Yes.' "[17] Through his penetrating endeavors to apply the method of analysis outlined above, Moore demonstrated convincingly the extreme difficulty of stating *exactly* the sense of many everyday assumptions and expressions, and his great carefulness and caution kept him from formulating far-reaching hypotheses or maintaining definite views. But his acute, painstaking endeavor itself exercised a profound influence on a large number of his pupils in England, among whom may be mentioned C. D. Broad, L. S. Stebbing, F. P. Ramsey, J. T. Wisdom, A. E. Duncan-Jones, A. J. Ayer, M. Black, H. B. Acton, R. B. Braithwaite, K. Britton, W. Kneale, H. Knight, M. MacDonald, C. A. Mace, A. M. MacIver, C. A. Paul, G. Ryle, J. W. Reeves, and, most important, Ludwig Wittgenstein, who attended Moore's lectures during the years 1912–14 and was later, from 1939 to 1948, his successor to the professorship at Cambridge.[18] As Wittgenstein has played a greater part than any other one philosopher in the development of the Vienna Circle, which seems not to have had any close knowledge of Moore, it will be necessary to deal a little more explicitly with his original philosophy.

7. Ludwig Wittgenstein's Logical-philosophical Treatise

The only published philosophical work by Wittgenstein, *Tractatus logico-philosophicus*, is in many respects a highly remarkable achievement. Appearing first in Oswald's *Annalen der Naturphilosophie* in 1921, it was published the following year in London as an independent book, containing the original German text together with an English translation, the latter being carefully revised by the author himself. Its contents are formulated as a series of aphorisms with comments. The comments contain specifications of the main propositions and more or less detailed justifications or illustrations of them. There is no proper deductive context, and often it may be difficult to see whether a proposition is put forward as a mere postulate or as the result of an unformulated argument. Consequently, the book is anything but easy to read, and to this day several parts of it are not completely understood. When, in spite of this, it has aroused such vital interest in expert circles, this is due to the fact that it contains, beyond doubt, remarkable discoveries and ideas of a logical and epistemological nature and that altogether it bears witness to a rare originality and acuteness. It is extremely regrettable that a commentary by Friedrich Waismann, announced for several years, has not been published. However, within the Vienna Circle, where Waismann and Schlick were periodically in touch with Wittgenstein, the book was thoroughly discussed; and through the publications of the Circle, as well as through Russell's Introduction to the English edition, certain of its fundamental new ideas gradually became more widely known. The most important of these, which may be considered largely as a critical development of Russell's thought, are contained in the main propositions of the book:

"1. The world is everything that is the case.

"2. What is the case, the fact, is the existence of atomic facts.

"3. The logical picture of the facts is the thought.

"4. The thought is the significant proposition.

"5. Propositions are truth-functions of elementary propositions. (An elementary proposition is a truth-function of itself.)

"6. The general form of truth-function is: $[\bar{p}, \bar{\xi}, N(\bar{\xi})]$. This is the general form of proposition.

"7. Whereof one cannot speak, thereof one must be silent."

In order to understand these propositions, it is necessary to make clear what problem it is that Wittgenstein tries to solve in his treatise. To use the words of Russell, "What relation must one fact (such as a sentence) have to another in order to be *capable* of being a symbol for that other?"[19] To which Wittgenstein answers as follows:

The symbolizing fact must be a picture of what is symbolized, in the sense that it must be of the same form or structure as that which is symbolized. To every element in the one must correspond one and only one element in the other, and the elements of the two facts must be similarly arranged. They must be related to each other as a figure to its projection or as a gramophone record or the musical thought or the score or the waves of sound are related to one another, so that they can be deduced from each other mutually by means of a kind of "law of projection" (4.014; 4.0141). In the natural languages this relation of projection is highly imperfect, and that is just why our everyday language gives rise to many misunderstandings and senseless philosophical problems. "Most propositions and questions, that have been written about philosophical matters, are not false, but senseless. We cannot, therefore, answer questions of this kind at all, but only state their senselessness. Most questions and propositions of the philosophers result from the fact that we do not understand the logic of our language. (They are of the same kind as the question whether the Good is more or less identical than the Beautiful.) And so it is not to be wondered at that the deepest problems are really *no* problems" (4.003). "All philosophy is 'critique of language' (but not at all in Mauthner's sense). Russell's merit is to have shown that the apparent logical form of the proposition need not be its real form" (4.0031).

This basic thought and its consequences are further illustrated by the comments on the first six main propositions. As to No. 1, the comment simply says that the world consists of facts and that these are independent of one another. As to No. 2, it is observed that atomic facts are combinations of objects (entities, things) that are simple. The way in which objects hang together in an atomic fact is the form of the atomic fact. To the atomic facts correspond atomic propositions, the forms of which must be identical with those of the corresponding facts. "We make to ourselves pictures of facts" (2.1). "The picture is a model of reality" (2.12). "To the objects correspond in the picture the elements of the picture" (2.13). "The picture consists in the fact that its elements are combined with one another in a definite way" (2.14). "In order to be a picture a fact must have something in common with what it pictures" (2.16). "What the picture must have in common with reality in order to be able to represent it after its manner—rightly or falsely—is its form of representation" (2.17). "The picture, however, cannot represent its form of representation; it shows it forth" (2.172). "The picture has the logical form of representation in common with what it pictures" (2.2). "The picture agrees with reality or not; it is right or wrong, true or false" (2.21). "What the picture represents is its sense" (2.221). "In the agreement or disagreement of its sense with reality, its truth or falsity consists" (2.222). "In order to discover whether the picture is true or

The Vienna Circle: Its Program and Presuppositions

false we must compare it with reality" (2.223). "It cannot be discovered from the picture alone whether it is true or false" (2.224). "There is no picture which is apriori true" (2.225). A distinction must therefore be made between the truth of a picture and its sense: the sense is that which it represents, but whether it is true or false depends on whether it represents a fact or not, which cannot be decided a priori.

As to No. 3, Wittgenstein observes that "the totality of true thoughts is a picture of the world" (3.01) and that "in the proposition the thought is expressed perceptibly through the senses" (3.1). "In the proposition the name represents the object" (3.22), but "only the proposition has sense, only in the context of a proposition has a name a meaning" (3.3). "If we change a constituent part of a proposition into a variable, there is a class of propositions which are all the values of the resulting variable proposition. This class in general still depends on what, by arbitrary agreement, we mean by parts of that proposition. But if we change all those signs, whose meaning was arbitrarily determined, into variables, there always remains such a class. But this is now no longer dependent on any agreement; it depends only on the nature of the proposition. It corresponds to a logical form, to a logical prototype" (3.315). In order to avoid the errors due to the imperfection of our everyday language, we must employ a symbolism which excludes them, "a symbolism, that is to say, which obeys the rules of *logical* grammar—of logical syntax" (3.325). "In logical syntax the meaning of a sign ought never to play a rôle . . ." (3.33).

In the comments on No. 4 Wittgenstein develops his theory of the logical correspondence between propositions and reality. "The proposition is a picture of reality, for I know the state of affairs presented by it, if I understand the proposition. And I understand the proposition, without its sense having been explained to me" (4.021). "The proposition *shows* its sense. The proposition *shows* how things stand, *if* it is true. And it *says*, that they do so stand" (4.022). "To understand a proposition means to know what is the case, if it is true. (One can therefore understand it without knowing whether it is true or not.) One

Ludwig Wittgenstein

understands it if one understands its constituent parts" (4.024). "The meanings of the simple signs (the words) must be explained to us, if we are to understand them. By means of propositions we explain ourselves" (4.026). "One name stands for one thing, and another for another thing, and they are connected together. And so the whole, like a living picture, presents the atomic fact" (4.0311). "The possibility of propositions is based upon the principle of the representation of objects by signs. My fundamental thought is that the 'logical constants' do not represent. That the *logic* of the facts cannot be represented" (4.0312). "In the proposition there must be exactly as many things distinguishable as there are in the state of affairs, which it represents. They must both possess the same logical (mathematical) multiplicity (cf. Hertz's *Mechanics*, on Dynamic Models)" (4.04). "This mathematical multiplicity naturally cannot in its turn be represented. One cannot get outside it in the representation" (4.041). "Reality is compared with the propositions" (4.05). "Propositions can be true or false only by being pictures of the reality" (4.06). "Every proposition must *already* have a sense: assertion cannot give it a sense, for what it asserts is the sense itself. And the same holds of denial, etc." (4.064). "A proposition presents the existence and non-existence of atomic facts" (4.1). "The totality of true propositions is the total natural science (or the totality of the natural sciences)" (4.11). "Philosophy is not one of the natural sciences. (The word 'philosophy' must mean something which stands above or below, but not beside, the natural sciences.)" (4.111). "The object of philosophy is the logical clarification of thoughts. Philosophy is not a theory but an activity. A philosophical work consists essentially of elucidations. The result of philosophy is not a number of 'philosophical propositions,' but to make propositions clear. Philosophy should make clear and delimit sharply the thoughts which otherwise are, as it were, opaque and blurred" (4.112). "Propositions can represent the whole reality, but they cannot represent what they must have in common with reality in order to be able to represent it—the logical form. To be able to represent the logical form, we should have to be able to put ourselves with the propositions outside logic, that is, outside the world" (4.12). "... That which expresses *itself* in language, *we* cannot express by language. The propositions *show* the logical form of reality ..." (4.121). "What *can* be shown *cannot* be said" (4. 1212).

These more or less obscure assertions were eagerly discussed within the Vienna Circle, and, as will appear from what follows, they have on essential points determined the view of the Circle on philosophy and its relation to the special sciences. However, for the time being, I will let this matter rest and pass to a short account of Wittgenstein's important theory of the truth-functions which is stated in the remaining part of the comments on No. 4 and in the comments on No. 5. He says here:

"The sense of a proposition is its agreement and disagreement with the possibilities of the existence and non-existence of the atomic facts" (4.2). "The simplest proposition, the elementary proposition, asserts the existence of an atomic fact" (4.21). "It is a sign of an elementary proposition, that no elementary proposition can contradict it" (4.211). "The elementary proposition consists of names. It is a connexion, a concatenation, of names" (4.22). "It is obvious that in the analysis of propositions we must come to elementary propositions, which consist of names in immediate combination ..." (4.221). "If the elementary proposition is true, the atomic fact exists; if it is false the atomic fact does not exist" (4.25). "The specification of all true elementary propositions describes the world completely. The world is completely described by the specification of all elementary propositions plus the specification, which of them are true and which false" (4.26). "The truth-possibilities of the elementary propositions mean the possibilities of the existence and non-existence of the atomic facts" (4.3).

If the truth-values (truth or falsehood) of the elementary propositions are combined in every possible way, a survey is obtained of the total number of truth-possibilities, which corresponds to a survey of the total number of possible combinations of all atomic facts. To every combination of atomic facts corresponds a combined molecular proposition, expressing

Ludwig Wittgenstein

which combinations of atomic facts exist and which do not exist, i.e., which combinations of truth-values of the corresponding atomic propositions exist and which do not exist. This may be presented by a truth-table which corresponds to a molecular proposition and may appear as follows:

p	q	
T	T	T
F	T	T
T	F	F
F	F	T

or shorter: $(TTFT)(p, q)$,

where 'p' and 'q' represent elementary propositions, and the 'T' and 'F' under each represent its possible truth-values, while the last column indicates whether the combinations of truth-values concerned exist or do not exist. Among the possible groups of molecular propositions, there are two extreme cases: the so-called "tautology," which is true for all truth-possibilities, and the so-called "contradiction," which is false for all truth-possibilities. They are without sense, but not senseless. "Tautology and contradiction are not pictures of the reality. They present no possible state of affairs. For the one allows *every* possible state of affairs, the other *none* . . ." (4.462).

According to No. 5, every proposition is now a truth-function of the elementary propositions, which are the truth-arguments of the proposition. In his comments Wittgenstein develops his theory of probability, his theory of the logical relation of inference, and his theory that all logical propositions are tautologies and therefore say nothing of the reality. Further, he criticizes Russell's theory of the relation of identity and develops his theory that it is possible to construct any truth-function from the elementary propositions by the successive application of single logical operations. "Every truth-function is a result of the successive application of the operation (- - - T) $(\xi, . . .)$ to elementary propositions. This operation denies all the propositions in the right-hand bracket and I call it the negation of these propositions" (5.5). This development I shall now explain a little further.

As early as 1913 the American mathematician and logician, H. M. Sheffer,[20] showed that all the truth-functions used in *Principia mathematica* may be defined solely by means of the so-called "stroke-operation," which is written '$p|q$' and may be interpreted as 'not-p and not-q'. For instance, the negation of p and the disjunction of p and q may be defined as follows: $\sim p =_{Df} p|p$ and $p \vee q =_{Df} [(p|q)|(p|q)]$. Since the total number of other truth-functions of p and q may be defined by means of $\sim p$ and $p \vee q$, they may also be defined by repeated application of the stroke-operation. Wittgenstein's theory is a generalization of this from truth-functions with only one or two arguments to truth-functions with an arbitrary number of arguments. The principle is as follows:

If there is given only one elementary proposition, p, it is possible by means of the stroke-operation to construct: $p|p \,[=_{Df} \sim p]$, $(p|p)|p \,[=_{Df} p \cdot \sim p]$, $p|(p|p) \,[=_{Df} \sim p \cdot p]$, $(p|p)|(p|p) \,[=_{Df} p \cdot p], \ldots$

If two and only two elementary propositions, p and q, are given, it is further possible to construct: $q|q \,[=_{Df} \sim q]$, $(q|q)|q \,[=_{Df} q \cdot \sim q], \ldots p|q \,[=_{Df} \sim p \cdot \sim q]$, $(p|q)|(p|q) \,[=_{Df} p \vee q]$, $(p|p)|(q|q) \,[=_{Df} p \cdot q]$, $((p|p)|q)|((p|p)|q) \,[=_{Df} p \supset q], \ldots$

And it is possible to proceed in the same way no matter how many elementary propositions are given. Wittgenstein, writing instead of the above operation '$(---\text{T})(\xi, \ldots)$' its result '$N(\xi)$', i.e., the negation of the total number of variables of propositions ξ (5.502), expresses the method of construction in the general form of the truth-function $[\bar{p}, \xi, N(\xi)]$, where

'$\bar{p}$' stands for the class of all elementary propositions,
'ξ' stands for any class of propositions,
'$N(\xi)$' stands for the negation of all the propositions making up ξ.

The whole symbol '$[\bar{p}, \xi, N(\xi)]$' means whatever can be obtained by taking any selection of elementary propositions, negating them all, and then taking any selection of the class of propositions now obtained, together with any of the originals.[21] Or, in Wittgenstein's words: "This says nothing else than that every proposition is the result of successive applications of the operation $N'(\xi)$ to the elementary propositions" (6.001).

It is especially interesting that he also extends this method of construction to the so-called "generalized propositions," i.e., propositions of the form: "all x are f" (more exactly: "the propositional function fx is a true proposition for every value of x"), or of the form: "there are x's that are f" (more exactly: "the propositional function becomes a true proposition for at least one value of x"). In the current notation these propositions are written: '$(x) fx$' and '$(Ex) fx$', and Wittgenstein's theory is then expressed in the proposition: "If the values of ξ are the total values of a function fx for all the values of x, then $N(\xi) = {\sim}(Ex) fx$" (5.52). What this means, then, is that, by the application of the operation of negation $N'(\xi)$ to the class of propositions which are values of a given propositional function fx, one arrives at a proposition which says that it is false that there is at least one value of x for which fx is a true proposition. And by negation of this latter proposition one obtains the generalized existential proposition '$(Ex) fx$', that is, "there is at least one x, for which fx is a true proposition." Similarly, by starting from the negation of fx, not-fx, instead of from fx, it is possible to construct the generalized proposition '$(x) fx$', i.e., "fx is a true proposition for every value of x."

The remaining comments on No. 6 contain Wittgenstein's definition of natural numbers as exponents of operations and his theory that the propositions of mathematics are equations "and therefore pseudo-propositions" (6.2). It is impossible here to go into this question, but his view of logic must be briefly dealt with. He says:

"The propositions of logic are tautologies" (6.1). "The propositions of logic therefore say nothing. (They are the analytical propositions)" (6.11). "It is the characteristic mark of logical propositions that one can perceive in the symbol alone that they are true; and this fact contains in itself the whole philosophy of logic. And so also it is one of the most important facts that the truth or falsehood of non-logical propositions can *not* be recognized from the propositions alone" (6.113). "The fact that the propositions of logic are tautologies *shows* the formal—logical—properties of language, of the world . . ." (6.12). "The logical propositions describe the scaffolding of the world, or rather they present it. They 'treat' of nothing. They presuppose that names have meaning, and that elementary propositions have sense. And this is their connexion with the world. It is clear that it must show something about the world that certain combinations of symbols—which essentially have a definite character—are tautologies. Herein lies the decisive point. We said that in the symbols which we use much is arbitrary, much not. In logic only this expresses: but this means that in logic it is not *we* who express, by means of signs, what we want, but in logic the nature of the essentially necessary signs itself asserts. That is to say, if we know the logical syntax of any sign language, then all the propositions of logic are already given" (6.124). "Whether a proposition belongs to logic can be determined by determining the logical properties of the *symbol*. And this we do when we prove a logical proposition. For without troubling ourselves about a sense and a meaning, we form the logical propositions out of others by mere *symbolic rules*. We prove a logical proposition by creating it out of other logical propositions by applying in succession certain operations, which again generate tautologies out of the first. (And from a tautology only tautologies *follow*.) Naturally this way of showing that its propositions are tautologies is quite unessential to logic. Because the propositions, from which the proof starts, must show without proof that they are tautologies" (6.126). "Proof in logic is only a mechanical expedient to facilitate the recognition of tautology, where it is complicated" (6.1262). "All propositions of logic are of equal rank; there are not some which are essentially primitive and others deduced from these. Every tautology itself shows that it is a tautology" (6.127).

The remaining part of the comments on No. 6 are of a more sporadic character and are often merely short aphoristic remarks on various philosophical questions. I quote only the more

important ones, which have exercised a certain influence on the philosophy of the Vienna Circle.

"Logical research means the investigation of *all regularity*. And outside logic all is accident" (6.3). "The law of causality is not a law but the form of a law" (6.32). "If there were a law of causality, it might run: 'There are natural laws . . .' " (6.36). "A necessity for one thing to happen because another has happened does not exist. There is only *logical* necessity" (6.37). "As there is only a *logical* necessity, so there is only a *logical* impossibility" (6.375). "It is clear that ethics cannot be expressed . . ." (6.421). "Death is not an event of life. Death is not lived through. . . . Our life is endless in the way that our visual field is without limit" (6.4311). "Not *how* the world is, is the mystical, but *that* it is" (6.44). "For an answer which cannot be expressed the question too cannot be expressed. *The riddle* does not exist. If a question can be put at all, then it *can* also be answered" (6.5). "The solution of the problem of life is seen in the vanishing of this problem . . ." (6.521). "There is indeed the inexpressible. This *shows* itself; it is the mystical" (6.522). "The right method of philosophy would be this: To say nothing except what can be said, i.e., the propositions of natural science, i.e., something that has nothing to do with philosophy: and then always, when someone else wished to say something metaphysical, to demonstrate to him that he had given no meaning to certain signs in his propositions. This method would be unsatisfying to the other—he would not have the feeling that we were teaching him philosophy—but it would be the only strictly correct method" (6.53). "My propositions are elucidatory in this way: he who understands me finally recognizes them as senseless, when he has climbed through them, on them, over them. (He must so to speak throw away the ladder, after he has climbed up on it.) He must surmount these propositions; then he sees the world rightly" (6.54).

And then the book concludes with No. 7 without comments: "Whereof one cannot speak, thereof one must be silent" (7).

The fascinating effect of this book on the members of the Vienna Circle will be understood, when it is kept in mind that it contained a series of important logical discoveries as well as a wealth of new philosophical views, the grounds for and consequences of which were often barely indicated and so left to be worked out in full by its readers. And, simultaneously, it contained an element of irritation because of its strange mixture of lucid clearness and obscure profundity. Logic and mysticism, elucidation and obscuration, were here found side by side and deeply impressed the members of the Circle and in particular Moritz Schlick, whose thoughts had already in several respects taken a similar trend. The book was eagerly discussed at the meetings of the Circle and contributed essentially to the formation of logical positivism and provoked both agreement and disagreement. In connection with the other influences formerly mentioned (see pp. 2–3), it led, in the course of the twenties, to the crystallization of the philosophical view characteristic of the Vienna Circle, to which Wittgenstein himself did not belong.

8. Rudolf Carnap's Theory of The Constitution of Concepts

Another influence of considerable importance in the formation of the views of the Circle was Carnap's "theory of constitution," put forward in his *Der logische Aufbau der Welt* ("The Logical Construction of the World") (1928), the main lines of which I shall now state briefly. Carnap (born 1891), who in 1926 became lecturer in Vienna and, later, professor in Prague and, since 1936, has been a professor in Chicago, had earlier published several contributions to the philosophy of geometry and physics, among which may be mentioned *Der Raum: Ein Beitrag zur Wissenschaftslehre* (1922) and *Physikalische Begriffsbildung* (1926). In these he had shown himself to be an exceptionally stringent and lucid thinker, and he soon became one of the leading figures within the Vienna Circle. His great systematic gifts bore their first large fruit in the above-mentioned work, *Der logische Aufbau der Welt*, to which were added, as supplementary writings, some minor publications of the same year, namely, *Scheinprobleme in der Philosophie: Das Fremdpsychische und der Realismusstreit* (Berlin, 1928) and *Abriss der Logistik, mit besonderer Berücksichtigung der Relationstheorie und ihrer Anwendungen* (Vienna, 1928). In the first of these, certain applications of the theory of constitution propounded in the main work are explained and treated, and the latter contains a brief and clear account of the logistic method used in the formulation of theories.

The purpose of the theory of constitution will perhaps be best understood if viewed in the light of its philosophical applications and results. These results, which may be described as a continuation and clarification of certain ideas of Mach, Russell, and Wittgenstein, go to show, positively, that all the concepts of the natural and social sciences may be defined by means of so-called "elementary experiences," so that all statements of those sciences may be tested or checked by means of such elementary experiences and, negatively, that many traditional philosophical problems are merely pseudo-problems, since, being based on untestable assertions, they are, strictly speaking, senseless. More accurately, Carnap defines his criterion of meaning as follows:

"The meaning of a statement consists in its expressing a (thinkable, not necessarily also an actual) state of affairs. If an (alleged) statement expresses no (thinkable) state of affairs, it has no meaning and hence is only apparently an assertion. If a statement expresses a state of affairs, it is at all events meaningful, and it is true if this state of affairs exists, and false if it does not. One can know whether a statement is meaningful before one knows whether it is true or false.

"If a statement contains only concepts which are already known or recognized, it derives its meaning from these. On the other hand, if a statement contains a new concept or one whose legitimacy (scientific applicability) is in question, one must specify its meaning. In order to do this, it is necessary and sufficient to state the (only thinkable) experiential situations in which it would be called true (not: 'in which it is true'), and those in which it would be called false."[22]

In order to be factual, statements must be founded on an experience: nonfounded statements are empty or meaningless. This principle is acknowledged and practiced in all the natural

The Vienna Circle: Its Program and Presuppositions

and social sciences (natural science, psychology, cultural science). But this means that the objects of these sciences must be "constituted" in such a way that every statement about them can be written as, or "translated" into, a founded statement that is equivalent with, i.e., that has the same truth-value as, the original one. To show how this may be done is the aim of the theory of constitution.

To facilitate the understanding of Carnap's method, it may be expedient to recall a few of the logistic concepts used in the theory of constitution. There is, in the first place, the concept "propositional function," by which is understood an expression that contains one or more variables and which, by substitution of suitable arguments for these, becomes a true or a false proposition. Propositional functions with only one variable may be called properties, and their extension is then constituted by the objects satisfying them, that is to say, the names of which, when inserted instead of the variable, make the propositional function a true proposition. The totality of these objects is also called the class of objects defined by the propositional function. If two or more propositional functions are satisfied by exactly the same arguments, they are said to be of the same extension or to be coextensive; and, by the introduction of a special "sign of extension" for a group of coextensive propositional functions, it is possible to formulate propositions of the whole group without regarding the conceptual content ('red', for instance) contained in the propositional functions, but retaining the truth-values of the propositions resulting from the functions. Although not objects, the extensions are often spoken of as if they were, and Carnap therefore uses the designation "quasi-objects" as a convenient manner of speaking.

By means of these concepts Carnap is able to formulate his theory of constitution as follows: To constitute an object means to reduce it to other objects, i.e., to formulate a general rule (a "rule of constitution" or a "constitutional definition") indicating the way in which a statement containing the name of the first object may be replaced by an equivalent statement not containing it.[23] In simple cases this consists of a rule to the effect that, whenever the name of the first object appears, a certain expression containing the names of other objects but not that of the first object be substituted for it (explicit definition).[24] If an explicit definition in this sense is not possible, a contextual definition may be used, i.e., a rule of transformation stating generally how statements in which the expression which is not explicitly definable occurs may be replaced by other statements where it does not occur. Both explicit and contextual definitions may thus be used for the elimination of certain expressions, whether these are explicitly definable or not.

As, according to the definition just given, constitutional definitions concern only extensions, the formulation of constitutional definitions may be designated as an extensional method of definition. "It depends on the 'thesis of extensionality.' In every statement about a concept, the concept should be interpreted extensionally, i.e., it should be represented by its extension (class, relation); or, more precisely, in every statement about a propositional function, the propositional function may be replaced by its sign of extension."[25]

It is now the task of the theory of constitution to arrange the objects of every science according to their reducibility. The system forms, as it were, a genealogy of objects, the roots of which are the objects which cannot be reduced to others, and the trunk and branches show to which other objects any given object may be reduced. What Russell and Whitehead did in *Principia mathematica* with regard to mathematics (reduced all mathematical concepts to the logical fundamental concepts) Carnap in his theory of constitution attempts to do with regard to the natural and social sciences, although, as far as the greater part is concerned, only in outlines and with a limited application of symbolic logic.

As the various sciences do not generally avail themselves of the logistic language in which Carnap's definitions are formulated, but use a more everyday realistic language, he is obliged to replace his logistic criterion on the reducibility of objects by the following criterion of reducibility in realistic formulation: "We call an object a 'reducible to objects $b, c \ldots$' if for the existence of every state of affairs with regard to $a, b, c \ldots$ a *necessary and sufficient condition* may be given which depends only on objects $b, c. \ldots$."[26] By means of this criterion he is able to find out whether a given object is capable of being reduced to another object or not, and he can thus ascertain the order in which the objects must be constituted to form a connected and all-inclusive system of constitution. As this order is not uniquely determined on every point, however, by the said criterion of reducibility, Carnap also uses epistemological priority as a principle of arrangement; and this he defines as follows: "One object (or type of object) is called epistemologically prior with respect to another if the second is known by means of the first and, therefore, knowing the first object is a precondition to the knowing of the second object."[27] In consequence of the latter principle of arrangement, Carnap may also conceive of his whole system of constitution as a "rational reconstruction of the formation of reality, a formation which in the actual process of cognition is made intuitively."[28]

Being of the opinion that the four main kinds of objects are cultural (*geistige*) objects, other minds (*fremdpsychische*), physical objects, and data of our own minds (*eigenpsychische*), Carnap finds that between these objects reducibility is possible in the order mentioned,[29] so that cultural objects may be reduced to other minds, these may be reduced to physical objects, and these again to the data of one's own mind. Briefly, his course of reasoning is as follows: cultural objects (i.e., historical, sociological objects, such as religion, ways and customs, state, etc.) are known partly through their "mental manifestations" (human ideas, feelings and acts of volition), partly through their "documentations" (i.e., physical products, such as things, documents, and the like), and may therefore be constituted on the basis of these. And the objects of other minds are known partly—and mainly—through expressions of emotions and thought, partly—although, so far, very imperfectly—through the brain processes corresponding to the mental phenomena, and may therefore be constituted on the basis of physical objects. And the latter, finally, are known by observation, i.e., by data of our own minds, on the basis of which they may therefore be constituted.[30]

It should continuously be kept in mind, however, that the independence of the various kinds of objects is by no means eliminated by constitution. The higher objects are not composed of the lower but belong to quite different types of objects, which is shown by the fact that they cannot meaningfully be substituted for one another in given statements.[31] The constitution merely shows that statements of higher objects may be translated into statements of lower objects without their truth-value being altered and that statements of any kind of objects may accordingly be tested by means of statements of the lowest kind, the data of our own minds. Likewise, it should be emphasized that the order of arrangement here chosen is not the only possible one. It is, as already mentioned, based on epistemological priority. But if for other reasons it is found expedient, one may very well use the physical objects (i.e., the material things of our everyday life) as the basic element, since in principle the objects of our own mind may be constituted from the brain processes by means of the psychophysical relation. In view of the knowledge of the various kinds of objects and their mutual relations which actually exist in the sciences, Carnap chooses the data of our own minds as a basis for his system of constitution, and he describes them in the following way:

"The egocentric basis we shall also call the *'solipsistic' basis*. This does not mean that solipsism itself is here presupposed in the sense of regarding only one subject and his experiences as the sole reality, consequently denying the reality of other subjects. The distinction between real and unreal objects is not made at the beginning of the system of constitution. At the beginning there is no distinction made between those experiences which are, on the basis of later constitution, distinguished as perception, hallucination, dream, etc. This distinction as well as the consequent distinction between real and unreal objects occurs only at a rather high level of constitution. . . . The basic region can also be called 'the given'; it must be noted, however, that there is no intention to presuppose something or somebody to whom the given is given. . . .[32] The given is without a subject."[33]

Having chosen the data of the "own mind" as basis, Carnap determines the so-called "elementary" experiences as basic elements within this sphere and by elementary experiences he understands "experiences in their totality and closed unity."[34]

The function of elementary experiences within the system is similar to that of sensations within Mach's system, but they differ from the latter in not being the results of an analysis, but concrete, complicated units of experience. As such, they cannot be divided up but only be submitted to a so-called "quasi-analysis" on the basis of similarities and other relations holding among them.[35] As the basic relation Carnap uses the recollection of similarity, by which he understands the relation subsisting between two elementary experiences, when a comparison between a recollection of the first elementary experience and the second elementary experience shows that there is an approximate or complete agreement between a certain quality in the one and a certain quality in the other.[36] And from this fundamental relation between the elementary experiences the various objects and kinds of objects are constituted as outlined below.

It should be observed, to begin with, that in building up his system of constitution Carnap employs primarily the logistic symbolic language in the formulation of his constitutional definitions. To make them more easily understood, however, he writes them simultaneously in three other languages, viz., our everyday word-language, the realistic language which is the one current in the empirical sciences, and a fictitious constructive language containing the operational rules for the construction of the objects defined.[37] Although the logistic language is more exact, the following examples of Carnap's constitutional definitions will be given in the realistic language, which does not require so much specific knowledge in order to be understood and which seems sufficient to give an impression of the character of the system.

First, 'elementary experiences' are defined as the members of the relation "recollection of similarity," and next 'part-similarity' is defined as the relation subsisting between two elementary experiences, either of which contains a constituent part similar to a constituent part of the other one. Then 'a region of similarity' is defined as the greatest possible class of qualities between which a part-similarity exists, and 'a quality-class' as the quasi-object that represents something common to elementary experiences; further, he defines 'sense-classes' as classes of abstractions of chains of similarity of qualities, i.e., as what is common for a series of qualities passing evenly into one another. The sense of sight is thereupon defined as a sense-class having the dimensional number five (namely, color tone, saturation, lightness, height, and width). Then he defines 'sensation', 'place of field of vision', 'being in the same place', and 'neighborhood', as well as 'equicolored', 'color class', 'neighboring colors', and 'preceding in time'. And this concludes Carnap's treatment of the lowest stage, the data of the own mind in the system of constitution, from which he passes to the intermediate stages, beginning with physical objects.

By 'physical objects' he understands the material objects of our everyday life, which are characterized, in the first place, by filling a certain part of space at a certain point of time: "Place, shape, size, and position belong to the set of determinators of every physical thing. In addition, at least one sense-quality— e.g., color, weight, temperature—also belongs to this set of determinators."[38] Their constitution starts with the constitution of the space-time world, which is defined as the class of world-points to which are assigned colors (or other sense-qualities), i.e., the points in the n-dimensional space of real numbers in so far as they serve for the assignment of the qualities mentioned. For such assignments twelve rules are given, of which we shall mention here only Nos. 9 and 10, since they concern a controversial point in positivistic theories: "9. In so far as there is no reason to the contrary, it is presumed that a point of the external world that is seen once exists before and after it is seen; its positions form a continuous world line. 10. It is further presumed, in so far as there is no reason to the contrary, that such points of the external world have the same or similar color at other times as they had at the time they were seen."[39] The visual objects are defined as bundles of world-lines, the neighborhood relations of which remain much the same for a long period, and *my body* as a visual object with a series of special characteristics. With the help of these concepts, tactual-visual objects and the remaining senses and sense-qualities are defined, whereupon the whole domain of the own mind is determined as the sum total of elementary experiences thus arranged plus the unconscious objects constituted in analogy to the color points not seen at the present moment, so that these objects "consist of nothing but an appropriate rearrangement of immediately presented objects."[40]

The *world of perception* constituted in the whole space-time world by the attribution of sense-qualities to the individual world-points is completed by analogical attribution in a way that in a sense corresponds partly to a postulate of causality, partly to a postulate of substance. Between the world of perception and *the physical world* there is this difference: while the former is constituted by the attribution of sense-qualities to the world-points, the latter is constituted by the attribution of numbers, the physical quantities; this makes it possible to formulate laws mathematically and to achieve a unique noncontradictory intersubjectivation. Within the physical world *biological objects* may then be constituted, including especially *human beings* with their *expressive movements*, and they form the basis of the higher stage: other minds and cultural objects.

For the relation of expression is used the relation between certain observable physical processes in *my body* and a class of data frequently occurring at the same time in *my mind;* the mind of another person can then be constituted by the attribution of the latter class to similar processes in the body of another person. Accordingly, it is stated that "there are no other minds without bodies" and "the whole of the *experience of other people consists*, therefore, in nothing but *a reordering of my experiences and their constituent parts.*"[41] Also the communications of other persons and the utterances of factual statements may be constituted on the basis of the signs generally applied to these processes. And thus the road is open for the constitution of *the world of the other person*, which, by comparison with my own world of observation, gives rise to the constitution of *the intersubjective world* that forms the proper domain of the objects of science—all of it, however, only as certain ramifications of "my" system of constitution, which does not mean, of course, that such ramifications exist only in my mind or in my body but merely that they may be constituted from objects in my own mind, i.e., that statements of them are capable of being transformed into statements of my own mind without any change in the truth-values of the statements. The same applies to the cultural objects constituted from their manifestations, i.e., from the mental processes in which they are actualized or make themselves known. Thus the object "state," for instance, may be constituted as follows: "A *state* is a system of relations among people characterized in such and such a way by its manifestations, viz., the mental behavior of these people and their dispositions for such behavior, especially the behavior dispositions of one individual as conditioned by the actions of other people."[42] As to *the values*, these may be constituted from an earlier point in the system of constitution, viz., from *experiences of value*, such as experiences of bad or good conscience, or duty, or responsibility, or aesthetic experiences, etc. "This does not mean that values are psychologized any more than the constitution of physical objects meant that these were psychologized. The system of constitution does not speak this realistic language, but is neutral with respect to the metaphysical components of realistic statements. However, it translates statements about the relation between value and value-feelings into the constitutional language in a way analogous to the way propositions concerning the relation between physical objects and perceptions are translated. . . ."[43] With this we close our outline of the system of constitution."[44]

What, now, is achieved by this system? That it has been carried through in detail only as far as the fundamental part is concerned Carnap himself emphasizes repeatedly and that, accordingly, its universal application may involve several changes; but,

The Vienna Circle: Its Program and Presuppositions

apart from that, the question arises: What would be achieved by carrying it through completely?

The answer is that, if carried through, the system would show *that* and *how* the totality of statements about objects forming the subject matter of the various sciences are capable of being transformed into statements about immediate experiences having the same truth-values as the original statements. In other words, it would show that all scientific statements are capable of being verified or falsified by means of immediate experiences. This is the positive side of the matter. Negatively, it would show that it is superfluous to assume or apply other sources or means of knowledge than logic and immediate experience. Indeed, Carnap goes so far as to say that the allegation of such other sources of knowledge leads merely to metaphysical assumptions which are meaningless, i.e., incapable of being tested by experience. Only statements consisting solely of logical constants and terms capable of being constituted on the basis of experience have a meaning in the strict sense of this word. Therefore, the theory of constitution may be used to purge science and philosophy of meaningless statements and pseudo-problems. In principle all meaningful questions can be answered—in the affirmative or the negative. There are no insoluble riddles; the apparent insolubility of certain problems is due to the fact that they are based on meaningless assumptions.

"It is sometimes said that the answers to many questions cannot be put into concepts, that they cannot be expressed. But in that event even the question itself cannot be expressed. In order to see this, we will investigate more precisely *what constitutes the answer to a question*. In a strictly logical sense, the posing of a question consists in the presentation of a proposition and the setting of the task of establishing as true either this proposition itself or its negation. A proposition can be given only by the presentation of its sign, the sentence, which is composed of words or other symbols. It frequently occurs, especially in philosophy, that a series of words is given which is considered a sentence but which, in fact, is not. A series of words is not a sentence if it contains a word that is without meaning or (and this is more frequently the case) when all the individual words have a meaning but these meanings do not fit into the context of the sentence. . . . If a real question is presented, what is the situation with respect to the possibility of answering it? In that case a proposition is given, expressed in conceptual signs connected in a formally permissible manner. Every legitimate concept of science has, in principle, its definite place in the system of constitution ('in principle,' i.e., if not at present, then in a possible future stage of scientific knowledge); otherwise, it cannot be recognized as legitimate. Since we are concerned here only with answerability *in principle,* we disregard the momentary condition of science and consider the stage in which the concepts which appear in the given proposition are incorporated into the system of constitution. On the basis of its constitutional definition, we substitute for the sign of each of the concepts in the given sentence the defining expression and make, step by step, the further substitutions of constitutional definitions. . . . The sentence given in the posing of the question is thus so transformed that it expresses a definite (and, indeed, a formal and extensional) state of affairs in respect to the basic relation. We assume in the theory of constitution that it is in principle determinable whether or not a specified basic relation holds between two elementary experiences. However, the state of affairs mentioned is composed of such particular relational propositions; and, further, the number of elements among which the basic relations hold, viz., elementary experiences, is finite. From this it follows that the existence or nonexistence of the state of affairs in question is in principle determinable in a finite number of steps and thus the *question posed is in principle answerable.*"[45]

On these cardinal points the members of the Vienna Circle were in 1928 fairly well agreed. The discussions continued, however, and a further examination of the problems gave rise to difficulties which not only made Carnap modify his standpoint considerably but also resulted in certain divergencies of opinion within the Circle.[46] But before these divergent tendencies had made themselves felt, the Circle had become so firmly established and so convinced that its methods and fundamental views

The Vienna Circle: Its Program and Presuppositions

were basically correct that, after 1930, it decided to get into touch with similar-minded groups and persons in other countries, and its development during the decade which followed showed an increasing international activity and growing response from many different quarters. This led to an extension of the external frame, and the very fact that the circle of the participants in the discussions was so widened resulted, necessarily, in a broadening of the basis of discussion, since the persons attracted by the general attitude and program of the movement had, in many respects, very different standpoints and opinions regarding the details of *logical empiricism*, as the movement now came to be called; its adherents wanted to emphasize that they did not consider themselves tied to positivistic views in the more narrow and dogmatic sense. In the following chapter this energetic and comprehensive development, intensive as well as extensive, will be dealt with.

II. Logical Empiricism: Its Expansion and Elaboration

1. Publications, Congresses, and International Connections

Logical positivism was first introduced to an international forum of philosophical experts at the Seventh International Congress of Philosophy held at Oxford in 1930. Here Schlick read a paper on "The Future of Philosophy," in which, with as much enthusiasm for, as confidence in, the new method of philosophy, he heralded a new era in the history of philosophy. ". . . It appears that by establishing the natural boundaries of philosophy we unexpectedly acquire a profound insight into its problems; we see them under a new aspect which provides us with the means of settling all so-called philosophical disputes in an absolutely final and ultimate manner. This seems to be a bold statement, and I realize how difficult it is to prove its truth and, moreover, to make anyone believe that the discovery of the true nature of philosophy, which is to bear such wonderful fruit, has already been achieved. Yet it is my firm conviction that this is really the case and that we are witnessing the beginning of a new era of philosophy, that its future will be very different from its past, which has been so full of pitiful failures, vain struggles, and futile disputes."[1]

The new view of philosophy advocated was that of Wittgenstein, which Schlick expressed in two assertions, one negative and one positive: (1) philosophy is not a science and (2) it is the mental activity of clarification of ideas. Clarifying our thoughts means discovering or defining the real meaning of our propositions, which must be done before their truth can be established. This latter part is the task of the special sciences, with which philosophy cannot compete. All metaphysical attempts to do so have been vain and have only led to mutual conflicts between varying systems. And the reason for this is now understood: "Most of the so-called metaphysical propositions are no propositions at all, but meaningless combinations of words; and the rest are not 'metaphysical' at all, they are simply concealed scientific statements the truth or falsehood of which can be ascertained by the ordinary methods of experience and observation.[2]

"How will philosophy be studied and taught in the future?

"There will always be men who are especially fitted for analysing the ultimate meaning of scientific theories, but who may not be skillful in handling the methods by which their truth or falsehood is ascertained. These will be the men to study and to teach philosophizing, but of course they would have to *know* the theories just as well as the scientist who invents them. Otherwise they would not be able to take a single step, they would have no object on which to work. A philosopher, therefore, who knew nothing except philosophy would be like a knife without a blade and handle. Nowadays a professor of philosophy very often is a man who is not able to make anything clearer, that means he does not really philosophize at all, he just talks about philosophy or writes a book about it. This will be impossible in the future. The result of philosophizing will be that no more books will be written about philosophy, but that *all* books will be written in a philosophical manner."[3]

Schlick's prophecies, however, caused no great stir among the other members of the congress, and, if someone had foretold the

Logical Empiricism: Its Expansion and Elaboration

immensely rapid development and the response which the movement was to evoke in the course of the coming decade, he would no doubt have been met with a skeptical shake of the head. Nevertheless, the movement gained speed very rapidly during the next few years. This was particularly due to the publication, begun in 1930, of the periodical *Erkenntnis* (edited by Hans Reichenbach and Rudolf Carnap) and to the various series of writings, among which must be especially mentioned the series "Schriften zur wissenschaftlichen Weltauffassung" (edited by Philipp Frank and Moritz Schlick) and "Einheitswissenschaft" (edited by Otto Neurath, Rudolf Carnap, Philipp Frank, and Hans Hahn until the death of the latter in 1934; thereafter by Neurath, Carnap, and Joergen Joergensen and, from 1938, Charles Morris). In the first series the following ten books were published:

R. VON MISES, *Wahrscheinlichkeit, Statistik und Wahrheit* (1928); Eng. trans.: *Probability, Statistics, and Truth* (New York, 1939).
R. CARNAP, *Abriss der Logistik* (1929).
M. SCHLICK, *Fragen der Ethik* (1930); Eng. trans.: *Problems of Ethics* (New York, 1939).
O. NEURATH, *Empirische Soziologie* (1931).
P. FRANK, *Das Kausalgesetz und seine Grenzen* (1932).
O. KANT, *Zur Biologie der Ethik: Psychopathologische Untersuchungen über Schuldgefühl und moralische Idealbildung, zugleich ein Beitrag zum Wesen des neurotischen Menschen* (1932).
R. CARNAP, *Logische Syntax der Sprache* (1934); Eng. trans.: *Logical Syntax of Language* (London and New York, 1937).
K. POPPER, *Logik der Forschung: Zur Erkenntnistheorie der modernen Naturwissenschaft* (1935).
J. SCHÄCHTER, *Prolegomena zu einer kritischen Grammatik* (1935).
V. KRAFT, *Die Grundlagen einer wissenschaftlichen Wertlehre* (1937).

In the second series the following seven monographs appeared:
H. HAHN, *Logik, Mathematik und Naturerkennen* (1933).
O. NEURATH, *Einheitswissenschaft und Psychologie* (1933).
R. CARNAP, *Die Aufgabe der Wissenschaftslogik* (1934).
P. FRANK, *Das Ende der mechanistischen Physik* (1935).
O. NEURATH, *Was bedeutet rationale Wirtschaftsbetrachtung* (1935).
NEURATH, BRUNSWIK, HULL, MANNOURY, and WOODGER, *Zur Enzyklopädie der Einheitswissenschaft. Vorträge* (1938).
R. VON MISES, *Ernst Mach und die empiristische Wissenschaftsauffassung* (1939).

Publications, Congresses, and International Connections

In 1938 this series was supplemented by the "Library of Unified Science Series," in which only two volumes have appeared:

R. VON MISES, *Kleines Lehrbuch des Positivismus: Einführung in die empiristische Wissenschaftsauffassung* (1939).

H. KELSEN, *Vergeltung und Kausalität* (1941); Eng. trans.: *Society and Nature* (Chicago, 1943).

In 1938 was begun also the publication of the large *International Encyclopedia of Unified Science* (University of Chicago Press) long planned by Otto Neurath; a number of monographs in this work had appeared when World War II seriously slowed down the development of the enterprise. The monographs published are as follows:

OTTO NEURATH, NIELS BOHR, JOHN DEWEY, BERTRAND RUSSELL, RUDOLF CARNAP, and CHARLES MORRIS, *Encyclopedia and Unified Science* (1938).
V. F. LENZEN, *Procedures of Empirical Science* (1938).
C. MORRIS, *Foundations of the Theory of Signs* (1938).
L. BLOOMFIELD, *Linguistic Aspects of Science* (1939).
R. CARNAP, *Foundations of Logic and Mathematics* (1939).
J. DEWEY, *Theory of Valuation* (1939).
E. NAGEL, *Principles of the Theory of Probability* (1939).
J. H. WOODGER, *The Technique of Theory Construction* (1939).
G. DE SANTILLANA and E. ZILSEL, *The Development of Rationalism and Empiricism* (1941).
O. NEURATH, *Foundations of the Social Sciences* (1944).
P. FRANK, *Foundations of Physics* (1946).

In addition, the followers of the movement, in various parts of the world, published in the course of the thirties a number of works of varying size, the most important of which will be mentioned below, and, at the initiative of Otto Neurath, the indefatigable organizer, co-operation was initiated between empiricist and logicist periodicals in various countries.

This extensive publishing activity contributed greatly to the development of the movement, as did also the arrangement of a number of international congresses that gave the members of the Vienna Circle an opportunity of stating and discussing their ideas with other philosophers and scientists feeling a need for international co-operation on the basis of empiricist-scientific fundamental views advocated by the movement. Detailed re-

Logical Empiricism: Its Expansion and Elaboration

ports of all these congresses have been published in *Erkenntnis*, in the *Journal of Unified Science* (the periodical continuing *Erkenntnis*), and in a special report of the congress at Paris in 1935, *Actes du congrès international de philosophie scientifique, Sorbonne, Paris, 1935* (Paris, 1936).

The first two of these congresses (called "Tagungen") were kept within rather narrow limits and were attended by a relatively small number of participants from Austria, Czechoslovakia, and Germany. The first was held in Prague in 1929 and comprised, besides a number of papers (by Hahn, Neurath, and Frank) containing general information on the views of the Vienna Circle, a series of papers and discussions on causality and probability (Reichenbach, von Mises, Paul Hertz, Waismann, and Feigl) and on the foundations of mathematics and logic (Adolf Fraenkel and Carnap). The latter subject again formed the main subject at the second conference, held at Königsberg in 1930. Here Carnap lectured on the logicistic, Arend Heyting on the intuitionist, and Johann von Neumann on the formalist foundation of mathematics, while Otto Neugebauer read a paper on pre-Greek mathematics, Reichenbach one on the physical concept of truth, and Werner Heisenberg one on the principle of causality and quantum mechanics. Furthermore, there were at the two meetings vivid and stimulating discussions on the subjects and problems dealt with.

The next congress was held at Prague in 1934. It was called a preparatory meeting (the Paris congress was being planned for the following year under the name of the "Congrès international de philosophie scientifique"). Attended by people from various countries who later became more or less intimately connected with the movement and who met here for the first time, the preparatory meeting achieved a more international character than the preceding meetings had. Among the favorably interested participants were Lukasiewicz, Tarski, Ajdukiewicz, Janina Hosiasson, and Marja Kokoszynska, Poles; Ernest Nagel and Charles Morris, Americans; Louis Rougier, Frenchman; Eino Kaila, Finn; and Joergen Joergensen, Dane, all of whom read papers and took part in the discussions. The members of

Publications, Congresses, and International Connections

the group also took an active part in the Eighth International Congress of Philosophy held at Prague during the following days. Here Neurath read a paper on unified science, Schlick on the concept of wholeness, Carnap on the method of logical analysis, Reichenbach on the significance of the concept of probability for knowledge, and Joergensen on the logical foundations of science. These details are mentioned because they convey an impression of the kinds of problems with which the group was concerned.

This impression will become more complete if we consider the main subjects discussed the following year at the large congress at Paris: scientific philosophy and logical empiricism (Enriques, Reichenbach, Carnap, Morris, Neurath, Kotarbinski, Wiegner, Chwistek), unity of science (Frank, Du Nouy, Brunswik, Gibrat, Neurath, Hempel and Oppenheim, and Walther), language and pseudo-problems (Tarski, Kokoszynska, Massignon, Masson-Oursel, Richard, Chevalley, Padoa, Greenwood, Rougier, Matisse, Feigl, Vouillemin), induction and probability (Reichenbach, Schlick, Carnap, De Finetti, Zawirski, Hosiasson), logic and experience (Ajdukiewicz, Benjamin, Renaud, Petiau, Destouches, Métadier, Habermann, Chwistek, Braithwaite, Tranekjaer Rasmussen, Grelling), philosophy of mathematics (Gonseth, Lautman, Juvet, Bouligand, Destouches, Mania, Jaskowski, Raymond, Becker, Schrecker), logic (Tarski, Helmer, Sperantia, Lindenbaum, Bachmann, Padoa, Malfitano, Honnelaitre, Bollengier, Bergmann), and history of logic and scientific philosophy (Scholz, Jasinowski, Raymond, Bachmann, Padoa, Tegen, Hollitscher, Ayer, Zervos, Joergensen, Frank, Heinemann). At this congress also the above-mentioned *International Encyclopedia of Unified Science* was planned, at the initiative of Neurath, and a committee was set up for the drafting of a uniform international logical notation.

The following year, in 1936, the Second International Congress for the Unity of Science was held at Copenhagen and had the problem of causality as its main theme. This congress included a paper by Niels Bohr on causality and complementarity, while Frank spoke on philosophical interpretations and mis-

Logical Empiricism: Its Expansion and Elaboration

interpretations of the quantum theory, Lenzen on the interaction between subject and object in observation, J. B. S. Haldane on some principles of causal analysis in genetics, Rashevsky on physicomathematical methods in biological and social sciences, Rubin on our knowledge of other men, Neurath on sociological predictions, Somerville on logical empiricism and the problem of causality in social science, Hempel on a purely topological form of non-Aristotelian logic, and Popper on Carnap's logical syntax. During the congress, news was received of the assassination of Moritz Schlick, who had sent in a paper on the quantum theory and cognizability of nature.

The next year, in 1937, a Unity of Science of Congress was held again in Paris in connection with the Ninth International Congress of Philosophy (Congrès Descartes). As, in the arrangement of its sections, this congress had shown itself particularly interested in the representatives of logical empiricism and had devoted a special section to the unity of science, the congress of the logical empiricists was confined to a conference on the problems of scientific co-operation, especially in connection with the *Encyclopedia* and the unification of logical symbolism. At the main congress (Congrès Descartes), Carnap spoke on the unity of science based on the unity of language; Neurath on prediction and terminology in physics, biology, and sociology; Reichenbach on the principal features of scientific philosophy; Frank on modern physics and the boundary between subject and object; Grelling on the influence of the antinomies in the development of logic in the twentieth century; Hempel on a system of generalized negations; Tarski on the deductive method; and Oppenheim on class concepts and order concepts. Several representatives of movements allied to logical empiricism took an active part. This was the last of the international congresses of philosophy before the outbreak of World War II.

But the movement of logical empiricism found time for two more congresses before the great catastrophe. The first was held in 1938 at Cambridge, England, and the second in 1939 at Harvard University, Cambridge, Massachusetts. The Cambridge congress of 1938 had for its main theme the language of

Publications, Congresses, and International Connections

science, and it included papers on language and misleading questions (L. S. Stebbing), relations between logical positivism and the Cambridge school of analysis (M. Black), the diverse definitions of probability (M. Fréchet), languages with expressions of infinite length (Helmer), mathematics as logical syntax and formalization of a physical theory (Strauss), the logical form of probability-statements (Hempel), the language of science (M. Fréchet), experience and convention in physical theory (Lenzen), autonomy of the language of physics (Rougier), the realistic interpretation of scientific sentences (Donald C. Williams), the formalization of a psychological theory (Woodger), the function of generalization (Arne Ness), the concept of Gestalt (Grelling and Oppenheim), the departmentalization of unified science (Neurath), propositional logic in the Middle Ages (K. Durr), the scope of empirical knowledge (Ayer), logic as a deductive theory (Waismann), two ways of definition by verification (Braithwaite), physics and logical empiricism (Frank), significant analysis of volitional language (Mannoury), and imperatives and logic (Joergensen).

The Harvard congress, the fifth and last congress before the war, was quite naturally attended predominantly by Americans, although some European philosophers and scientists were there. Further, in consequence of the anticultural and anti-Semitic politics of naziism, several of the leading figures of the movement had, in the course of the thirties, emigrated to the United States, which had thus become the new center of logical empiricism. The interest of the Americans had been stimulated by Morris and Nagel as well as by the men from Europe, among whom were Carnap, Reichenbach, Frank, von Mises, Feigl, Kaufmann, and Hempel. Some of the subjects of the papers read and discussed were: aims and methods for unifying science (Sarton, Bridgman, Kallen, Langer, Feigl, Nagel, Joergensen, von Mises, Gomperz), scientific method and the language of science (Swann, Carnap, Reichenbach, Hempel, Wundheiler, Williams, Senior, Felix Kaufmann, J. Kraft, Montague, Benjamin, Quine), methodology of the special sciences (Lindsay, Rougier, Pratt, Stevens, Leonard, Gerard, Henderson, Neurath, Morris,

Logical Empiricism: Its Expansion and Elaboration

Dennes, Somerville), problems in exact logic (Curry, Rosser-Kleene, Tarski, Church, Copeland, Margenau), science and society (Wirth, Zilsel, Brewster, Oboukhoff, Karpov, Byrne), and history of science (Jaeger, De Lacy, Santillana, Parsons, Davis, Kelsen, Frank). Although the outbreak of World War II, two days before the opening of this congress, made itself felt, the congress was carried through according to its program, and the lively and objective discussions of the subjects treated indicated a widespread interest in the views and methods of logical empiricism that promised well for the future of the movement in its new home. However, in consequence of the development of the war, and particularly when America joined in, conditions became so difficult that a slowing-down was inevitable. As I am yet uninformed as to details, I shall confine myself in the following exposition to the development of logical empiricism until the first of September, 1939, the date of the beginning of the war.

I shall, therefore, now go back to the twenties, or still further, and speak about the various circles with which the Vienna Circle gradually came to co-operate, owing to their common interest in one or several essential questions. They are principally the following: the Berlin group; the Lwow-Warsaw group; the Cambridge analysts, pragmatists, and operationalists; the Münster group, as well as various more isolated investigators in different countries.

2. The Berlin Group

Simultaneously with the gathering by Schlick of the Circle at Vienna, a similar group was formed in Berlin, which in 1928 was organized as the "Gesellschaft für empirische [later, following a proposal by David Hilbert, 'wissenschaftliche'] Philosophie." Among the leaders were Hans Reichenbach (born 1891), Alexander Herzberg, and Walter Dubislav; some other members of the society may be mentioned—Kurt Grelling (1886–1943?), Kurt Lewin (1890–1947), Wolfgang Köhler (born 1887), and Carl Gustav Hempel (born 1905). Its object was to promote scientific philosophy, by which was understood "a philosophical method which advances by analysis and criticism of the results of the special sciences to the stating of philosophical questions and their solutions."[4] The significance of such a scientific-analytical method had been emphasized by Reichenbach as early as 1920;[5] and, true to their program, he and those who agreed with him concerned themselves mainly with specific investigations of fundamental concepts, theories, and methods within the individual sciences, while they had some reservations about the tendency of the Vienna Circle to form systems and set up strict prescriptions and prohibitions.[6] Among their investigations may be mentioned Dubislav's detailed analysis of various methods of definition (*Über die Definition* [3d ed., 1926]); Grelling's inquiries into the paradoxes of the theory of sets and logic; Lewin's work on genidentity and scientific method; Köhler's on physical Gestalts; and Reichenbach's inquiries into the theory of relativity, the concepts of space and time, causality, probability, and the problem of induction. Being especially characteristic of the thought of the Berlin group, Reichenbach's work will be dealt with in more detail.

Through his inquiries into the general assumptions and the epistemological content of the theory of relativity, Reichenbach had reached the conclusion that the Kantian theory of the a priori character of space and time—as well as of other concepts of the natural and social sciences—was untenable. It is true that in his treatise on the theory of relativity and a priori knowledge he maintains that the world of experience is first constituted by means of a priori principles, but these are neither eternal nor deducible from an immanent scheme: "Our answer to the critical question is: there are, indeed, a priori principles which make the correlation of knowledge and observations univocal. But these may not be deduced from an immanent scheme. We must discover them only in the gradual labor of the analysis of science and cease questioning the duration of the validity of their special form."[7] In his remarkable work, *Philosophie der Raum-Zeit-Lehre* (1928), which contains a thorough epistemological analysis of the Euclidean and the non-Euclidean geometries and their relation to experience, he formulated the important principle of the relativity of geometry: "From this it follows that to say that a geometry is *true* is meaningless. We get only a proposition which characterizes something objective if, in addition to the geometry G of the space, we also specify the universal field of force K, which is connected with it. . . . Only the combination $G + K$ is an assertion of cognitive value."[8] This is partly due to the circumstance that all knowledge of reality presupposes so-called "correlative definitions" (*Zuordnungsdefinitionen*), i.e., statements as to what real things are designated by the concepts previously defined—a fact which had already been strongly stressed by Schlick in his *Allgemeine Erkenntnislehre* ([1918], pp. 55 f.) and by Reichenbach himself in his first book on the theory of relativity (pp. 32 f.). The first and most fundamental correlatives are a matter of definition and, in so far, arbitrary and of no epistemological value (which means that it is meaningless to regard them as true statements of the objects), but, on the basis of them, statements may be formulated, the truth and falsehood of which must be decided by experience. Formerly this fact was not fully realized, but the analysis of the theory of relativity has made it unambiguously clear "that correlative definitions are needed at many more places than the old theory of space-time believed; especially for the comparison of length at different places and in different inertial systems and for simultaneity. The core of the theory consists in the hypothesis that measuring bodies obey different correlative definitions from those which the classical theory of space-time assumed. This is, of course, an assertion of an empirical character and can be true or false; with it only the *physical theory of relativity* stands or falls. The *philosophical theory of relativity*, however, as the discovery of the definitional character of the system of measurement in all its particulars, is unaffected by any experience; to be sure, it was acquired through physical experiments; it is, however, a philosophical cognition, not subject to criticism from the special sciences."[9]

Unfortunately, it is impossible to enter into a detailed consideration of the many interesting and thorough analyses undertaken by Reichenbach in the work mentioned; and likewise

The Berlin Group

space does not permit of a detailed account of his *Axiomatik der relativistischen Raum-Zeit-Lehre* (1924). However, a short exposition of his view on the relation between causality, probability, and induction is indispensable. His Doctor's thesis (1916) was *Der Begriff der Wahrscheinlichkeit für die mathematische Darstellung der Wirklichkeit*, and henceforth his interest has constantly centered on this subject, which he has treated in numerous papers and books, the most important of which are *Wahrscheinlichkeitslehre: Eine Untersuchung über die logischen und mathematischen Grundlagen der Wahrscheinlichkeitsrechnung* (1935) and *Experience and Prediction: An Analysis of the Foundations and the Structure of Knowledge* (1938). His fundamental thought is that natural science never confines itself merely to describing events of the past but also predicts coming events, which can never be done with absolute certainty but only with a smaller or greater degree of probability. The concept of probability, therefore, of necessity enters into the concept of knowledge of natural science. Even so-called "causal" statements are merely border cases of statements of probability: "For this reason, we must replace the strictly causal proposition by two propositions: (I) If an event is described by a certain number of parameters, a later event likewise characterized by a certain number of parameters can be predicted with probability p. (II) This probability p approaches 1 as more and more parameters are taken into consideration."[10] Accordingly, statements concerning the future are neither simply true nor simply false but more or less probable. In order to value their probability, a graduated scale for sentences must be constructed that, on the basis of previous facts, ascribes to every possible sentence about the future event a certain degree of truth. In the theory of statements concerning the future, two-valued logic, which operates only with the values truth and falsehood, should be replaced by a continuous scale of probability, and the theory of the Vienna Circle that the meaning of propositions consists in their method of verification should therefore be generalized; instead of maintaining that meaningful propositions must be either true or false, one should assert that they have a certain probability; and, instead

Logical Empiricism: Its Expansion and Elaboration

of maintaining that propositions that are verified in the same way have the same meaning, one should assert that propositions to which any observable facts give the same value of probability have the same meaning. Only such a generalized probability-logic, containing two-valued logic as a boundary case, is capable of affording a satisfactory explanation of the statements of the natural and social sciences and their meaning. Reichenbach therefore developed a logic of probability, the basic concepts of which are definable by means of truth-tables that are generalizations of those of two-valued logic and contain these as special cases.[11] However, the basic elements of this probability-logic are not propositions but sequences of propositions, i.e., logical constructions obtained by co-ordinating with a propositional function a series of its arguments. In order to meet the difficulties arising when it is desired to fix the probability of a statement of a single future event, Reichenbach thinks it necessary to give a new interpretation of the meaning of statements of single events, and what he proposes is to assert such statements not as being true or false but as a "posit," the evaluation of which is fixed by the probability of the whole class of events of which the single event concerned is a member.[12] Having to choose among several relevant possibilities, we will choose the most probable and "posit" that one. The aim of the whole theory, which has been much debated and thoroughly discussed, is, then, in brief, to give an account of the meaning of a statement based not on its verifiability but on its probability, the latter being of such nature as to comprise verification and falsification as special cases. So far the theory has not, however, won the general assent of the adherents of logical empiricism.

The same applies to Reichenbach's theory of induction, which assumes that probability-logic can be applied to reality. But what right have we to assume that this is so? In answering this question Reichenbach attempts, first, to show that all the assumptions of probability-logic may be reduced to one, viz., the existence of a limit of relative frequency in a series of observable facts. If such limit exists, all the laws of the calculus of probability become tautological, and the question of the applicability of probability-logic is reduced to the question of whether the series of observable facts approach a limit or not. The assumption that they do so is decidedly no tautology, and already Hume has shown that the correctness of this assumption cannot be proved. In this Reichenbach agrees, but, arguing as follows, he still thinks there is a certain rational justification in maintaining the following assumption: Since we know neither whether the assumption is true nor whether it is false, we are justified in defending it in the same sense in which we make a "wager." We want to foresee the future, and we can do so if the assumption is justified—and so we wager on this assumption. Thus we have at least a *chance* of success, while, if we are skeptical and cautious and hold back, we are certain of obtaining nothing. "We are in the same situation as a man who wants to fish in an uncharted place in the sea. There is nobody to tell him whether or not there are fish in this place. Shall he cast his net? Well, if he wants to fish I would advise him to cast his net, at least to take the chance. It is preferable to try even in uncertainty than not to try and be certain of getting nothing."[13] This is his principal reply to the problem of induction, which he amplifies by considerations on the procedure of correction, according to which one does not merely consider a single series of inductions but connects it with the largest possible number of affiliated series, whereby it becomes possible to construct probabilities of higher order, which may increase the chance in every single case.[14] "The chances of our catching fish increase with the use of a more finely meshed net; we ought therefore to use such a net even if we do not know whether there are fish in the water or not. In these reflections, I submit, the problem of induction finds its solution. It does not presuppose a synthetic *a priori*, as Kant believed; for our characterization of induction as a necessary condition of prediction as well as the technique of refining inductive conclusions by the process of correction can be deduced from pure mathematics, that is, with tautological transformations only. This solution is due to a reinterpretation of the nature and meaning of scientific systems. A scientific system is not maintained as true, but only as our best wager on the

Logical Empiricism: Its Expansion and Elaboration

future. To discover what is our *best* wager in any situation of inquiry is the aim of all scientific toil; never can we arrive at predictions which are certain. Science is the net we cast into the stream of events; whether fish will be caught with it, whether facts will correspond to it, does not depend on our work alone. We work and wait—if without success, well then, our work was in vain."[15]

The work of the Berlin group came to an end when the Nazis came into power in 1933. Its members were dispersed; some of them died, and others emigrated to the United States, where a number of them, including Reichenbach, R. von Mises, and Hempel, are continuing their work in the analysis of science.

3. The Lwow-Warsaw Group[16]

Under the influence of Kazimierz Twardowski (1866–1938), a pupil of Brentano, a vigorous opposition arose in Poland against the irrationalistic metaphysics of the Polish romanticists. Members of this opposition who should be mentioned are: Jan Lukasiewicz (born 1878), Tadeusz Kotarbinski (born 1886), Stanislaw Lesniewski (1886–1939), Zygmunt Zawirski (1882–1946), Kasimierz Ajdukiewicz (born 1890) and Leon Chwistek (1884–1944); and among the younger ones were: Alfred Tarski (born 1901), Janina Hosiasson-Lindenbaum (1899–1941), Mordechaj Wajsberg (died 1942?), Adolf Lindenbaum (died 1941), Marja Kokoszynska, Stanislaw Jaskowski, Izydora Dambska, Henryk Mehlberg, Edward Poznański, Alexander Wundheiler, M. Presburger, and Boleslaw Sobocinski. These investigators were almost all well trained in symbolic logic, and several of them have made valuable contributions to the development of this discipline. Although none of them were adherents of logical positivism, several of them began, in the thirties, to co-operate closely with the Vienna Circle in the scientific analytic work in which they were keenly interested and which they pursued under the name of "metatheory," i.e., the theory of scientific theories. There was an especially lively and fruitful exchange of thought between Carnap and Gödel, on the one side, and Tarski, on the other. In this connection attention should be drawn to

Tarski's important treatise, "Der Wahrheitsbegriff in den Sprachen der deduktiven Disciplinen" (in German in *Studia philosophica*, I [Lwow, 1935]; in Polish in *Travaux de la société de sciences*, Cl. III, No. 34 [Warsaw, 1933]). In this he showed that the truth-concept in formal languages may be defined purely morphologically, i.e., solely by means of the external forms of the expressions and their relations, but that this definition presupposes a metalanguage, containing expressions of a higher logical type than the language whose truth-concept is being defined. Further, Tarski demonstrated that the semantics (i.e., the theory of the relation between signs and their designata) of any formalized language can be built up as a deductive theory with its own axioms and its own fundamental concepts based on the morphology of the language alone. That such investigations were bound to be of the greatest importance to the further development of logical empiricism will appear from the subsequent exposition of Carnap's view of philosophy as the syntactical and, later also, the semantical analysis of the language of science.

4. Pragmatists and Operationalists[17]

In America the development of pragmatism had led to a philosophical view resembling the general viewpoints of European logical empiricism in many respects and well suited to form a natural supplement to them. In Charles Sanders Peirce (1839–1914) we find the combination of an interest in empiricist philosophy and symbolic logic that is characteristic of the movement. Even Wittgenstein's theory of the meaning of propositions consisting in their verifiability was in a way anticipated by Peirce: "It appears, then, that the rule for attaining the third grade of clearness of apprehension is as follows: consider what effects, which might conceivably have practical bearings, we conceive the object of our conception to have. Then, our conception of these effects is the whole of our conception of the object."[18] Although this rule was considered principally with reference to morals and religion by William James (1842–1910), other American investigators used it in a purely epistemological

Logical Empiricism: Its Expansion and Elaboration

way. This is seen most clearly in the so-called "operationalists," whose most prominent representative is P. W. Bridgman, the physicist, who says in his *The Logic of Modern Physics* (1927): "In general, we mean by any concept nothing more than a set of operations; *the concept is synonymous with the corresponding set of operations*. If the concept is physical, as of length, the operations are actual physical operations, namely those by which length is measured; or if the concept is mental, as of mathematical continuity, the operations are mental operations, namely those by which we determine whether a given aggregate of magnitudes is continuous . . . the concepts can be defined only in the range of actual experiment, and are undefined and meaningless in regions as yet untouched by experiments. . . . Of course the true meaning of a term is to be found by observing what a man does with it, not by what he says about it."[19] This point of view, which puts the main stress on the practice and the acts of the investigator during his work of investigation, is characteristic of the whole pragmatic attitude. The way in which it was developed by John Dewey (born 1859) in, for instance, his *How We Think* (1910) and in *Experience and Nature* (1925) and *Logic, the Theory of Inquiry* (1939) gave this attitude a decidedly biosocial character that made the adoption of behavioristic viewpoints natural. In George Herbert Mead's (1863–1931) *Mind, Self, and Society* (1934) and *Philosophy of the Act* (1938), this tendency became dominant. By emphasizing the social nature of language and science, pragmatism led to a concept of meaning which, in Charles Morris' words, may be briefly stated as follows: "Seen in terms of the context of social behavior, meaning always involves a set of expectations aroused by the symbolic functioning of some object, while the object meant, whether past, present, or future, and whether confrontable by a particular person or not, is any object which satisfies the expectations. A self, as a social being, can for instance expect that other selves will verify its own expectations (a situation of constant occurrence in science), and in this sense at least meaning can outrun personal verification."[20] This view Morris himself later developed into a *semiotic* theory, according to

Pragmatists and Operationalists

which the meaning-situation is an organic whole with three closely interrelated dimensions: "the relation of sign to objects will be called M_E (to be read, 'the existential dimension of meaning,' or, in short, 'existential meaning'); the psychological, biological and sociological aspects of the significatory process will be designated M_P ('the pragmatic dimension of meaning,' or 'pragmatic meaning'); the syntactical relations to other symbols within the language will be symbolized by M_F ('the formal dimension of meaning,' or 'formal meaning'). The meaning of a sign is thus the sum of its meaning-dimensions: $M = M_E + M_P + M_F$."[21] Whereas the older form of empiricism concerned itself mainly with the first, pragmatism with the second, and logical positivism with the third of these dimensions of meaning, Morris thinks that, by considering all of them equally, a synthesis may be reached which signifies at the same time an expansion of the concept of meaning and an associated extended form of empiricism which he calls "scientific empiricism."

Of other American investigators working on related pragmatistic-operationalistic-scientific-analytic lines, among the best known are the following: Clarence Irving Lewis (born 1883), developed in his *Mind and the World Order* (1929) a "conceptualistic pragmatism" and undertook in his *Symbolic Logic* (1932), which he wrote together with C. H. Langford, significant investigations concerning the logic of modality; Morris R. Cohen (1880–1946), strongly influenced by Russell, expounded in his *Reason and Nature* (1931) a "realistic rationalism"; Victor F. Lenzen gave, in *The Nature of Physical Theory* (1931), an enlightening analysis of the concepts and theories of physics, emphasizing the importance of "successive definitions." Numerous other American philosophers and special scientists have worked along lines more or less related to the viewpoints of logical empiricism without having been in direct contact with this movement. Among its other adherents should be mentioned Ernest Nagel, A. E. Blumberg, Daniel J. Bronstein, and other members of the Harvard congress, and we must add to these the logical empiricists who have emigrated from Europe.

Logical Empiricism: Its Expansion and Elaboration

5. The Uppsala School[22]

Although the contact between logical empiricism and the members of the Uppsala school has so far been comparatively slight, this distinctive trend within Swedish philosophy should be mentioned because it is, in several essential respects, closely related to logical empiricism and because the connection between the two seems to be growing. The Uppsala school was founded about 1910 by Axel Hägerström (1868–1939) and his colleague Adolf Phalén (1864–1931) and gathered a number of adherents and pupils, among whom were: Karl Hedvall, Harry Meurling, Ejnar Tegen, Vilhelm Lundstedt, Karl Olivecrona, Gunnar Oxenstjerna, Konrad Marc-Wogau, Ingemar Hedenius, and Anders Wedberg. Although the reasoning and the views of the two movements are not identical, there is a far-reaching agreement between the Uppsala school and logical empiricism, in that they are both decidedly antimetaphysical and for both the main task of philosophy consists in the analysis of concepts. Further, both are opposed to epistemological idealism ("subjectivism," the nature and existence of that which is conceived depends on our conception thereof) and are adherents of the theory that statements of valuations are not true statements but merely expressions of certain feelings and, accordingly, have no factual meaning. Especially with regard to the two last points, the Uppsala school has performed a comprehensive and commendable piece of work which historically anticipates the work of logical empiricism without, however, having influenced it. As has already been mentioned, a certain contact was established during the course of the thirties, and there is every reason to expect a closer co-operation between the two movements to their mutual inspiration and a further development of the basic views. In this connection Marc-Wogau's recent study, *Die Theorie der Sinnesdaten: Probleme der neueren Erkenntnistheorie in England* (1945), should be mentioned.

6. The Münster Group

As the last of the groups working with logical empiricism, the logistic school in Münster, created by Heinrich Scholz (born

1884), may be mentioned. Scholz, who worked originally in theology and philosophy of religion, became interested in logistics; and in the thirties he inspired a number of young investigators —Bachmann, Hermes, and others—to undertake significant inquiries into the foundations of logic and mathematics, while he himself was eagerly engaged in the study of the historical development of logic, stressing in particular the work of Leibniz and Frege (*Geschichte der Logik* [1931]). He was not an adherent of the ideas of logical empiricism, and the co-operation was strictly limited to formalistic-logistic problems, with no mention of the positivistic applications and viewpoints condemned in Nazi Germany. Scholz and his school have resumed their work since the war.

7. Individuals

Besides the above-mentioned groups entering into a limited or extensive collaboration with logical empiricists, there were in the various countries a number of individuals who joined the movement and took an active part in its development. Among these were the following: Eino Kaila (born 1890 in Finland), developed logistic-empiricistic ideas in a series of remarkable writings (such as, for instance, *Über den physikalischen Realitätsbegriff* [1942]) and expounded his theory of knowledge based on those ideas in his *Den mänskliga Kunskapen* (1939); his pupil, Georg Henrik von Wright, besides making intensive studies in *The Logical Problems of Induction* (1941) and *Über Wahrscheinlichkeit* (1945), also wrote a simple and lucid exposition of the fundamental thought of logical empiricism (*Den logiska Empirismen* [1943]); the Frenchman, Louis Rougier (born 1889), has published writings on *Les Paralogismes du rationalisme* (1920), on *La Structure des théories deductives* (1921), on *La Scolastique et le thomisme* (1925), and various other subjects of scientific theory; the Englishman, J. H. Woodger, after having undertaken an epistemological analysis of biological concepts and theories in his *Biological Principles* (1929), has made valuable contributions to the development of formal theories with biological interpretations in his *Axiomatic Method in*

Logical Empiricism: Its Expansion and Elaboration

Biology (1937) and in his monograph in this *Encyclopedia* entitled *The Technique of Theory Construction;* Alfred Jules Ayer (also English), in his *Language, Truth, and Logic* (1936), gave a penetrating exposition of the fundamental principles and main results of logical empiricism and in numerous articles and papers defended them against various English critics. Later he expounded the theory in a revised form in his *The Foundations of Empirical Knowledge* (1940). In Germany, P. Oppenheim dealt with the systematization of science and (together with C. G. Hempel) wrote *Der Typusbegriff im Lichte der neuen Logik* (1936). The Swiss, F. Gonseth, formed an "idoneistic" theory of his own concerning the nature of mathematics; and Karl Dürr dealt with the logic of Leibniz and other historical predecessors of some of the fundamental thoughts of logical empiricism. The Norwegian, Arne Ness (born 1912), put forward a behavioristic theory of knowledge in terms referring to the verbal and nonverbal behavior of the scientist (*Erkenntnis und wissenschaftliches Verhalten* [1936]). In his work *'Truth' as Conceived by Those Who Are Not Professional Philosophers* (1938), he studied the actual use of the term 'truth' by psychological methods (questionnaires and interviews). He later developed a special form of philosophical analysis of language which he calls "precision analysis." It is elaborated in his forthcoming work, *Interpretation and Preciseness*. The Dane, Joergen Joergensen (born 1894), has written *A Treatise of Formal Logic*, Volumes I–III (1931), as well as a survey of the various sciences in their systematic contexts from encyclopedic points of view, and has used logical-empiristic viewpoints and methods in his *Psykologi paa biologisk Grundlag* ("Psychology Based on Biology") (1941–45).

Many other investigators in various countries have in various fields worked more or less along the lines of logical empiricism: the philosopher B. von Juhos in Austria, the logistician Uuno Saarnio in Finland, and, in Denmark, Alf Ross and Bent Schultzer, professors of law, and the sociologist, Svend Ranulf. It is impossible to make this an inclusive list because there is difficulty in deciding just where to draw the line.

8. The Question of the Nature of Philosophy

After this outline of the external development of logical empiricism, I shall now consider its internal development. As has already been indicated, important divergencies arose toward the end of the twenties within the Vienna Circle because of various doubts as to some of its own presuppositions. These divergencies concerned the question as to how their philosophical work should be rightly characterized on the basis of their own principles, on the question of the verifiability of statements, and, accordingly, on the theory of meaning as synonymous with verifiability.

As to the nature of philosophy, Wittgenstein maintained that the task of philosophy is a clarification of thought, not a theory but an activity, and that philosophical propositions are, strictly speaking, logically meaningless and "inexpressible," for which reason they should be discarded when their purpose has been attained, in the same way as a scaffolding is thrown away when a building is completed. While, to begin with, Schlick and most of the other members of the Vienna Circle immediately accepted this view, Neurath raised strong opposition against it toward the end of the twenties, as he feared that it would lead to a revival of metaphysics as "the philosophy of the inexpressible." In this he was strongly supported by Carnap, who gave the objections a precise form and put forward a new view of the nature of philosophy that was clearly expressed in his article "On the Character of Philosophical Problems."[23] According to Carnap, *philosophy is the theory of science* or *"the logic of science,* i.e., the logical analysis of the concepts, propositions, proofs, theories of science," and its propositions are not meaningless mediums for elucidation but constitute a legitimate field of study, which he called the "logical syntax of the language of science" and treated in detail in his great work *Logische Syntax der Sprache* (1934),[24] which we shall now consider.

Logical Empiricism: Its Expansion and Elaboration

9. Carnap's Logical Syntax of Language*

Carnap's concept of the logical syntax of a language is a generalization of Hilbert's metamathematics, in which, as is well known, the meaning of mathematical signs and formulas is completely disregarded and they are considered solely in a "formalistic" way, i.e., as figures written down and transformed according to certain definite rules. In other words, metamathematics is a theory the object of which is mathematical signs and formulas. Similarly, the logical syntax of language is a purely formal theory of the linguistic signs and their composition into sentences, proofs, and theories, particularly a theory of the signs or sign combinations occurring or acceptable in the sciences, including, of course, those occurring in mathematics; for this reason Carnap's syntax comprises Hilbert's metamathematics as a special part. While it was the object of Hilbert to establish through metamathematics the consistency of classical mathematics, Carnap's purpose is not so much to prove that all science is noncontradictory as to establish the following two theses: (*a*) an investigation of the logic of science need never pay regard to the meaning but only to the formal rules of linguistic expressions, and (*b*) the fixation of the formal rules of any language and the investigation of the consequences of such rules can be built up in exactly the same way as a scientific theory, namely, as a logical syntax of the language concerned, and can usually be formulated in that very language. Thus, considering philosophy as the syntax of the language of science, Carnap refutes Wittgenstein's view of philosophy as an activity that is able only to express itself in meaningless sentences; and at the same time he sharply delimits philosophy as something apart from the special sciences, since philosophy does not deal with the *objects* but only with the *sentences about the objects of such sciences*. The special sciences comprise all "object-questions," whereas philosophy is concerned only with the "logical questions" dealing with scientific concepts, propositions, the-

---

* [In fairness to Professor Joergensen it should be stated that considerations of space made it necessary to omit portions of the analysis of Carnap's earlier views.—The Editors.]

ories, etc., considered formally as complexes of signs constructed in accordance with certain rules for combinations of signs. These rules are partly rules of formation, partly rules of transformation. The former are the rules for the composition of the various kinds of signs of a language into sentences (i.e., corresponding roughly to usual grammar); the latter are rules for the deduction of a sentence from other sentences (i.e., rules of inference, so that the logical syntax will comprise what is generally called "logic"). For the different (from a logical point of view) languages, these two kinds of rules are different and may be fixed arbitrarily, because they, so to speak, define the language to which they are to apply. Here the "principle of tolerance" applies: "*It is not our business to set up prohibitions, but to arrive at conventions.... In logic, there are no morals.* Everyone is at liberty to build up his own logic, i.e. his own form of language, as he wishes. All that is required of him is that, if he wishes to discuss it, he must state his methods clearly, and give syntactical rules instead of philosophical arguments."[25] Thus we may, for instance, construct one language restricted to finitist mathematics and another language the mathematical part of which contains all of classical mathematics (and physics), and so reduce any dispute between intuitionists and formalists in mathematics to a mere disagreement as to which form of language they wish to use.

Carnap then proceeds to illustrate the syntax by means of two languages serving as instances of formal languages. Since it is a very complicated matter, although in principle possible, to set up the formal rules of our everyday language, Carnap chooses two artificial languages, viz., the language of finitist mathematics and the language of classical mathematics. He calls them "language I" and "language II," formulates the syntactical rules for each, and shows that the syntax of language I can be expressed in that language itself, so there is nothing to prevent a language in this sense describing its own form or structure (which had been declared impossible by Wittgenstein). Carnap demonstrates this by means of the method of arithmetization, introduced by Gödel into metamathematics, according to which a number is co-ordinated to every sign of the system in such a way that every expression can be translated into a corresponding arithmetical expression. And as language I contains arithmetic, this means that the syntax of this language can be expressed in the language itself.

In his investigation of the two model languages Carnap states a number of instances worked out in detail and confirming the above-mentioned thesis *b*. But, however thoroughly and subtly worked out, instances cannot, of course, prove the thesis generally, and Carnap accordingly undertakes a series of fundamental inquiries into general syntax, i.e., into syntactical rules concerning either all languages or comprehensive classes of languages. In these he defines and discusses a number of logical-syntactical concepts—the most important is the concept of "consequence," which for any language is defined by the rules of transformation of that language and which, therefore, varies from one language to another. Roughly speaking, it may be said that a sentence in a given language is a consequence of certain other sentences if, and only if, it can be constructed from these latter by application of the rules of transformation of the language concerned. As the rules of transformation are purely formal, the concept of "consequence" is so, too, and by means of the latter it is then possible to define various other important syntactical concepts, such as the concepts "analytic," "contradictory," and "synthetic," which give an exhaustive classification of all sentences occurring in the different branches of science, and also the concept "the content of a sentence," besides many other concepts that are worked out with extreme penetration and mathematical precision. For that very reason they are too complicated to be stated here, but an impression of Carnap's way of procedure may perhaps be obtained by considering his simple and lucid exposition in *Philosophy and Logical Syntax* (1935).

"Given any language-system, or set of formation rules and transformation rules, among the sentences of this language there will be true and false sentences. But we cannot define the terms 'true' and 'false' in syntax, because whether a given sentence is true or false will generally depend not only upon the syntactical form of the sentence but also upon experience; that is to say, upon something extra-linguistic. It may be, however, that in certain cases a sentence is true or false only by reason of the rules of the language. Such sentences we will call *valid* and *contravalid* respectively. Our definition of validity is as follows: a sentence is called *valid*, if it is a consequence of the null class of premises (i.e. if it presupposes no premise) . . . a sentence 'A' of a certain language-system is called *contravalid* if every sentence of this system is a consequence of 'A'. . . ."[26]

By means of the concepts here defined it is then possible to give a purely formal definition of the "sense" or "content" of a sentence. "If we wish to characterize the purport of a given sentence, its content, its assertive power, so to speak, we have to regard the class of those sentences which are consequences of the given sentence. Among these consequences we may leave aside the valid sentences, because they are consequences of every sentence. We define therefore as follows: the class of the non-valid consequences of a given sentence is called the *content* of this sentence."[27] The logical-philosophical significance of such definitions is that they show that all factual sentences may be submitted, by means of them, to a logical analysis without its being necessary at any point to consider anything but the purely formal properties of the sentences concerned. Their "sense" in the usual vague and undefined meaning of the word is logically irrelevant and may be replaced, according to Carnap's theory, in all logical investigations by the formal concept of "content" here defined.

There are, however, certain sentences with regard to which this is anything but evident, and as to these Carnap proceeds in a special way. They are the sentences which he calls "pseudo-object-sentences," i.e., sentences which *seem* to deal with the objects mentioned in them but which, upon a closer inspection, appear to be purely syntactical (e.g., 'The rose is a thing'). As these very sentences play an important part in current philosophy, Carnap attaches considerable weight to them, it being possible to maintain his above-mentioned thesis *a* only if it can be established that the pseudo-object-sentences are syntactical in character. He contrasts them with the *syntactical sentences* mentioned above and with *real object-sentences* (e.g., 'the rose is red'), which concern extra-linguistic objects and belong to the special sciences.

Although a pseudo-object-sentence may have the same grammatical subject as an object-sentence, it asserts no quality of the subject. We can, moreover, discover its truth without observing the object to which we refer but only by considering its syntactical status. Thus we see that a pseudo-object-sentence is really syntactical and can be translated into a syntactical sentence having the same content (e.g., 'The word 'rose' is a thing-word').

Syntactical sentences are also said to be sentences of *the formal mode of speech*, while pseudo-object-sentences are said to be sentences of *the material mode of speech*. According to Carnap, the material mode of speech often gives rise to pseudo-problems or disputes that may be avoided by translating the sentences concerned into the formal mode of speech.[28] Indeed, all traditional metaphysical problems seem to arise from the very circumstance that they have been discussed in the material mode of speech instead of having been analyzed syntactically. An example will illustrate this: "One frequent cause of dispute amongst philosophers is the question what *things* really are. The representative of a positivistic school asserts: 'A thing is a complex of sense-data.' His realistic adversary replies: 'No, a thing is a complex of physical matter'; and an endless and futile argument is thus begun. Yet both of them are right after all: the controversy has arisen only on account of the unfortunate use of the material mode. Let us translate the two theses into the formal mode. That of the positivist becomes: 'Every sentence containing a thing-designation is equipollent* with a class of sentences which contain no thing-designations, but sense-data-designations,' which is true; the transformation into sense-data-references has often been shown in epistemology. That of the realist takes the form: 'Every sentence containing a thing-designation

---

* Two sentences are *equipollent* if each is a consequence of the other.

Carnap's Logical Syntax of Language

is equipollent with a sentence containing no thing-designation, but space-time-coordinates and physical functions,' which is obviously also true. . . . There is no inconsistency. In the original formulation in the material mode the theses *seemed* to be incompatible, because they *seemed* to concern the essence of things, both of them having the form: 'A thing is such and such.' "[29]

In other cases the problem is solved by our showing that apparently contradictory theses do not belong to the same syntactically defined language. This applies, for instance, to the controversy between the logicists (Frege, Russell) and the axiomaticists (Peano, Hilbert) on the nature of numbers. The former assert: "Numbers are classes of classes of things," while the latter assert: "Numbers are a unique kind of entities." Translating these assertions into the formal mode, we get: "Numerical symbols are class-symbols of the second order," and "Numerical symbols are symbols of individuals (i.e., symbols of zero order that occur only as arguments)." These sentences may be conceived either as belonging each to its own separate arithmetical language or as proposals for separate languages, i.e., for different ways of talking about numbers. In either case the discussion is no longer a controversy about what is true and what is false but is reduced to a question of what language is best suited for talking about arithmetics.

On the basis of similar analyses of a long series of philosophical problems and assertions of various kinds, Carnap thinks himself justified in asserting that all the theorems of philosophy can be treated syntactically, that is to say, can be translated into the formal mode of speech whereby the problems attached to them will either be automatically revealed as being illusory pseudo-problems or be reduced to proposals for different languages, the expediency, but not the correctness, of which may be discussed. He finds no need to eliminate completely the material mode of speech: "This mode is usual and perhaps sometimes suitable. But it must be handled with special caution. In all decisive points of discussion it is advisable to replace the material by the formal mode; and in using the formal mode, reference to the language-system must not be neglected. It is not neces-

Logical Empiricism: Its Expansion and Elaboration

sary that the thesis should refer to a language-system already put forward; it may sometimes be desired to formulate a thesis on the basis of a so far unknown language-system, which is to be characterized by just this thesis. In such a case the thesis is not an assertion, but a proposal or project, in other words a part of the definition of the designed language-system. If one partner in a philosophical discussion cannot or will not give a translation of his thesis into the formal mode, or if he will not state to which language-system his thesis refers, then the other will be well-advised to refuse the debate, because the thesis of his opponent is incomplete, and discussion would lead to nothing but empty wrangling."[30]

The main result is, therefore, that every indicative, meaningful sentence either is an object-sentence which, as such, belongs to one special science or another or is a syntactical sentence which belongs to logic or mathematics, and that, accordingly, philosophy may be defined as the sum total of the true syntactical sentences concerning the languages of the special sciences. This again leads to various new problems—or old problems in a new formulation—such as: Do the various special sciences speak the same language, and, if not, is it possible to construct a language common to all? And what is the criterion of the truth—or merely meaningfulness—of an object-sentence? The first of these questions leads to the discussion of one of the main points of logical empiricism: *the unity of science* and the associated thesis of *physicalism*, while the second is important with regard to the *theory of verifiability* and to the problem of the *basis of the system of constitution*. As these problems overlap to a large extent, a constant interaction took place in their treatment from the beginning of the thirties; but, for the purposes of clarity, they will here, as far as possible, be treated separately, and we shall start with the last problem: the problem of basis and verification.

10. Protocol-Sentences and Substantiations ("Konstatierungen")

In his *Der logische Aufbau der Welt* Carnap had, as we know, chosen as basis for his theory of constitution the immediately given experiences which he asserted were subjectless. This starting point was not, however, acceptable to Neurath. He was afraid that it might lead to a return to metaphysical absolutism, and, besides, he found the connection between the experiences and the sentences that were to describe them, and to be checked by them, metaphysical.

He consequently maintained that propositions were checked only by other propositions. A new proposition is compared with those already accepted and is called correct if it can be incorporated into the system. Sometimes one may, although this decision is not easily made, change the whole previously accepted system of propositions to allow for the new one. "Within unified science there are significant tasks of transformations,"[31] whereas *outside* unified science there is nothing with which a relation may be established. Not even direct statements of observation can be compared with the objects concerned but merely with other statements of observation or with statements of other kinds, and their truth does not depend on their agreement with the objects observed but solely on their agreement with the totality of all statements accepted at the given time. Neurath now proceeded to look for purely formal, syntactical characteristics of direct statements of observation, which he called (following a suggestion of Carnap) *protocol-sentences*, as he wanted to stress that these sentences were of the same kind as the ones which natural scientists use in making protocols (records of observations) and which form the starting point for their hypotheses and theories and the criterion for their validity.

As the debate proceeded, the prevailing view became that from a philosophical-epistemological standpoint there was no difference in principle between protocol-sentences and other legitimate scientific sentences; and the discussion concerning the syntactical form of protocol-sentences therefore subsided, the whole question then being considered a matter of convention.

The above "most radical form" of logical empiricism did not, however, win the general approval of all the followers of the movement. Schlick was in direct opposition. He maintained that, by introducing the concept "protocol-sentence," the aim had been from the beginning to sort out a group of sentences capable of serving as an absolutely firm basis for knowledge and as a means of testing all other sentences. And, since noncontradictoriness or incorporability in a system of sentences cannot enable us to distinguish between knowledge of reality and fairy tales that are consistently built up, the sentences characteristic of knowledge must be distinguished by special properties. But, as he admits that even protocol-sentences are hypothetical because for various reasons they *may* be doubted (the observer may, for instance, be guilty of a slip of the pen, or he may have lied) and are sometimes rejected (as, for instance, a single measurement that cannot be brought to agree with a certain series of measurements of the same magnitude), he thinks that knowledge—certain knowledge—cannot be based on protocol-sentences but must be based on certain sentences of observations or "Konstatierungen," by which he understands statements of what is being observed. These are always of the form "so-and-so here now." What these sentences have in common is that they fulfil the function of pointing. What 'here' and 'now', etc., mean cannot generally be given in verbal definitions but must be specified by gesture, pointing, etc. The meaning of a substantiation can be understood if, and only if, it is compared with the facts. However, as in the case of analytic judgments, establishing the meaning of a substantiation is not distinguishable from establishing its truth. "It makes as little sense to ask whether I can be mistaken about its truth as about that of a tautology. Both are absolutely valid. However, the analytic, tautological sentence is without content, while the substantiation provides us the satisfaction of genuine knowledge of fact."[32] Strictly speaking, however, substantiations cannot be written down at all, because when we do so the "pointing" words 'here' and 'now' lose their sense.[33]

Against this view Neurath asked how it would ever be possible to ascertain that Schlick had had an experience which he could not write down[34] and also called attention to the fact that the absolutely certain knowledge sought by Schlick is not an empirical fact but wishful thinking connected with certain meta-

Verifiability and Testability

physical ideas of a difference between "the real world" and knowledge of it. Referring to the detailed and penetrating criticism of this metaphysical duplication which Frank had set forth in his *Das Kausalgesetz und seine Grenzen* (1932), chapter x, Neurath said: "Thus the attempt to achieve knowledge of fact is reduced to the attempt to bring the sentences of science into agreement with as many protocol-sentences as possible."[35] And as to consistent fairy tales versus knowledge of reality, he refers to the fact that "the practice of life" very quickly reduces the number of the systems of sentences having an equal right *from a logical point of view*, as most of them soon appear unsuited for predictions.[36] But this does not make the rest absolutely certain. "*There is no way to make absolutely certain protocol-sentences the point of departure for the sciences.*" There is no *tabula rasa*. We are like sailors who have to rebuild their ship on the open sea without ever being able to tear it down in a dry dock to rebuild it with new parts.[37]

As to the further course of this discussion, which was cut short by the death of Schlick in 1936, readers are referred to the instructive articles by C. G. Hempel, "On the Logical Positivists' Theory of Truth"[38] and "Some Remarks on 'Facts' and Propositions,"[39] in which he defends the standpoint of Neurath and Carnap and criticizes that of Schlick. It is impossible here to go into details, but a single aspect of the matter, namely, the development of the question of verifiability, will be dealt with below, as it signifies an essential generalization of the logical-empiricist view of the truth and meaning of sentences.

11. Verifiability and Testability

Keeping in mind that logical positivists identified the meaningfulness of reality-sentences with their verifiability, it will be understood that the question of how reality-sentences can be verified must be of the utmost interest to them. Reality-sentences that cannot be verified or falsified are, according to this view, meaningless. But now it became apparent that not even protocol-sentences, by means of which the truth of all other reality-sentences was to be tested, were capable of being verified in the strict sense of the word so that they become absolutely certain. And matters are still worse, of course, with regard to more complicated sentences, as, for instance, the general sentences of which the natural laws form a part, since from a logical point of view they are "general implications" in the simplest case of the form: for all x, if x has the property f, then x has the property g. As Popper says, "logical positivism destroys not only metaphysics but also natural science."[40] As a first way out of this difficulty Schlick had proposed a different conception of natural laws: "Natural laws are not (in the language of the logician) 'general implications,' because they cannot be verified for *all* cases; they are rather rules or directions for the investigator to find his way through the real world, to discover true sentences, to predict certain occurrences."[41] This way of escape, however, had not won the approval of the other logical empiricists, who felt bound to acknowledge natural laws as general implications. But how then could they be made to agree with the theory that the meaningfulness of sentences consists in their verifiability?

This could be done only by amending the theory. A first proposal in that direction was made by Popper in his *Logik der Forschung* (1935), where, as the criterion of the meaningfulness of a sentence, he uses not the verifiability but the falsifiability of the sentence. "Our formulation depends on an asymmetrical relation between verifiability and falsifiability, which is connected with the logical form of universal sentences; viz., these are never derivable from particular sentences but can be contradicted by particular sentences."[42] By this criterion of meaning, he proposed to sort out empirical-scientific sentences from a priori–analytical sentences (logic and mathematics) as well as from nonfalsifiable reality-sentences (metaphysics). But this suggestion was not approved either because universal sentences, logically viewed, seem to parallel existential sentences, which latter can never be falsified but in certain cases may be verified, and because some scientifically recognized sentences contain a combination of the peculiarities of universal and existential sentences (they contain both a universal and an ex-

Verifiability and Testability

istential quantifier) and, accordingly, can be neither verified nor falsified. This applies, for example, to statements concerning the limit of the relative frequency of a certain event in a series of events, that is, concerning probability-statements according to a commonly held view. Some logical empiricists were for a time inclined to regard these statements as "pseudo-sentences," or they sought another interpretation of sentences of probability. As this gave rise to great difficulties, the view was gradually accepted that scientific sentences may very well contain both universal and existential quantifiers, and consequently it became necessary to look for a new and more liberal criterion of meaning than that mentioned above. As he had done so often before, Carnap pulled the loose ends together, worked the matter through, and outlined a theory and a proposal that have since formed the starting point for the further discussion of this problem.

Carnap's exposition was published in a treatise called "Testability and Meaning."[43] Popper, in his *Logik der Forschung*, had strongly emphasized the necessity of distinguishing between various "degrees of testability (*Prüfbarkeit*)"; and Carnap, at the congress in Paris (1935), had stressed the importance of distinguishing between "truth" and "confirmation" (*Bewährung*): while truth is an absolute concept independent of time, confirmation is a relative concept, the degrees of which vary with the development of science at any given time. Further, he distinguished between two different kinds of reality-sentences, viz., those that are directly testable and those that are merely indirectly testable. "By a directly testable sentence we mean one for which, under imaginable conditions, on the basis of one or a few observations, we can with confidence regard either as so strongly confirmed that we accept it or as so strongly disconfirmed that we reject it. . . . Indirect testing of a sentence consists in directly testing other sentences which have a certain relation to it."[44] The most important testing operations are (*a*) confrontation of a sentence with observation and (*b*) confrontation of the sentence with sentences that have been previously recognized. Of these, the former operations are the more important, for in their absence there is no confirmation at all, while the latter are merely auxiliary operations, which mostly serve to eliminate unsuited sentences from the system of sentences of the science concerned.

These views are now further implemented and defined in "Testability and Meaning," which contains the following introductory remarks: "If by verification is meant a definitive and final establishment of truth, then no (synthetic) sentence is ever verifiable, as we shall see. We can only confirm a sentence more and more. Therefore we shall speak of the problem of *confirmation* rather than of the problem of verification. We distinguish the *testing* of a sentence from its confirmation, thereby understanding a procedure—e.g. the carrying out of certain experiments—which leads to a confirmation in some degree either of the sentence itself or of its negation. We shall call a sentence *testable* if we know such a method of testing for it; and we shall call it *confirmable* if we know under what conditions the sentence would be confirmed. As we shall see, a sentence may be confirmable without being testable; e.g. if we know that our observation of such and such a course of events would confirm the sentence, and such and such a different course would confirm its negation without knowing how to set up either this or that observation."[45]

Reichenbach thinks he has found a measure for the degree of confirmation in the limit of the relative frequency of the cases of confirmation, so that any sentence may be said to be a probability-sentence; this being a controversial point, however, Carnap prefers to distinguish between probability (in the frequency sense) and degree of confirmation;[46] he also advises us not to discuss matters in the material mode of speech, as this mode serves to veil the fact that the answering of certain pertinent questions depends on the choice of the structure of the language applied, which appears evident when the formal mode of speech is used. He therefore develops a logical-syntactical analysis of the pertinent concepts, which is too technical to be quoted here. It must suffice to state that the investigation results in various proposals or requirements, the fulfilment of which signifies more or less radical forms of empiricism and may be said to define different concepts of what empiricism is or should be. He makes four requirements in all, of which the first is the most rigid and the last the most liberal one. Being formulated in the formal mode of speech, the requirements concerned define four different empiricist languages. The four requirements are as follows:

"*Requirement of Complete Testability:* Every synthetic sentence must be completely testable." I.e., if any synthetic sentence S is given, we must know a method of testing for every descriptive predicate occurring in S.[47]

"*Requirement of Complete Confirmability:* Every synthetic sentence must be completely confirmable." I.e., if any synthetic sentence S is given, there must be for every descriptive predicate occurring in S the possibility of our finding out for suitable points whether or not they have the property designated by the predicate in question.[48]

"*Requirement of Testability:* Every synthetic sentence must be testable." This requirement admits incompletely testable sentences—these are chiefly universal sentences to be confirmed incompletely by their instances.[49]

"*Requirement of Confirmability:* Every synthetic sentence must be confirmable." Here both restrictions are dispensed with. Predicates which are confirmable but not testable are admitted; and generalized sentences are admitted. This is the most liberal of the four requirements. But it suffices to exclude all sentences of a nonempirical nature, e.g., those of transcendental metaphysics, inasmuch as they are not confirmable, even incompletely. Therefore, it seems to Carnap that it suffices as a formulation of the principle of empiricism; in other words, if a scientist chooses any language fulfilling this requirement, no objection can be raised against this choice from the point of view of empiricism.[50]

The main result is, then, that the discussion as to what sentences may be considered meaningful and what sentences meaningless, from the point of view of empiricism, has led, on the one hand, to a more precise definition of and distinction between various empirical languages and so to various concepts of meaning in an empirical sense and, on the other, to the acceptance of the most liberal of the alternatives compatible with empiricism. And this, Carnap thinks, has helped to smooth the way for the development of converging views and approaches to *scientific empiricism* as a movement comprising all allied groups—an ever more scientific philosophy. This aim is closely connected with the idea of a unity of science that has already been mentioned several times but which we shall now carry a little further.

12. Unity of Science and Physicalism

The expression 'unity of science' was introduced into logical empiricism by Neurath. He wanted thereby to mark his opposition to the view that there are different *kinds* of sciences (and, corresponding to them, different kinds of reality or being), such as natural sciencés (*Naturwissenschaften*) versus the humanities (*Geisteswissenschaften*), or factual sciences (*Wirklichkeitswissenschaften*) versus normative sciences (*Normwissenschaften*). He also wanted, by the words 'unity of science', to sum up the objective aimed at by logical empiricists, viz., the formation of a science comprising all human knowledge as an epistemologically homogeneous ordered mass of sentences being of the same empiricist nature in principle, from protocol-sentences to the most comprehensive laws for the phenomena of nature and human life.[51] To use a traditional expression, unity of science might also be called "monism free from metaphysics." A first manifestation of this attitude in the Vienna Circle was Carnap's theory of constitution, which Neurath, however, for the above-mentioned (p. 69) reasons found unacceptable. He thought it very important that the unification of the various special sciences into a unity of science should take place through the formation of a universal language of science, i.e., a language the logical syntax of which permitted sentences from the most different special sciences to be combined with one another so as to form a logical context. "The universal language of science becomes a self-evident demand, if it is asked, how can certain singular predictions be derived; e.g., 'the forest fire will soon subside'. In order to do this we need meteorological and botanical sentences and in addition sentences which contain the terms 'man' and 'human behavior'. We must speak of how people react to fire, which social institutions will come into play. Thus, we need sentences from psychology and sociology. They must be able to be placed together with the others in a deduction at whose end is the sentence: 'Therefore, the forest fire will soon subside'."[52] *"We must at times be able to connect all types of laws with one another.* All, whether they be chemical, climatological, or sociological laws, *must be conceived as parts* of one system, viz., unified science."[53] Without this, the practical application of science would be excluded in many domains, and the unity of science therefore forms the basis of the applications of science, depending on the combination of premises from different scientific disciplines into connected chains of inference.

In science as well as in our everyday life we do actually avail ourselves of a kind of "universal slang," whenever we want to reason or to think things over, and the aim of unified science is to make this universal slang homogeneous and universal, eliminating merely metaphysical absurdities. This, however, again raises the question: What language would be best suited for the performance of this task? In his theory of constitution Carnap used, as we know, an egocentric, phenomenological language, thinking that by constitution he would be able to reduce all other concepts to phenomenological basic concepts. But he and Neurath soon agreed that it would be more expedient to use a so-called "physical" or "physicalistic" language or, as it was later called, a "thing-language," by which they understood the language in which we, both in physics and in everyday life, speak of physical things (which again approximately means: material things, in the everyday understanding of that expression). The task then became to formulate the rules of formation and of transformation of such language so that all concepts and sentences can be expressed in it, if necessary, by suitable translations and so that all scientific theories can by means of it be reduced to as few deductive systems as possible, preferably to a single one. "In our discussions in the *Vienna Circle* we have arrived at the opinion that this physical language is the basic language of all science, that it is a universal language comprehending the contents of all other scientific languages. In other words, every sentence of any branch of scientific language is equipollent to some sentence of the physical language, and can therefore be translated into the physical language without changing its content. Dr. Neurath, who has greatly stimulated the considerations which led to this thesis, has proposed to call it the thesis of *physicalism.*"[54]

The physical language, Carnap says further, is characteristic, in that it consists of sentences that give in their simplest form a quantitative description of a definite space-time-place (e.g., 'At such and such space-time-point the temperature is so and so many degrees'), or, expressed formally: Sentences that attribute to a certain series of values of space-time-co-ordinates a certain value of a definite physical function. In so far as rules are known for a unique translation of sentences of qualitative characteristics into sentences of quantitative characteristics, there is nothing to prevent the physical language from containing characteristics of the former kind.[55]

The reason for choosing such a language as that of unified science is that it is *intersensual, intersubjective, and universal.* What this means will now be outlined.

That the physical language is *intersensual* means that its sentences can be tested by means of various senses, because actually there is no physical function that can be co-ordinated solely with qualitative characteristics from a single sphere of sense. The characteristic "tone of such and such pitch, timbre, and loudness" may, for instance, be co-ordinated with the following characteristic in the physical language: "Material oscillation of such and such basic frequency with such and such harmonic frequencies with such and such amplitudes," which, by application of certain apparatuses, may be tested by means of the sense of sight or of touch. And, similarly, qualitative characteristics of color may be co-ordinated to physical characteristics of electromagnetic oscillations, which may, for instance, be tested by means of their place in the spectroscope, that may again, by suitable devices, be demonstrated by contact with an indicating needle or by ascertainment of a tone by listening, so that a blind physicist will very well be able to test the qualitative protocol-sentence, 'Here is now green of that and that shade'. It is therefore possible in principle to construct a physical language of such a kind that the qualitative characteristics of the protocol-language depend functionally and uniquely on the distribution of values of physical functions, so that *the physical characteristics may be said to apply intersensually*.[56]

That the physical language is *intersubjective* means that its sentences can be tested by various subjects and thus hold a meaning for all of them. This appears from the fact that a given subject (individual) can observe by means of experiments under what physical conditions various other subjects react by certain qualitative protocol-sentences, e.g., 'I now see green of that and that shade'. Thus a correspondence may be established between every single physical characteristic, on the one hand, and the qualitative characteristics contained in the protocol-sentences of the various subjects, on the other, so that *the physical characteristics may be asserted to apply intersubjectively*.[57]

That the above co-ordinations between physical and qualitative characteristics can be established is no logical necessity but depends on empirical "happy circumstances" connected with "a very general structural feature of experience."[58]

Finally, that the physical language is *universal* means that every scientifically acceptable sentence, whether originating from our everyday language or from a branch of science, can be translated into it. When investigating this view, it is necessary to distinguish between the question of the translatability of protocol-sentences and the question of the translatability of other sentences of the natural and social sciences.

As to the protocol-sentences, the assertion that they are in principle translatable depends on the so-called "logical behaviorism,"[59] which says that sentences concerning mental phenomena (experiences, observations, recollections, emotions, etc.) possess a meaning that can be intersubjectively tested only if they are conceived as sentences concerning the bodily condition and/or behavior of the individual concerned, such as, for example, the condition of his nervous system or his appearance and movements (including also movements of speech).

As regards the remaining sentences belonging to the natural and social sciences, it appears that the translation into the physical language cannot be accomplished solely by explicit definitions but also requires the application of the "reduction" defined by Carnap.[60] This operation has a function similar to that of "constitution" in *Der logische Aufbau der Welt*, but, contrary to constitution, reduction is defined in the formal mode of speech, and the definition is expressed exactly by means of logistic symbols. To go into details would take us too far, but, roughly speaking, it may be said that the content of the definition is that a term 'a' is "reducible" to other terms 'b', 'c', . . . , if it is possible by means of the latter to formulate the characteristics concerning the conditions under which we are going to use the term 'a'. "The simplest method of reducing, in this sense, one concept to another is by definition. If 'a' can be defined by 'b', 'c', . . . , then obviously 'a' is reducible to 'b', 'c'. . . . It can, however, be shown that the method of definition is not the only one but is the simplest special case of reduction. E.g., the concept 'electrical field' is reducible to the concepts 'body,' 'mass,' 'electric charge,' and spatiotemporal determinations. We can, by the use of these concepts, formulate rules for the application of the concept 'electrical field,' viz., describe an experimental test for this concept. On the other hand, we cannot give a definition of 'electrical field' which contains only those concepts. Therefore, we must distinguish the broader concept 'reducibility' from the narrower concept 'definability.' "[61]

While reduction by definition cannot be carried through even with regard to the concepts of physics, nothing seems to prevent the reduction of the total number of concepts of the natural and social sciences to the physical language, if reduction is taken in its wider and more liberal sense, and this procedure is therefore suggested for unified science. The crucial points, where special difficulties might be expected to arise, concern the translations of biological, psychological, and sociological sentences into the physical language. As is well known, the material mode of speech has often led us to conceive the objects of those sciences as different in principle and (in a not specified sense) mutually irreducible. But the translation into the formal mode of speech of the sentences about these sciences shows that a reduction of their concepts to the physical language is possible in principle, and that, accordingly, the advantages attached to the realization of the idea of the unity of science are within reach, although to carry it out in detail would, of course, require both much more special investigation and a greatly extended co-operation among the investigators of the special sciences, mutually, and between them and logicians. In order to convey an idea of the view of the logical empiricists, their attitude to the three crucial points mentioned should be dealt with briefly.

In regard to biological sentences, logical empiricists think that the possibility of their translation into the physical language is evident, considering that all biological concepts capable of being empirically tested concern conditions and processes in bodies that may be characterized by space-time-co-ordinates. The vitalistic concepts, such as "entelechy," etc., that are incapable of being tested must, of course, be dropped, while the analysis of concepts such as "whole" and "purposiveness" has not as yet been performed in detail but will hardly give rise to difficulties in principle.

As regards the translatability of psychological sentences, logical behaviorism is invoked. If this is tenable, the translatability in principle of psychological sentences into the physical language is evident. And, having once gone so far, there seems no possibility of insurmountable difficulties in connection with the translation of sociological sentences, which describe the relation of persons and other organisms to one another and to their surroundings.

In addition to these considerations concerning general principles, logical empiricists also, in support of the idea of a unity of science, refer to the many border sciences growing up in an increasing number and bearing witness to formerly unheeded cross-connections between the traditional branches of science, such as biophysics, biochemistry, psychophysiology, social psychology, etc.; and the result of their deliberations is that they think themselves entitled to assert that "the concepts of the thing-language provide a common basis to which all concepts of all the parts of science can be reduced"[62]—only, of course, in the above-mentioned sense of "reduction."

This result only justifies a continuation of the work of realizing the idea of the unity of science. A road has been opened for a detailed analysis of the concepts of the individual sciences for the purpose of showing how the sentences of every one of them may be reduced to the thing-language. But the analysis itself is, of course, a gigantic piece of work that can be performed only by the co-operation of logicians and the specialists within the various special sciences. Such co-operation has indeed also been eagerly sought by logical empiricists from the early days of the Vienna Circle, and the ever increasing number of special scientists participating in the congresses is impressive evidence of the fact that this need for co-operation is widely felt. Its most conspicuous expression has been, perhaps, in the *International Encyclopedia of Unified Science*, where scientists of the special sciences and philosophers work together in harmony, although they are completely free to express varying opinions on questions of doubt. Strictly speaking, the thesis of physicalism cannot be considered proved until the reduction to the thing-language of the total number of the concepts of the natural and social sciences is made, which means, of course, never. But this in no way makes the work on the creation of an ever greater connection within the sphere of sciences superfluous, let alone useless. And should it appear that concepts actually exist which cannot be reduced to the thing-language—well, then, that does not make the idea of unity less valuable but merely shows that it is necessary to choose another language than the thing-language as the language of unity, which may very well be possible, although care should be taken, of course, that a reasonable meaning can always be attached to the sentences of any such language.[63]

As regards the question of the reduction of scientific theories to a few or even a single deductive system, the prospects are, in the opinion of logical empiricists, much darker than where the question of the reduction of concepts to the physical thing-language is concerned. Not even all physical laws can at present be included in a single deductive theory, and the prospects for a derivation of biological from physical laws—let alone a derivation of psychological or sociological laws from the physical plus the biological laws—are distant, although not hopeless. Efforts are being made to create more comprehensive syntheses, and no limits can be set beforehand to these endeavors. Yet, in spite of the great advantage of a unity of laws, its importance is not so fundamental as that of the unity of language,[64] which is more easily achieved.

13. Present Tendencies and Tasks

In this exposition of the development of logical empiricism I have kept largely to the main lines of development, and I hope that I have succeeded in making them clear. I have had to leave completely out of consideration a great many penetrating individual analyses, some of which have been the conditions and others the fruits of this development. So far logical-mathematical and physical concepts, theories, and methods have been treated, whereas biological, psychological, and sociological subjects, as well as concepts and theories of value, have been only occasionally touched upon. But the very idea of a unity of science implies that all spheres of knowledge should be treated, and the predilection for the exact sciences is a defect, against which the gradually growing connection with the views developed within pragmatism should now serve as a useful remedy. As yet, we are in these domains at the beginner's stage, which is to some extent due to the relative backwardness of these sociohumanistic sciences. However, from the co-operation with pragmatists and operationalists especially interested in biology, psychology, and sociology results may be expected which are necessary in order to create a proper balance of things. At the Harvard congress of 1939 this tendency made itself plainly felt and also came to expression in Morris' paper, "Semiotic, the Sociohumanistic Sciences, and the Unity of Science," in which he showed that the so far neglected spheres of knowledge can, in principle, be incorporated into unified science via a comprehensive theory of signs, or semiotic, a point which he later developed in his *Signs, Language, and Behavior* (1946). The same tendency was also pronounced in Joergensen's paper at the Harvard congress, "Empiricism and Unity of Science," in which especially the incorporation of the formal sciences into unified science was sketched and an attempt made to establish this contact through psychology; this conception was later expounded in his *Psykologi paa biologisk Grundlag* ("Psychology Based on Biology") (1941–45). Since the precise apparatus of concepts and the refined methods which have resulted from the work with the analysis of the exact sciences have proved highly useful in the further realization of the program of the unity of science, it is possible that the development in this direction may proceed more quickly than might have been expected, in view of the relatively great complication of these spheres. Prospects seem bright for the further development of logical empiricism, which has had the good luck to be stimulated by the metaphysical verbosity re-emerging in the wake of the last war, in almost the same way as the Vienna school and its predecessors were in their day stimulated by the unverifiable nebulous speaking of speculative metaphysicians.

Another tendency came to expression at the Harvard congress, namely, an increasing interest in semantics, which had, in particular, been developed by the Lwow-Warsaw school but which, so far, in the works of the logical empiricists had been overshadowed by logical syntax. While syntax is exclusively concerned with purely formal relations between linguistic expressions *qua* mere figures, semantics treats of the relations between the expressions of a given language and their "designata," i.e., that which they designate. In his paper, "Science and Analysis of Language," Carnap stressed the great significance of semantics and characterized as semantical several main concepts which he had formerly regarded as syntactical. This applies, for example, to concepts like "consequence," "analytic," "contradictory," and others, all of which are based on the important semantical concept of truth. As to the connection between them, Carnap said: "I have explained the semantical analysis of a language as exhibiting the relation of designation. We might equally well regard it as exhibiting the truth-conditions of the sentences of the language in question. This is merely a different formulation of the aim of semantics. Suppose a sentence of the simplest form is given, consisting of a proper name combined with a one-place predicate (e.g. 'Switzerland is small'); if, now, we know which object is designated by the name and which property is designated by the predicate then we also know the truth-condition of the sentence: it is true if the object designated by the name has the property designated by the predicate. Thus the concept of *truth* turns out to be one of the fundamental concepts of semantics. We may say that the result of a semantical analysis of a sentence is the understanding of the sentence. To understand a sentence is to know what is designated by the terms occurring in the sentence and, hence, to know under what conditions it will be true. But the understanding of a sentence does not suffice, in general, for knowing whether those conditions are fulfilled, in other words, whether the sentence is true or not. But sometimes there is such a relation between two sentences that a semantical analysis of them, in other words, the understanding of the sentences, suffices to show that if the first sentence is true the second must also be true. In this case the second is called a *logical consequence* of the first. This concept, the basic concept of the theory of logical deduction and thereby of logic itself, is thus based upon a certain relation between truth-conditions, and hence is a semantical concept. The same holds for other logical concepts which are often applied in the logical analysis of science, e.g. logically true (analytic), logically false (contradictory), logically indeterminate or factual (synthetic, neither logically true nor logically false), logically compatible, etc."[65] In consequence of the above view, Carnap later, in his *Introduction to Semantics* (1943), replaced his earlier syntactical definitions of the concepts mentioned by semantical definitions and also found it necessary, in general, to supplement many of the former discussions and analyses by corresponding semantical ones. They were not incorrect, to be sure, but they were incomplete. Perhaps the awakening interest in the pragmatic views developed by Morris and others will show that semantical analyses are not exhaustive either; but this question belongs to the future.

To characterize in brief the value of the contribution of logical empiricism to the development of human knowledge can best be done, I believe, by emphasizing that it has led to the appearance of entirely new points of view as regards philosophical problems. These must today be posed in a way that differs in principle from the ones hitherto used, and their treatment requires much more exactness than has been exercised heretofore. The very fact that we have grown accustomed to ask for the *meaning* of words and sentences and have found useful criteria has intensified our criticism of statements made by ourselves and by others and has thus furthered the critical attitude which, combined with inventiveness and imagination, is the basic condition for a sensible approach to the practical problems of our day and to the promotion of scientific investigation. To return to past ways of thinking would be like ignoring the quantum theory in physics. Or, in other words, it is, as matters stand, impracticable. And to have made a contribution which it is impossible to ignore if scientific investigation is to proceed is presumably the utmost that may be expected from the pursuers of science. But this expectation the pioneers of logical empiricism have already fulfilled. And if today the still unsolved problems within the sphere of philosophy can be formulated and treated with a precision and clarity formerly unknown, the merit is theirs. They have not created a new philosophical system, which, indeed, would have been contrary to their highest intentions, but they have paved the way for a new and fruitful manner of philosophizing.

Notes and Bibliography

Chapter I

1. See Postscript, bringing this material up to date.
2. H. Feigl, "Logical Empiricism," in *Twentieth Century Philosophy*, ed. Dagobert D. Runes (New York, 1947), pp. 406–8. Compare Otto Neurath, *Le Développement du cercle de Vienne et l'avenir de l'empirisme logique* (Paris, 1935), chap. v, where he attempts to show the reason why the movement originated just in Vienna, where liberalistic and empiricist trends had made themselves felt for several decades, which had not been the case in Germany.
3. *Wissenschaftliche Weltauffassung*, pp. 16–17.
4. Neurath, *Le Développement du cercle de Vienne*, p. 58.
5. See, e.g., P. Frank, "Logisierender Empirismus in der Philosophie der U.S.S.R.," *Actes du congrès international de philosophie scientifiques, Sorbonne, Paris, 1935* (Paris, 1936), VIII, 68–76.
6. As a curiosity it may be noted that Comte is not mentioned at all in Russell's large *A History of Western Philosophy* (London, 1946). Even Ernst Mach is not mentioned.
7. Cf. Jean Nicod, "Les Tendences philosophiques de M. Bertrand Russell," *Revue de mét. et de mor.*, XXIX (1922), 77.
8. Concerning Mach's relation to logical empiricism see R. von Mises, "Ernst Mach und die empiristische Wissenschaftsauffassung," *Einheitswissenschaft* ("Library of Unified Science," No. 7 ['s Gravenhage, 1938]).
9. B. Russell, *Our Knowledge of the External World as a Field for Scientific Method in Philosophy* (Chicago, 1914), chap. ii.
10. *Ibid.*
11. B. Russell, "Logical Atomism," *Contemporary British Philosophy: Personal Statements, First Series* (London and New York, 1924), p. 363.
12. Russell, *Our Knowledge*, p. 112.
13. *Ibid.*, p. 111.
14. *Ibid.*, p. 78.
15. *Ibid.*, p. 89.
16. *Ibid.*, pp. 111–12.
17. G. E. Moore, *Principia ethica* (Cambridge, 1903), p. ix.
18. See, e.g., R. B. Braithwaite, "Philosophy", in *Cambridge University Studies*, VII (1933), pp. 1–32.
19. Russell's Introduction to Wittgenstein, *Tractatus* (London, 1922), p. 8.
20. H. M. Sheffer, "A Set of Five Independent Postulates for Boolean Algebras, with Application to Logical Constants," *Trans. Amer. Math. Soc.*, XIV (1913), 488–89.
21. Cf. Russell's Introduction to *Tractatus*, pp. 13–15.
22. Carnap, *Scheinprobleme*, pp. 27–29.
23. Carnap, *Der logische Aufbau der Welt*, p. 2.
24. *Ibid.*, p. 47.
25. *Ibid.*, pp. 57–58.
26. *Ibid.*, p. 65.
27. *Ibid.*, p. 74.

Notes and Bibliography

28. Ibid., p. 139.
29. Ibid., p. 79.
30. Ibid., p. 80.
31. Ibid., p. 86.
32. Ibid., p. 87.
33. Ibid., p. 92.
34. Ibid., pp. 93–104.
35. Ibid., p. 102.
36. Ibid., pp. 109–10.
37. Ibid., p. 133.
38. Ibid., p. 23.
39. Ibid., p. 169.
40. Ibid., p. 176.
41. Ibid., pp. 186–87.
42. Ibid., p. 202.
43. Ibid., p. 204.
44. Ibid.
45. Ibid., pp. 245–55.

46. A brief survey of the first stages of this internal criticism will be found in A. Petzäll, *Logistischer Positivismus* ("Göteborgs Högskolas Årsskrift," Vol. XXXVII Göteborg, [1931]). Incidentally, it may be noted that the first thoroughgoing criticism of Carnap's *Der logische Aufbau der Welt* was advanced by another Scandinavian philosopher, Eino Kaila, who, like Petzäll, had studied in Vienna, in his penetrating essay, *Der logistische Positivismus: Eine kritische Studie* (Turku, 1930). Kaila later gave valuable contributions to certain parts of the theory of constitution in his *Das System der Wirklichkeitsbegriffe* (Helsingfors, 1936) and his *Den mänskliga Kunskapen* ("Human Knowledge") (Helsingfors, 1939). A comprehensive critical study which also considers the later development of the movement is J. R. Weinberg's *An Examination of Logical Positivism* (London, 1936).

Chapter II

1. M. Schlick, "The Future of Philosophy," *Seventh International Congress of Philosophy, Oxford, 1930* (Oxford, 1931), p. 112. A more detailed discussion under the same title, "The Future of Philosophy," was published in *Publications in Philosophy*, ed. P. A. Schilpp, Vol. I (College of the Pacific, 1932). This lecture was reprinted in *Gesammelte Aufsätze* (Vienna, 1938) and in *Basic Problems of Philosophy*, ed. D. J. Bronstein et al. (New York, 1947).
2. "The Future of Philosophy," p. 115.
3. Ibid., p. 116.
4. See *Erkenntnis* I (1930), 72.
5. H. Reichenbach, *Relativitätstheorie und Erkenntnis apriori* (Berlin, 1920), p. 71.
6. H. Reichenbach, "Logistic Empiricism in Germany and the Present State of Its Problems," *Journal of Philosophy*, XXXIII (1936), 114.
7. Reichenbach, *Relativitätstheorie und Erkenntnis apriori*, p. 74.
8. Reichenbach, *Philosophie der Raum-Zeit-Lehre*, p. 45.
9. Ibid., pp. 205–6.
10. Reichenbach, *Ziele und Wege der heutigen Naturphilosophie* (Leipzig, 1931), pp. 38–39.
11. Reichenbach, *Wahrscheinlichkeitslehre* (Leiden, 1935), p. 381.
12. Ibid., p. 387.
13. Reichenbach, "Logistic Empiricism," p. 157; cf. also his *Experience and Prediction*, p. 363.
14. See Reichenbach, *Wahrscheinlichkeitslehre*, p. 305, and his *Experience and Prediction*, p. 363.
15. Reichenbach, "Logistic Empiricism," pp. 158–59.

Notes and Bibliography

16. Cf. Ajdukiewicz, "Der logistische Antiirrationalismus in Polen," *Erkenntnis*, V, 151; and Rose Rand, "Kotarbinski's Philosophie auf Grund seines Hauptwerkes: 'Elemente der Erkenntnistheorie, der Logik und der Methodologie der Wissenschaften,'" *Erkenntnis*, VII, 92. See also Z. Jordan's book (Postscript).
17. See, e.g., C. Morris, "Some Aspects of Recent American Scientific Philosophy," *Erkenntnis*, V, 142.
18. C. S. Peirce, "How To Make Our Ideas Clear," *Popular Science Monthly*, January, 1878, here quoted from Peirce, *Chance, Love, and Logic: Philosophical Essays* (London, 1923), p. 45.
19. P. W. Bridgman, *The Logic of Modern Physics* (New York, 1927), pp. 5-7; see also two articles by Herbert Feigl on operationism and explanation in *Psychological Review*, LII, 195; reprinted in *Readings in Philosophical Analysis* (see Postscript).
20. C. Morris, "The Concept of Meaning in Pragmatism and Logical Positivism," *Actes du huitième congrès international de philosophie à Prague, 2–7 septembre, 1934* (Prague, 1936), p. 133.
21. C. Morris, *Logical Positivism, Pragmatism, and Scientific Empiricism* (Paris, 1937), p. 65. Morris has recently given a comprehensive exposition of his semiotic in *Signs, Language, and Behavior* (New York, 1946).
22. See, e.g., K. Marc-Wogau's article, "Uppsala Filosofien och den logiska Empirismen," *Ord och Bild* (1944), p. 30, where similarities and differences between the two movements have been clearly stated.
23. In *Philosophy of Science*, I (1934), 5.
24. Published in a revised and enlarged English translation entitled *The Logical Syntax of Language* (1936). In his *Die Aufgabe der Wissenshaftslogik* (in the collection "Einheitswissenschaft," No. 3 [1934]) and in his London lectures, *Philosophy and Logical Syntax* (London, 1935), Carnap has given more popular expositions of his theory.
25. Carnap, *Logical Syntax of Language* (London, 1937), pp. 51–52.
26. Carnap, *Philosophy and Logical Syntax*, pp. 47–49.
27. *Ibid.*, p. 56.
28. This point of view Carnap had already advanced in his article, "Die physikalische Sprache als Universalsprache der Wissenschaft," *Erkenntnis*, II (1931), 432.
29. Carnap, *Philosophy and Logical Syntax*, pp. 81–82.
30. *Ibid.*, pp. 80–81.
31. O. Neurath, "Soziologie im Physikalismus," *Erkenntnis*, II (1931), 403; cf. also O. Neurath, "Physikalismus," *Scientia*, 1931, p. 299.
32. M. Schlick, "Über das Fundament der Erkenntnis," *Erkenntnis*, IV (1933), 96–97.
33. *Ibid.*, p. 98.
34. O. Neurath, "Radikaler Physikalismus und 'wirkliche Welt,'" *Erkenntnis*, IV (1933), 361.
35. *Ibid.*, p. 356.
36. *Ibid.*, p. 352.
37. O. Neurath, "Protokollsätze," *Erkenntnis*, III (1932), 206.
38. In *Analysis*, II (1935), 49.
39. *Ibid.*, p. 93.
40. K. Popper, *Logik der Forschung* (Vienna, 1935), p. 9.
41. M. Schlick, "Die Kausalität in der gegenwärtigen Physik," *Naturwissenschaften*, XIX (1931), 156.

Notes and Bibliography

42. Popper, *Logik der Forschung*, p. 13.
43. Published in *Philosophy of Science*, III (1936), 419, and IV (1937), 1.
44. R. Carnap, "Wahrheit und Bewährung," *Actes du congrès international de philosophie scientifique, Paris, 1935* (Paris, 1936), IV, 19.
45. *Philosophy of Science*, III, 20-21.
46. This question was discussed later in detail by C. G. Hempel in his "A Purely Syntactical Definition of Confirmation," *Journal of Symbolic Logic*, Vol. VIII (1943), and in "Studies in the Logic of Confirmation," *Mind*, LIV (1945), 1 and 97.
47. *Philosophy of Science*, IV, 33.
48. *Ibid.*, p. 34.
49. *Ibid.*
50. *Ibid.*, pp. 34-35. As to the view here mentioned, see also C. G. Hempel, "Le Problème de la vérité," *Theoria*, 1937, p. 206.
51. See, e.g., O. Neurath, *Empirische Soziologie: Der wissenschaftliche Gehalt der Geschichte und Nationalökonomie* (Vienna, 1931), p. 2.
52. O. Neurath, *Einheitswissenschaft und Psychologie* (Vienna, 1933), p. 7.
53. O. Neurath, "Soziologie im Physikalismus," *Erkenntnis*, II (1931), 395.
54. R. Carnap, *Philosophy and Logical Syntax*, p. 89.
55. R. Carnap, "Die physikalische Sprache als Universalsprache der Wissenschaft," *Erkenntnis*, II (1931), 441-42.
56. *Ibid.*, p. 445.
57. *Ibid.*, p. 447.
58. *Ibid.*
59. See, e.g., C. G. Hempel, "Analyse logique de la psychologie," *Revue de synthèse*, X (1935), 27; and R. Carnap, "Les Concepts psychologiques et les concepts physiques sont-ils foncièrement différentes?" *Revue de synthèse*, X (1935), 43.
60. R. Carnap, "Testability and Meaning," *Philosophy of Science*, III, 434.
61. Carnap, "Einheit der Wissenschaft durch Einheit der Sprache," *Travaux du IX⁰ congrès international de philosophie* (Paris, 1937), IV, 54. Cf. Carnap, "Ueber die Einheitssprache der Wissenschaft: Logische Bemerkungen zum Projekt einer Enzyklopädie," *Actes du congrès international de philosophie scientifique* (Paris, 1936), II, 60.
62. Carnap, "Einheit der Wissenschaft," p. 57.
63. I could imagine, for instance, that one might go so far as to give up intersubjectivity and accordingly admit sentences as meaningful, if only they are introspectively testable (and so not mere sound-complexes with no designations) or, at any rate, introspective sentences that agree to such an extent as to fulfil the requirements generally made by psychologists for the admittance of their universal validity in psychology. In case a criterion of meaning as liberal as this is accepted, logical behaviorism will no longer be a necessary condition of such extended unity of science but merely a special means of testing, side by side with introspection. However, actual metaphysical sentences of untestable entities would be excluded as meaningless.
64. Cf. R. Carnap, *Logical Foundations of the Unity of Science*, in *Encyclopedia of Unified Science*, I, No. 1 (Chicago, 1938), 60-62.
65. Here quoted from a separate print distributed at the congress. A similar reaction to the prevalent formal-syntactical view came simultaneously to expression in J. Joergensen's "Reflexions on Logic and Language. I. Languages, Games, and Empiricism; II. Semantical Logic," *Journal of Unified Science (Erkenntnis)*, VIII (1939), 218.

Postscript

By Norman M. Martin

World War II caused considerable disturbance in the movement of logical empiricism. Most of the European philosophers survived, and many of them left the Continent for Great Britain or the United States. Hosiasson and Lindenbaum died in Poland; Kurt Grelling and Karl Reach were deported by the Nazis and died or were killed. The *Journal of Unified Science* and the "Library of Unified Science" were discontinued because of the war. The work on the *International Encyclopedia of Unified Science* was hampered, although a number of monographs were issued (see chap. ii, part 1).

The war did not, however, put an end to the work of the logical empiricists. On the contrary, this work continued along several lines. The Sixth International Congress for the Unity of Science was held at the University of Chicago, September 2–6, 1941. Some of the main topics were the unification of science, the theory of signs, psychology, and valuation. Since then no congresses have been held.

Considerable progress has been made in semantics. Especially important here are the contributions of Carnap. His *Introduction to Semantics* (Cambridge: Harvard University Press, 1942) presents the problems involved in the construction of semantical systems, especially with the construction of L-concepts, i.e., concepts which are applicable on merely logical reasons as opposed to factual reasons, and with the relations between syntax and semantics. He there explains in detail how he would modify the views expressed in his *Logical Syntax of Language*. Further attention to the relation between semantics and syntax is paid in Carnap's *Formalization of Logic* (Cambridge: Harvard University Press, 1943). By "formalization" is meant the construction of a syntactical concept which applies whenever a given semantical concept applies in any semantical system which is a true interpretation of the constructed calculus. For example,

Postscript

C-implication (derivability) in logical syntax is intended as a formalization of L-implication. The problem of the book is whether the calculi common today are full formalizations of logic and, if not, whether such a formalization can be made. Carnap shows that the usual propositional calculus is not a full formalization of propositional logic but that, with the introduction of a new type of syntactical concept called "junctives," a full formalization can be achieved. Similar results hold for functional logic.

In *Meaning and Necessity* (Chicago: University of Chicago Press, 1947) Carnap suggests the substitution of the method of extension and intension for the method of the name-relation, which had dominated earlier semantical discussion. By this method, instead of considering an expression as the name of an entity, it would be considered to have an intension and an extension; e.g., the predicate 'red' has the property of being red as its intension and the class of red things as its extension. Carnap proposes to use the concepts of intension and extension, which occurred now and again in the old logic, as key concepts in semantical analysis. He discusses the possibility of an adequate extensional metalanguage for semantics and finds it, in general, possible, although there are some doubtful features. He also outlines a system of modal logic which he constructs in greater detail in "Modalities and Quantification," *Journal of Symbolic Logic*, XI (1946), 33–64.

Several interesting contributions to semantic theory are contained in the "Symposium on Meaning and Truth" which appeared in Volumes IV (1944) and V (1945) of *Philosophy and Phenomenological Research*. C. I. Lewis, in "Modes of Meaning" (*ibid.*, Vol. IV), gives an analysis of language similar in many respects to the intension-extension distinction made by Carnap. He distinguishes (as terms): denotation—the class of all actual things to which a term applies; comprehension—the class of all consistently thinkable things to which a term applies; connotation—which is identified with a correct definition of the term; and signification—the comprehensive character such that everything that has that character is correctly namable by the term.

Postscript

Analogous distinctions are made for sentences. G. Watts Cunningham, in "On the Linguistic Meaning-Situation" (*ibid.*, Vol. IV), attempts to specify the limits of conventionalism in semantics by asserting that, while the words and rules of syntax of a language are conventional, the syntactical structure is determined by the referent. Felix Kaufmann, in "Verification, Meaning, and Truth" (*ibid.*, Vol. IV), attempts to define truth in terms of agreement with the rules of scientific procedure—a position not unlike that of Neurath. C. J. Ducasse, in "Propositions, Truth, and the Ultimate Criterion of Truth" (*ibid.*, Vol. IV), defends the view that ultimate "undisbelievability" is the criterion of truth. Alfred Tarski, in "The Semantic Conception of Truth" (*ibid.*, Vol. IV), presents in English the main features of the definition of truth which he had presented earlier in Polish and German; he clarifies the nature of this concept and defends his views against his critics. Norman Dalkey, in "The Limits of Meaning" (*ibid.*, Vol. IV), gives an analysis of vagueness, pointing out three elements which he terms "confusion," "obscurity," and "incomplete determination." These views were discussed by the symposiasts and by Ernest Nagel, who came out strongly against Ducasse's formulations, in later issues of the journal.

Another significant line of work, which was pursued throughout the war years, was the analysis of science. A collection of articles by Philipp Frank, dating from 1908 to 1938, which dealt with the philosophy of physics was published under the name *Between Physics and Philosophy* (Cambridge: Harvard University Press, 1941). Felix Kaufmann presented his theory of scientific procedure in *Methodology of the Social Sciences* (New York: Oxford University Press, 1944). He emphasizes particularly the reliance of scientific procedure on rules (often implicit) of procedure. Thus, for him, the reversibility of the decision to accept a proposition into the body of knowledge (the principle of permanent control) and the necessity of having grounds for the acceptance of a proposition are extremely important. Rules of scientific procedure may in his opinion be changed, but only in connection with "rules of higher order." In line with this ap-

Postscript

proach, Kaufmann discusses methodological issues, first of empirical science in general, and then, in particular, of problems in social science, such as value-statements, behaviorism, and the nature of social law.

Another important work is Hans Reichenbach's *Philosophical Foundations of Quantum Mechanics*, in which he discusses the mathematics of quantum mechanics and the problems of its interpretation, suggesting that a three-valued logic is more suitable for this purpose than the usual two-valued logic. Quantum mechanics can be formulated in one of three ways, in a wave language, a corpuscle language, or a neutral (three-valued) language. In the first two, sentences expressing causal anomalies appear. These do not appear in the neutral language; however, sentences about interphenomena do appear when this language is used.

In *Elements of Symbolic Logic* (New York: Macmillan Co., 1947) Reichenbach attempts to characterize the logic of scientific laws. He does this with the help of the concept of "original nomological statement," which he defines as "an all-statement that is demonstrably true, fully exhaustive, and universal." Then he is able to describe the common character of all laws. In the same book he also gives an analysis of grammar from the standpoint of modern logic.

An interesting contribution to the logical analysis of science is "Studies in the Logic of Explanation," by Carl G. Hempel and Paul Oppenheim, in *Philosophy of Science*, XV (1948), 135–75. Hempel and Oppenheim attempt to examine explanation by looking at the conditions that the explanans must fulfil. The principal requirements are: the explanandum must be a logical consequence of the explanans; the explanans must contain general laws, and these must actually be required in the derivation of the explanandum; the explanans must be capable, at least in principle, of test by experiment or observation, and the sentences constituting the explanans must be true. The authors hold that these criteria are general throughout science. In this connection they discuss the concept of "emergence," concluding that it must be purged of its connotations of absolute unpredictability. In line with these views they construct a precise logical theory of explanation.

A great deal of discussion on the philosophy of probability has occurred. In the "Symposium on Probability" which took place in *Philosophy and Phenomenological Research*, Volumes V (1945) and VI (1946), Donald Williams defends the Laplacean conception, which was attacked from a frequency point of view by Reichenbach, von Mises, and Margenau. Carnap, in "The Two Concepts of Probability" (*ibid.*, Vol. V [1945], 513-32), defends the view that there are actually two distinct concepts used under the name of "probability," both of which have a right to scientific treatment. The first of these concepts is sometimes also called "degree of confirmation," the second, "relative frequency in the long run." Carnap then illustrates at length the differences in logical nature between the two concepts. The first of these concepts is a semantical one dealing with relations between sentences; the second is an empirical concept. A basic sentence of the first is true by logic alone and one of the second by virtue of the facts. In "On Inductive Logic," *Philosophy of Science*, XII (1945), 72-97, Carnap elaborated his system of probability in the sense of degree of confirmation. The exposition of his system of inductive logic will constitute the bulk of his forthcoming two-volume work, *Probability and Induction*. Felix Kaufmann held, in "Scientific Procedure and Probability," in *Philosophy and Phenomenological Research*, VI (1945), 47-66, that degree of confirmation should be defined in terms of the process of accepting propositions into the body of accepted knowledge. For this reason he wants to distinguish sharply between the confirmation of a proposition not yet accepted and the corroboration of one already accepted. An alternative definition of degree of confirmation to that offered by Carnap was presented by Hempel and Oppenheim in "A Definition of 'Degree of Confirmation,'" *Philosophy of Science*, XII (1945), 98-115, and by Olaf Helmer and Oppenheim in "A Syntactical Definition of Probability and Degree of Confirmation," *Journal of Symbolic Logic*, X (1945), 25-60. This definition is of particular interest, since, when so defined, the degree of confirma-

Postscript

tion function is not a probability function, i.e., it does not have all the mathematical properties commonly associated with probability in mathematical theory. In the discussions centering around the symposium on probability, Nagel and Bergmann participated actively.

In addition to the above-mentioned works on more or less specific topics, several works of a more general nature on the theory of signs and theory of value were written by logical empiricists. Russell wrote *An Inquiry into Meaning and Truth* (New York: W. W. Norton & Co., 1940), in which he defends a causal theory of language. He holds the view that the proper individuals of an epistemologically correct language are universals. He maintains the necessity of basic propositions, i.e., propositions which are caused (and justified) by perception and which are known to be true. He defends the correspondence theory of truth against Dewey's "warranted assertibility" and similar opinions. Russell also published *A History of Western Philosophy and Its Connections with Political and Social Circumstances* (New York: Simon & Schuster, 1945), in which he attempts to analyze the major philosophers from the standpoint of the philosophy of logical analysis. In addition, Russell wrote *Human Knowledge: Its Scope and Limits* (New York: Simon & Schuster, 1948), in which he deals with problems of epistemology, semiotic, and the philosophy of science. For the first time he deals with the problem of probability; he holds that scientific inference needs some statement of the inductive principle which would be a synthetic statement but could not be established by any argument from experience. He concludes from his general study of knowledge that empiricism is not an adequate theory of knowledge, although less inadequate than previous theories. He also holds that these inadequacies can be discovered by adherence to the doctrine that "all human knowledge is uncertain, inexact and partial."

Charles Morris wrote *Paths of Life* (New York: Harper & Bros., 1942), in which he analyzes the principal patterns of value-preferences and suggests, as a possible means of uniting them in dynamic interaction, one which involves features of all

Postscript

of them. *The Open Self* (New York: Prentice-Hall, 1948) continues his empirical study of value-patterns. In *Signs, Language, and Behavior* (New York: Prentice-Hall, 1946) Morris analyzes meaning-phenomena at length. He distinguishes four modes of signifying: the designative (e.g., "the coin is round"), the appraisive (e.g., "the coin is good"), the prescriptive (e.g., "Come here"), and the formative (e.g., "the coin is a coin"). In addition, four uses of language (informative, valuative, incitive, and systemic) are distinguished. On the basis of these distinctions Morris classifies types of discourse. His point of departure is behavioral (more in the sense of Tolman and Mead than of Watson), and one of his principal results is the formulation of the theory of signs, or semiotic, in behavioral terms. He considers at length the importance and role of signs in individual and social life.

Another important contribution to the theory of meaning is C. I. Lewis' *Analysis of Knowledge and Valuation* (La Salle, Ill.: Open Court Publishing Co., 1946). Lewis begins with a general theory of meaning derived from Peirce, together with the distinction between empirical and analytic statements: the analytic ones are those which relate to meanings alone. Empirical sentences are of three types: first, expressive statements, which express an experience directly and which are, therefore, indubitable to the one who utters them, although they may be false in the case of a lying report—they are thus much like Schlick's substantiations; second, terminating judgments, which make predictions concerning experience specific as to time and place; and, finally, nonterminating judgments, which make predictions concerning experience general as to time and place. Lewis analyzes all knowledge into these types of empirical and analytic sentences. He also presents an analysis of value-sentences so that they are a species of empirical sentence.

Another study concerning the nature of valuation is Charles L. Stevenson's *Ethics and Language* (New Haven: Yale University Press, 1944). Stevenson attempts to distinguish between differences in belief and differences in attitude; valuational statements are analyzed into cognitive and prescriptive com-

Postscript

ponents (e.g., 'this is good' is interpreted as 'I approve of this, do so likewise'), and it is maintained that ethical differences are ultimately differences in attitude rather than in belief.

Within the "Library of Living Philosophers," edited by Paul A. Schilpp, two volumes were published under the titles of *The Philosophy of G. E. Moore* (Evanston: Northwestern University, 1942) and *The Philosophy of Bertrand Russell* (Evanston: Northwestern University, 1944). Each of these volumes contains a series of descriptive and critical essays by several authors, together with a reply by the philosopher concerned, and a complete bibliography. Among the contributors are C. D. Broad, C. L. Stevenson, Paul Marhenke, C. M. Langford, John Wisdom, Susan Stebbing, Hans Reichenbach, Kurt Gödel, Max Black, and Ernest Nagel.

An excellent summary of the work done by the Polish groups is presented in *The Development of Mathematical Logic and Logical Positivism in Poland between the Two Wars*, by Z. Jordan (New York: Oxford University Press, 1945). A good summary of the position of logical empiricism, including a selected bibliography of empiricist publications, can be found in Herbert Feigl's article on "Logical Empiricism," in *Twentieth Century Philosophy: Living Schools of Thought*, edited by Dagobert D. Runes (New York: Philosophical Library, 1943). This article and many others by writers of the logical-empiricist movement are reprinted in *Readings in Philosophical Analysis*, edited by Herbert Feigl and Wilfrid Sellars (New York: Appleton-Century-Crofts, 1949). This volume contains sections on semantics, confirmability, logic and mathematics, the a priori, induction and probability, logical analysis of philosophy, philosophy of science and ethics, from viewpoints allied to logical empiricism. Among the authors included, in addition to the editors, are Quine, Tarski, Frege, Russell, Carnap, Lewis, Schlick, Ajdukiewicz, Nagel, Waismann, Hempel, Broad, Ducasse, Reichenbach, and Stevenson, as well as a number of other empiricist philosophers.

The "Discussion on the Unity of Science," in which, among others, Neurath, Morris, and Horace Kallen participated, ap-

Postscript

peared in *Philosophy and Phenomenological Research*, Volume VI. In 1946, *Synthèse*, an international journal published in Holland, resumed the publication of its "Unity of Science Forum," which had been edited by Neurath until his death in 1945. *Analysis*, which represents, largely, the British analytic philosophers, has also resumed publication.

The movement of logical empiricism, having developed during the war even under unfavorable conditions, is now further expanding its activities.

EDITORS' NOTE: Since the Postscript written by Norman M. Martin early in 1949 a number of developments deserve notice. Among recent publications relevant to the field of this monograph, the following books may be mentioned: M. Black, *Language and Philosophy* (Ithaca: Cornell University Press, 1949); R. Carnap, *Logical Foundations of Probability* (Chicago: University of Chicago Press, 1950)—this is the first volume of the two-volume work, *Probability and Induction;* P. Frank, *Relativity—a Richer Truth* (Boston: Beacon Press, 1950); P. Frank, *Modern Science and Its Philosophy* (Cambridge: Harvard University Press, 1949)—this is an expanded version of his former work, *Between Physics and Philosophy;* A. Pap, *Elements of Analytic Philosophy* (New York: Macmillan Co., 1949); H. Reichenbach, *Theory of Probability* (Berkeley: University of California Press, 1949); P. Schilpp (ed.), *Albert Einstein: Philosopher-Scientist* (Evanston, Ill.: Library of Living Philosophers, 1949). A new journal, *Philosophical Studies*, edited by H. Feigl and W. Sellars, began publication in 1949 (Minneapolis: University of Minnesota).

Space does not permit reference to the recent developments of the philosophy of science in other countries, but the names of some new journals can at least be mentioned: *Methodos* (Italy); *Analisi* (Italy); *Sigma* (Italy); *Science of Thought* (Japan, and in Japanese); *British Journal for the Philosophy of Science*. The *Revue internationale de philosophie* devoted a special issue to logical empiricism (Vol. IV [1950]). There are articles by B. Russell, R. Carnap, C. G. Hempel, H. Feigl, and M. Barzin; and a

Postscript

selected bibliography of 216 items prepared by H. Feigl. There has just been received a book by V. Kraft, *Der Wiener Kreis: Der Ursprung des Neopositivismus* (Wien: Springer, 1950).

The Institute for the Unity of Science was incorporated in 1949 with Philipp Frank, of Harvard University, as president of the Board of Trustees. A grant from the Rockefeller Foundation made this incorporation possible. The *International Encyclopedia of Unified Science* will henceforth be owned and directed by the Institute for the Unity of Science. The Institute has been furnished quarters by the American Academy of Arts and Sciences, 28 Newbury Street, Boston 16, Massachusetts.

FUNDERBURG LIBRARY
MANCHESTER COLLEGE

**WITHDRAWN
from
Funderburg Library**

Special thanks to Jack Kolodny and Karl Weber.
Illustrations by Vicki Bocash.

The Art of Profitability by Adrian Slywotzky
Copyright ©2002 Mercer Management Consulting, Inc.

All rights reserved. No part of this book may be reproduced or transmitted in any form or by any means, electronic or mechanical, including photocopying, recording, or by any information storage and retrieval system, without permission in writing from Mercer Management Consulting.

Printed in the U.S.A.

MERCER
Management Consulting

The Art of Profitability

Adrian Slywotzky

Contents

Prologue 4
Lesson 1: Customer Solution Profit 10
Lesson 2: Pyramid Profit 16
Lesson 3: Multi-Component Profit 22
Lesson 4: Switchboard Profit 30
Lesson 5: Time Profit 38
Lesson 6: Blockbuster Profit 46
Lesson 7: Profit-Multiplier Model 56
Lesson 8: Entrepreneurial Profit 61
Lesson 9: Specialist Profit 68
Lesson 10: Installed Base Profit 74
Lesson 11: De Facto Standard Profit 78
Lesson 12: Brand Profit 83
Lesson 13: Specialty Product Profit 90
Lesson 14: Local Leadership Profit 95
Lesson 15: Transaction Scale Profit 102
Lesson 16: Value Chain Position Profit 108
Lesson 17: Cycle Profit 111
Lesson 18: After-Sale Profit 119
Lesson 19: New Product Profit 124
Lesson 20: Relative Market Share Profit 133
Lesson 21: Experience Curve Profit 140
Lesson 22: Low-Cost Business Design Profit .145
Lesson 23: Digital Profit 149
List of readings 156

Request to the Reader

Please read only one chapter per week. (One visit a week with my friend Zhao is more than enough.) Think about it a bit. Let it stew. Play with the ideas. Then go on to the next chapter.

. . .

> The pathway to profitability?
> It lies in fully understanding the customer.

. . .

Profit from the Art

As you read, continually re-focus on the implications for your organization. Make notes. Discuss with colleagues. Here are some questions to get started:

π How does profit happen for my company? For my competitors?

π How well do all my people understand our profit models? Is the organization aligned to help capitalize on them?

π Are there new profit models that we could apply to improve profitability?

π Which of our current initiatives could improve our profitability and should be accelerated? Which may actually impair it, and should be discontinued?

π Which specific actions can my organization take in the next ninety days to improve our profit position?

Prologue

September 21. Steve Gardner sat quietly in a forty-sixth floor office in downtown Manhattan.

The room was silent except for the steady tick of an antique rosewood clock hanging on the wall. It was 8:15 on a Saturday morning, and the offices of Storm and Fellows were nearly deserted. Steve himself would normally have been asleep at this hour, or perhaps sipping a first cup of coffee while skimming the *Times* at the kitchen table in his cramped Soho apartment. Despite four and a half years of working in "the real world" at the midtown headquarters of a multinational conglomerate, he'd never fully shaken the nightowl lifestyle of his undergraduate days, to which he happily reverted on weekends and holidays.

But today was different. Early Saturday morning, he'd been told, would be his only opportunity to meet David Zhao—"the man who understood how profit happens." Through determined effort and a lucky connection or two, Steve had worked his way to the fringe of one of the circles in which Zhao was known. So he'd not only heard of David Zhao but also had some inkling of the unique knowledge that Zhao possessed.

Suddenly the office door opened, and Steve rose to greet him.

"Good morning, Steve. I'm David Zhao. Thanks for accommodating me by coming here at this hour. It's quiet, and I find the view conducive to doing a little bit of thinking. I see you like it, too." He gestured toward Steve's chair, which had been turned from its place alongside the massive ornate oak desk to face the harbor view square-on.

Steve smiled. He quickly decided he liked this man. Zhao was a small, slender, slightly rumpled figure in a brown check jacket, khaki trousers, and battered loafers, resembling more a history professor at some little New England college than an astute businessman. His round face, topped by an unruly longish mop of coarse hair more gray than black, seemed almost unlined until he smiled, when a network of fine creases suddenly radiated from his deep brown eyes.

"It's a great view," Steve agreed. "But I'm surprised you have an office here at Storm and Fellows. I didn't know you were a lawyer."

Zhao laughed. He took his seat behind the desk, and Steve pulled up his own chair. "Not exactly," Zhao remarked. "It so happens I have a law degree from a previous life, but I don't practice law any more. I consult to Storm and Fellows on industry structure and other business issues related to anti-trust law. Frankly, it's a wonderful arrangement. They let me have this spectacular office, they pay me handsomely, and they basically leave me alone most of the time. But when they call on me—even if it's only once or twice a month—I have to be very, very good. Tens of millions—sometimes hundreds of millions—are at stake."

Steve was intrigued by Zhao's apparent openness. He gave the impression of being unguarded, completely at ease with himself. *Maybe I would be, too,* thought Steve wryly, *if I worked only a couple of times a month. What a deal!*

"You look impressed," Zhao commented. (*Am I that easy to read?* Steve wondered.) "You shouldn't be. I'm fortunate in being able to spend most of my time focusing on what interests me most."

"What interests you most?" asked Steve.

"Oh, a few things. For example, investing. When I left the research firm, they handed me a very nice nest egg. I realized I'd better figure out what to do with it—for the benefit of my wife and kids, if nothing else. So I made myself a student of the discipline of investing, and only recently have I graduated to some reasonable level of proficiency. It was both harder and more rewarding than I anticipated—and, oddly enough, I'm not talking about money."

"Is that right?" Steve asked. "How long did you feel clueless?"

"Out of ten years that I've been studying investing, I was lost for the first nine."

Steve laughed. "Not a job for the impatient, eh?"

Zhao smiled quietly. "You could say that."

"Why did it take so long? Doesn't investing use the same set of skills as business analysis?"

"That's a good question," Zhao responded. He was warming to Steve. "Look at it this way. Imagine a great lab scientist—a research cardiologist, let's say—a brilliant guy. Suppose that one day you learn you need a triple coronary by-pass. Are you going to let the lab guy perform the operation?"

"Never. I'd want a great surgeon—the more experienced the better."

"Naturally. Now, say the lab guy, who knows cardiology inside-out, decides to become a surgeon, because the compensation is ten times greater. How long do you think it would take him to learn?"

Steve pondered. *How long does a doctor's internship and residency usually last?* he wondered. He couldn't remember. "I don't know—five or six years?"

"Maybe. More like ten for my taste. I'm completely risk-averse, you know."

"I get it," Steve replied. He didn't really. He wondered where all this was leading. But for the moment, he felt happy to play along. "So what's the key to really mastering some new skill—like investing, say?"

"A ridiculous degree of persistence," Zhao answered. He paused, as if to mark a transition, and then leaned forward across the desk, looking closely at Steve. "So tell me," he said, "What brings you to see me today?"

Where to begin? "I heard your name at a cocktail party. Someone introduced me to a man named Otto Kerner. I told him I had to learn about profitability. And Mr. Kerner told me that if I wanted to learn about profit, I ought to meet you."

Zhao smiled. Kerner was Zhao's closest friend. A senior partner at Storm and Fellows, he was the person responsible for connecting Zhao to the firm. At age eighty-five, he still came into the office every day, even if only to spend half the afternoon chatting with Zhao. "I'm old enough to be Zhao's father," he liked to say to people at the firm who wondered about Zhao, "But when we talk, Zhao is the teacher and I'm the pupil. That's why we need him here at Storm and Fellows—he's my personal continuing education program."

"An introduction from Otto Kerner is like gold in my book," Zhao remarked. "But tell me—why?"

Steve was puzzled. "Why what?"

"Why do you have to learn profitability?"

Steve paused. A half dozen reasons were running through his mind. Why, indeed? He was tempted to say a couple of things, but he checked himself, realizing they were platitudes: *Because profit is the lifeblood of any organization . . . because the ultimate purpose of business is to create profits for shareholders . . .* Somehow, he sensed, the clichés he'd repeated in the workplace and even in business classes he was now taking at night, wouldn't work so well with David Zhao. He experienced an instant of panic, then consciously relaxed the tension that gripped him.

"It has to do with my job," he finally responded. "I work in strategic planning at Delmore, Inc." Steve glanced at Zhao, half-hoping for the raised-eyebrow look of respect he usually got when he mentioned the company name. But Zhao's expression betrayed nothing. Steve went on, "It's a big company with a great history, of course. And being in the planning department is a good opportunity for me. I get to look closely at all the various industries we're in, which is almost like getting a business-school education on the job. But as you probably know," he continued, "the company hasn't been doing very well lately. Profits are flat, and the stock price has been stagnant for about eighteen months."

"For two years, actually," Zhao remarked.

"I guess you're right," Steve said. "You must follow the stock."

"I find Delmore—*interesting* is the right word, I suppose," said Zhao. "And you're in strategic planning there. Tell me, Steve," he asked, "what sort of strategy do you plan?"

Was that an amused glint in Zhao's eye? "What I do is more like research—studying potential mergers, acquisitions, spin-offs—you know the sort of thing," he responded, immediately feeling that his answer sounded lame. "But I want to contribute more," he quickly added. "I want to learn how I can help the company get out of the doldrums. Does that make sense?"

"Why not?" Zhao answered. "But Delmore has been in business since 1904. It has revenues of $18 billion a year from forty different businesses. Surely the wise men and women who run the firm must know all about how to make profits? Or do you suppose they need Steve Gardner to teach them that?"

Steve reddened and sat for a moment in silence. He was thinking about some of the disturbing things he'd heard and seen around the offices at Delmore in the past six months. About the company-wide strategy conference, originally scheduled for April, that was first rescheduled twice, then postponed indefinitely, with no explanation as to why, causing rumors to swirl in the corridors . . . about the resignations that summer of three members of the executive committee, all within four weeks of one another. . . about the disparaging tone of recent comments by Wall Street analysts about Delmore, and the defensive tone of the company's public responses. And just this past week, people were whispering that the long-expected layoffs in three divisions would be a lot bigger than anticipated. Life at Delmore was feeling very different than it had when Steve joined the company.

Steve took a deep breath. "I guess I'm not necessarily convinced that the wise men and women at Delmore do know what profitability is all about," he finally admitted. He looked Zhao in the eye, wondering how Zhao would react.

Zhao merely turned his head slightly to stare more closely at Steve. A long moment passed. "Honesty," Zhao commented.

"Excuse me?"

"Honesty. I don't run into it very often."

Another pause, as Zhao stared through the glass wall, seemingly focused on a helicopter whirring across the water from New Jersey, nearly at a level with his own forty-sixth-floor perch.

Finally, he turned to Steve.

"If you really want to learn about profitability, I'm willing to teach you," he said. "But there are several conditions. First, we'll meet most Saturday mornings between now and next May. Second, every lesson will last exactly one hour. And I'll expect you to spend time between lessons reading and otherwise preparing. Is that acceptable?"

Steve bowed his head slightly. "Yes, it is."

"Are you doing anything other than working at Delmore? Moonlighting, or taking classes somewhere?"

"I *am* taking a night class this fall at NYU—financial management. I thought I'd take one or two courses a semester to help me decide whether to go on for an MBA. That's okay, right?" It had suddenly occurred to Steve that Zhao might consider him over-booked.

"It's fine," Zhao reassured him. "Your preparation time for me will be about four hours per week. I hope that works with your schedule?"

"I think so."

"Good. There's just one more thing. Did Otto tell you that I charge a fee?"

"No. How much is it?"

"A thousand dollars per lesson."

Steve sucked in his breath. Then his shoulders dropped, collapsing in defeat. He looked away, suddenly feeling frustrated and angry. He was tempted to speak his mind—or to simply storm out of the office, slamming the door behind him.

But instead, he simply said, quietly, "I can't afford that."

Zhao laughed, cutting the tension in the room. "Of course you can't," he replied. "You're a student. I'm not asking for the money now. You can pay the fee when you're able to—if you ever are."

Steve didn't know whether to feel relieved, embarrassed, or guilty. He thought about the usual four-digit balance in his bank account. "I might not be able to pay you for five or six years. Maybe longer."

"I know that," Zhao answered, a playful grin now spreading across his face. "Luckily for you, I've decided you're good for it."

Steve's mood turned to puzzlement and mild annoyance. Zhao, he vaguely felt, was being condescending, perhaps toying with him. *What makes Zhao think I'll ever pay him a penny?* he thought. *Maybe I'll take all his lessons, absorb all his ideas, then walk away and never see him again. That's probably what most people would do.*

"Do we have a deal?" Zhao asked.

Steve paused. "Yes, it's a deal," he found himself saying. Zhao reached across the desk, and the two men shook hands. And suddenly Steve sensed that he would never simply walk away from Zhao . . . that one day he would pay Zhao his total fee . . . and that Zhao had known all this before Steve himself did.

Zhao smiled as if he understood. "Very well then," he said. "Let's get started."

1
Customer Solution Profit

Zhao and Steve sat around the small table in the corner of Zhao's office. Zhao grabbed a yellow legal pad from his desk and placed it at the center of the table. In the upper right-hand corner of the top page, he wrote and circled the number 1.

"These pads have forty sheets," he remarked. "When the course is over, we should have two left."

Zhao reached into his jacket pocket and withdrew a sterling silver writing implement with which he drew three quick strokes and a zero, like this.

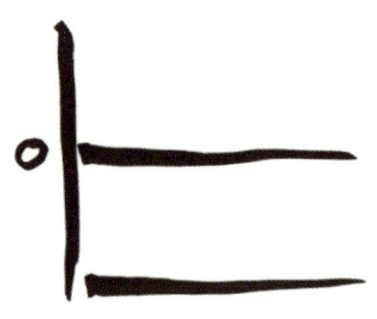

Zhao tossed the pad over to Steve and began to speak.

"I've thought a lot about profitability over the years, and studied a lot of companies that have found ways to achieve it. Hundreds of companies, no two exactly alike. Understanding the details that make a company unique is critical. It's easy to make general statements that sound convincing. But business consists of specific cases. What we need are general principles that are sturdy enough to fit specific cases. In thirty years, I think I've found a handful.

"Over the next several months, we're going to look at twenty-three ways a company can make a profit. I call them profit models. There's nothing sacrosanct about the number twenty-three. We could talk about twenty-four profit models, or maybe thirty. But for now, I've picked out twenty-three that I consider especially interesting and important. And one of the twenty-three is Customer Solution Profit.

"What's that?" Steve asked.

Zhao was about to reply, "Hold your horses," but he didn't. Instead, he paused a moment, then said, "Let me tell you a story. About Factset, a company in a very simple business. It sold financial information to money managers.

"The story starts in 1989. Back then, in my economic research days, I was working with a software company that got into the information business. They were a bunch of real rock-and-rolling financial buccaneers. They acquired a small firm—I'll call them Data House—that sold financial, corporate, and economic information to money managers, investment banks, corporate libraries, commercial banks, and professional service firms. Not a bad concept, but one that called for smart execution to generate consistent profits.

"Unfortunately, their execution was sloppy. After two years of thirty percent revenue increases, they found sales growth hitting the wall. Customers started churning, and profits plummeted. Eventually, the math got real simple. You didn't need a calculator to measure it: profitability was zero. The managers of the business broke up into warring camps, able to agree on nothing. The mood inside the company was becoming desperate. Then desperation turned into paralysis. Other than acrimonious debate, nothing much got done.

"Being around the company actually made me very uncomfortable. Conflict was everywhere, and I hate conflict. I was the facilitator at one meeting where three warring factions sat in separate corners, arms crossed, speaking to me and trying to ignore one another. When they did exchange words, they spat comments past each other rather than having a real conversation. Ever been in a meeting like that, Steve?"

Steve squirmed, recalling last Tuesday's budget session. Nor was last Tuesday unique. "A few times too many," Steve answered.

"Sorry to hear it. I hate those kinds of meetings—I just hate them.

"Then, at one of their strategy sessions, the marketing manager said something that captured my attention. She said, 'What I'd like to know is how those S.O.B.s at Factset have been able to out-compete us in the information business. What are they doing differently? How can they handle $24 million worth of business with a staff of thirty-six people, while we do $40 million with four hundred people?'"

"I sat up straight. 'Wow!' I thought, 'How can there be that huge a difference?' I realized that if we could answer that manager's question, we'd understand why Data House was in trouble, and what we could do about it.

"So I set out to find the answer. I interviewed dozens of customers to get a sense of how Factset operated. Piecing together fragments of information from all these conversations, I eventually put together a clear picture of how Factset had designed their business. Here's what I learned.

"The business information marketplace in which both Factset and my client, Data House, were operating involved close to a thousand major customers. But within that arena, to maintain a strong growth curve, Factset needed to capture only twenty new customers per year. Knowing this, they developed a powerful approach to make that happen.

"Once Factset identified a company as a potential customer for their information services, they'd send a team of two or three people to work there. They would spend two or three months, sometimes longer, learning everything they could about the customer—how they ran their business, how their systems worked (and didn't work), and what they really cared about. Based on this genuine knowledge of the customer, Factset then developed customized information products and services tailored to the specific characteristics and economics of the account. Once they landed the account, they spent a ton of time integrating their product into the customer's systems. During this process, Factset's revenues were tiny and their costs were huge. If you looked at a monthly P&L for a particular account, you'd see they were losing a ton of money. Costs of $10,000 might be charged against revenues of $3,000."

Zhao grabbed his yellow pad and pointed to the simple drawing he'd made. "See these lines?" he asked Steve. "These are two axes and a breakeven line."

"So the axes," Steve mused, "must represent time and profit."

"You're right," Zhao agreed. Then he handed the pencil to Steve. "Show me what Factset's profit curve looked like for the first three months of a typical new account."

Steve drew the curve. It was simple.

Zhao nodded. "That's it. But then things would begin to change. After three or four months, Factset's products would be woven into the daily flow of the customer's operations. Their software would be debugged and working fine. Now Factset didn't need three people working fulltime on the account. One person could maintain the service, probably part-time. And as the word spread among the client's employees about how powerful Factset's data was and how effectively Factset's service had been customized to their specific needs, they began taking more and more advantage of it. Factset's monthly costs fell from $10K to $8K, while monthly revenues started to grow, from $3K to $5K to $12K.

"Draw me what happened."

Steve thought for a moment, then drew a continuation of the curve.

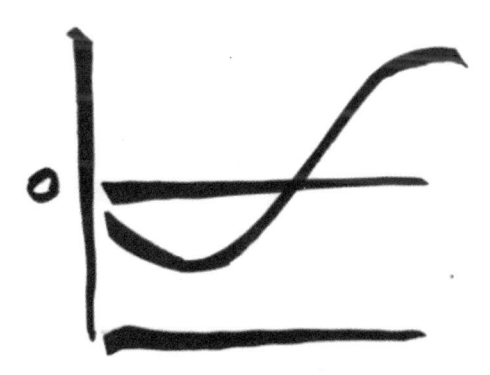

"You got it. That was the Factset secret. Beautifully simple, no?"

"I'll say. Did you tell your client?"

"Of course."

"Did they start to follow the Factset model?"

"They tried."

"And did it work?"

Zhao sighed. "You might say so. They went from losing money to a ten percent operating profit margin."

"So their profits rose from zero to $4 million?" Steve asked.

"Exactly right."

"What were Factset's margins?"

"How much do you think?"

"Hmm. Hand me that calculator."

"No, do it without the calculator," Zhao answered.

"Can I at least use pencil and paper?"

Zhao nodded.

Steve grabbed a pencil and began jotting down numbers. Let's see, he considered. Twenty-four million dollars in revenue generated by a staff of about forty people. How much would payroll costs be? These folks would probably be well paid. Some might make just sixty or seventy thousand, but a bunch would be in six figures. Steve seemed to recall hearing that benefits usually amounted to about fifty percent of salaries. So even well rewarded, the people would cost no more than, say, $200,000 apiece, counting salary, benefits, the whole nine yards. He multiplied. That makes eight million in payroll.

"How much would overhead be?" Steve wondered aloud.

"Use ten percent," Zhao suggested.

Okay, figure ten percent of revenue for overhead—$2.4 million. Then there would be licensing fees for the rights to the information being sold. Those might amount to another ten percent. Throw in a few more points for other costs... "I'll guess forty percent operating margin—about ten million bucks, all told."

Zhao smiled. "Very, very close."

"So Data House came nowhere near what Factset accomplished."

"That's true."

"I don't get it. You laid out the whole plan for them, didn't you? Are you saying that Data House didn't choose to follow the winning strategy, even after they *knew* it would work?"

"About right."

Steve shook his head. "Wow. I guess that must have been one of the worst organizations you've ever encountered. Did you ever work with any other company that simply refused to be successful?"

"Actually, it happens all the time. I can give you the complete recipe for the secret sauce, and the chances are good that you still won't use it."

"That's strange. Why visit the doctor, then ignore his advice?"

"It's a bit of a mystery. There's probably no one reason why people seem to prefer failure to success. We know that change can be psychologically threatening—that's part of the answer. In the case of Data House, they may have realized that following the Factset model would have taken a lot of hard work—much more than they were accustomed to. That's part of the answer, too. But I think the ultimate explanation is a simple one. To succeed in business, you have to have a genuine, honest-to-goodness interest in profitability. And most people don't." Zhao leaned back and spread his hands wide. "That's all there is to it."

Steve frowned. *Can that really be true?* he wondered. *It's hard to believe.* But then Steve thought about Delmore. Were all of the executives there truly interested in profitability? He remembered attending an off-site meeting with the leadership team of Delmore's paper-making division.

The division had been mired in a slow decline for over a year, as more and more of the market gradually shifted to competitors' more versatile products.

Yet, to judge by the contents of their discussions, most of the executives were focused on things the division was already doing well, whose impact on profits seemed to be small—incremental quality improvements and modest production efficiencies—rather than the needs of their customers. It was the kind of disturbing experience that had driven Steve to seek out Zhao's tutelage in the first place. *Maybe Zhao's right,* Steve mused. *Maybe some people in business just aren't very interested in profitability.*

Zhao sensed that he'd pushed Steve about as far as he could go in a single day. "That's all for now. Today's profit model was a simple one. But what is it, Steve? What's the *idea*?"

Steve thought for a moment. Then he said, "Invest time and energy in learning all there is to know about your customers. Then use that knowledge to create specific solutions for *them*. Lose money for a short time. Make money for a long time."

Zhao smiled. "You have it. But here's another question. Can you be profitable *without* knowing the customer?"

Steve hesitated. He thought about Delmore's paper division. The executives there didn't seem very clued in about their customers. . . but the division was still profitable, at least for the moment. "I think so," Steve finally answered, "but I'm not sure."

"Think about it," Zhao said. "Come back at the same time next Saturday. I'll have some breakfast for us. Bagels, juice, and coffee, okay?"

"Sure, fine."

"Great. We'll talk about pyramids."

"Pyramids—like in Egypt?"

"Not exactly."

"Any assignment?"

"Yes. Think about Factset's profit curve. And then think about where else the Customer Solution Profit model might apply. Make a list of the possibilities."

"Okay," Steve said. "But I don't think that'll take four hours."

Zhao chuckled. "Actually, it *could.*"

"Okay, I guess. See you next week."

"Right."

Steve left. Zhao went back to his desk and sat quietly for a few moments, gazing out the window. It was after nine o'clock, and a few of the firm's junior partners with Monday morning deadlines to meet could be heard stirring in the halls outside.

2
Pyramid Profit

September 28. It was raining—a drenching, miserable New York rain heavy with the chill of autumn. Three hours past dawn, the nearly empty streets were still almost as dark as night. At five minutes past eight, wet and feeling cold, Steve stuck his head into the doorway of Zhao's office. The overhead lights were off, leaving most of the office dark except for a warmly-lit circle of yellow light diffused by the brass lamp on Zhao's desk. Zhao was sitting there, dressed in the same check jacket he'd worn the week before, his head bent over a legal pad, eyes veiled with concentration as he wrote line after line in his meticulous black script, slowly, methodically, unpausing, gradually filling the page. It was fascinating to watch him working in such pure and unbroken silence.

Two minutes passed. Zhao reached the bottom of a page, flipped to another, and began to cover it with ink. Five minutes passed. Steve's eyes began to adjust to the near-darkness. He noticed the big windows streaked with moving rivulets of rain, and the faint gleam of the glass dial fronting the quietly ticking clock on the wall behind Zhao. Steve began to feel restless and a little embarrassed. When would Zhao come up for air? How much longer could he keep working without even a pause? Should Steve interrupt him? Would Zhao be annoyed to realize that Steve had been standing there, watching him, all that time?

Suddenly a gentle buzzer sounded. For the first time, Steve noticed the small, black Braun alarm clock at the corner of Zhao's desk. Zhao looked up, pressed down the off button on the clock, and noticed Steve.

"Come in! Sit down!" he greeted Steve, "It's good to see you." He rose and flicked a wall switch, filling the office with cool fluorescent light. The rain-gleaming windows turned into opaque walls in which the blurrily reflected images of Zhao and Steve and the office could barely be discerned.

"I didn't want to interrupt you—" Steve began to apologize.

"You didn't," Zhao laughed.

"Didn't you know I was here?" Steve asked, really curious.

Zhao pursed his lips and shrugged, in a half answer that was no answer. "Did you think about Factset and the Customer Solution Profit model?" he asked.

"Yes."

"Where can you apply it?"

"Practically everywhere, I think."

Zhao smiled. "As a matter of fact, you're right. Let me see your list."

Zhao studied Steve's list. It named five businesses.

Customer Solution Profit — potential applications:
Industrial plastics
Auto parts
Telecommunications equipment
Consumer financial services
Stock exchange

"No," Zhao remarked, "you can't do it on a stock exchange. A stock exchange is an auction, a pure auction. There's no relationship-building there."

Steve began to protest, but Zhao raised his hand for silence.

"This is good work. I want you to keep thinking about this, and next week bring me your list of situations where it will *not* work.

"By the way," Zhao added casually, as if it were merely a matter of idle curiosity, "is Delmore in any of the businesses you've listed here?"

"Sure," Steve answered. "All of the first three — plastics, auto parts, telecommunications equipment. That's how I knew to list them."

"I see," Zhao replied thoughtfully. "And how powerful are the businesses Delmore has created in each area?"

Steve was familiar with the numbers. "Sales in plastics and auto parts have drifted downward over the past year," he responded. "And so have profits. Of course, the management says that's purely a matter of the business cycle. They expect revenues to bounce back early next year, assuming the economy perks up. As for telecommunications equipment, it's been growing pretty fast — over twenty-five percent a year, compounded, over the past five years — with impressive margins. Tom Kennedy — the CEO, you know — likes to point to telecom as the big success story at Delmore."

"And what do *you* think, Steve?"

After a just-noticeable pause, Steve answered, "Honestly? I'm not sure I buy the logic behind our management's optimism."

Zhao raised his eyebrows. "Really? Tell me about it."

Steve had been trained not to gossip with outsiders about doings at Delmore. He had no reason to doubt Zhao's discretion, but somehow it felt disloyal to talk too freely about his misgivings about the company.

Zhao picked up on Steve's hesitation. "I don't want you to share any non-public information, of course," he said.

"I understand," Steve said. "It's not that. It's just that — well, I don't want to be disloyal. The people at Delmore have been very good to me."

Zhao bowed slightly. "I respect that, Steve. We don't have to talk about Delmore if it makes you uncomfortable."

Suddenly Steve realized that this was *not* what he'd wanted to hear. "No," he ventured, "I don't mean we can't talk about it. But I feel — well, I guess I feel a little torn."

"How so?"

Steve thought for a moment, then took a deep breath. "To tell the truth, I'm torn about how I feel about Delmore. I like the people there, I really do — they're good people. But I guess I wish I felt more confidence in them as business leaders."

"Is there any specific reason you feel that way?" Zhao asked.

"Well, the telecom business is actually a good example. It's been growing well, like I said, and the margins are still high. But over the past several months some small competitors have been eating away at the business. And from what I hear, the people in our telecom division don't have much of a clue as to what to do about it."

"Really." It was half a statement, half a question.

"Really. I'm no telecom expert, but I have lunch every couple of weeks with one of the guys in the division, and he says the focus is always on cutting costs — on whacking down the suppliers and trying to get the products made more cheaply."

"Isn't that important?" Zhao asked.

"Sure. But my buddy Frank says that whenever he tries to bring up other issues, such as expanding the range of customer services they offer — he gets ignored. Meanwhile, these new competitors are selling more than just equipment. They're sending consultants into smallish firms, like small financial companies, and helping them redesign their information systems. Delmore acts like this is small potatoes business, and maybe it is. But it keeps growing.

"It seems like the guys in telecom are just uncomfortable with the idea of redefining their business. Meanwhile, they just keep running a race against costs, as if that's all that matters. I really don't see where it'll end."

Zhao pondered Steve's words in silence for a moment. Then he said, "It's an interesting case. Have you spoken with Frank about it since our first class?"

"No, we're due to have lunch next Wednesday."

"I wonder whether Frank would agree with you that Delmore's telecom business ought to consider moving to a Customer Solution model."

"I don't know. I'd love to talk about it with him."

"I think you should," Zhao remarked. "Meanwhile, let's leave behind the Customer Solution model and travel to the other end of the profitability spectrum, to a profit model that can be applied in only a few situations."

"Hmm," Steve said. "Why do I want to learn *that?*"

"You're too impatient, Steve. Consider this: You may find that the Pyramid Profit model works only in one marketplace out of fifty. But if someday your company is operating in that one marketplace, you can make billions with the model. Is that worth learning?"

Steve grinned. "Billions? I suppose so."

"But there's always a better reason to learn a new profit model: to open your mind. To grasp principle. To absorb some of the modes of thinking that others have developed. Knowing these will help you think for yourself next time."

Zhao opened a desk drawer and pulled out the same yellow pad he'd used during their first lesson. He folded back the top page and tossed it in the center of his desk, between himself and Steve.

"Ten years ago, I gave a talk at a software company's marketing meeting, in Portland, Oregon. There were two hundred people in the audience. I was good, but the other guest speaker was better."

"Who was it?"

"A senior VP from Mattel. The CEO couldn't make it—she had to cancel at the last minute. That's what happens when you run a business, when you're the cardiologist, not the lab guy. Her replacement was a lab guy, name of Gary. He spoke for an hour, with no slides. I was spellbound. I wrote notes as fast as I could.

"When the talk was over, people flooded into the hall for coffee. I was asking them excitedly, 'What did you think about Gary's talk?' They hated it. '*Barbie* dolls!' they sniffed, 'We're a software company.'

"I was stunned. They didn't get it. They completely and thoroughly did not get it."

"Get what?" Steve asked.

"The pyramid."

"The pyramid?"

"Yes, the pyramid. Here's how it works at Mattel. You sell a Barbie doll for $20 to $30. But imitators can come in below you. So you build a firewall. You develop a $10 Barbie to seal off that space. It's barely profitable, but it prevents other companies from establishing a connection with your customers. And even girls who start with the $10 Barbie usually move on to buy accessories and other dolls that make them profitable for Mattel.

"But in order to achieve a real breakthrough, Mattel had to look in the other direction. Looking hard, they saw the opportunity for a $100 or $200 Barbie."

Steve was dubious. "Would parents really give their six-year-old daughter a $200 doll to play with?"

"Absolutely not, but that wasn't what Mattel envisioned. Forget about the little girl. Instead, think about her mother. She played with Barbies twenty or thirty years ago. She remembers those dolls with incredible fondness. And now she has money to spend. Maybe Mom will buy a designer Barbie—finely crafted, exquisite. Not a toy but a collector's item, like the china teapots or African sculptures or rare postage stamps that enthusiasts will pay a great deal to own. Providing enormous satisfaction to the customer and enormous margins to Mattel."

"A great concept for a toy that Baby Boomers are nostalgic about," Steve commented. "But how does it apply to other businesses?"

"Here's the real beauty in Mattel's idea," Zhao explained. "Suddenly, Barbie wasn't a product any longer, but a system, a carefully crafted, coordinated, and integrated system. A firewall of defensive product at the bottom of the pyramid and powerful profit-generators at the top. Brilliant!"

Zhao picked up his silver pen and drew. Four strokes, one long rectangle; then three smaller boxes, three strokes each.

He tossed the pen down. "Steve," he asked, "could Mattel have built the pyramid without understanding the customer? Without understanding *all* of the customers, current and potential?"

"I guess not," said Steve, suddenly remembering Zhao's customer questions from the week before.

"Where else do you see product pyramids at work, Steve?"

Steve pondered. "I'm not sure," he finally replied. "There are lots of companies that make products at more than one price point, but are they all pyramids?"

"Do you drive a car, Steve? If so, you encounter a product pyramid at least once a week. Think about it."

A light bulb went on. "At the gas pump," Steve said. "Regular, premium, super-premium—that's the idea, right?"

"That's right," Zhao nodded. "But it's a lousy pyramid."

"How come?"

"What kind of gas do you buy, Steve?"

"I don't know — the cheapest, I guess."

"And why is that?"

"I never thought about it."

"Exactly!" Zhao cried. "So the pyramid looks like this." He flipped the page and swiftly created another sketch:

"That's an awfully puny top end on that pyramid," Steve observed.

"That's the problem," Zhao agreed. "The high-end product is totally underpromoted! I have no reason to buy it — not one. So you see, even a potentially great idea can be destroyed by poor implementation."

"What makes the difference?" Steve asked.

"Great question," Zhao replied. "There are several factors. One is that your pyramid has to be more than just a collection of products at different price points. A true pyramid is a system in which the lower-priced products are manufactured and sold with so much efficiency that it's virtually impossible for a competitor to steal market share by underpricing you. That's why I call the lowest tier of the pyramid the firewall."

"I get it."

"But the most important factor is the nature of your customer set."

"How so?"

"Think about it. What is it about the customers for Barbie that enables Mattel to maintain such an effective product pyramid?"

Steve considered. "I guess the customers are a kind of pyramid, too," he said.

Zhao nodded vigorously. "That's the idea. The customers themselves form a hierarchy, with different expectations and different attitudes toward price. There are Mattel customers who absolutely won't spend more than $10 for a no-frills doll. There are others who'll pay top dollar for a unique product. The pyramid captures them both. But not every marketplace can be stratified in the same way."

"What other pyramids are there?" Steve asked.

"You tell me. Not now — next week. Bring me a list. And don't forget your umbrella."

3
Multi-Component Profit

October 5. As so often happens in the autumn in New York City, the weather had changed dramatically in the past week. The day outside was spectacular, filling Zhao's office with an intense, almost supernatural brightness. Zhao was getting up from his desk just as Steve arrived.

"Come in, Steve," Zhao said cheerfully. "Let me just turn off the overhead light. We don't need it."

As Zhao flicked the switch, they were both startled. No brightness was lost. The morning sun was so intense that the fluorescent light had added nothing. Only a certain indefinable quality of the light in the room had changed. The two of them sat in silence for a moment, drinking in the remarkable effect created by the sunshine that filled every nook and corner of the office. Steve felt they were in some sort of surreal aquarium, swimming not in water but in a very special kind of living light.

"Do you feel like a fish?" Zhao asked. Steve stared at him in surprise.

"Yes, but not an ordinary fish," Steve answered. He raised his right hand slowly, to watch the sunshine bathe it.

"A light fish," Zhao remarked.

Steve smiled. "That's it, of course."

Zhao smiled back. They let the atmosphere hold them for another long minute.

Finally, Zhao broke the silence. "We'd better get to work. You're not paying me to sit with you, watching a beautiful light. Do you have your list of Pyramid Profit companies?"

Steve pulled a sheet of paper out of his pocket:

Product Pyramids
Nokia phones
GM cars
American Express cards

Zhao frowned, though not with displeasure. "Good job, Steve," he remarked. "Very good job." He handed back the list. "You're right about Nokia. They have a complete line of digital phones at various price levels, including a very low-priced firewall version. General Motors, of course, invented the pyramid model back in the 1920s, under Alfred P. Sloan, with Chevrolet at the base and Cadillac at the apex."

Steve was secretly very pleased with himself. He wanted to keep this part of the conversation going. "Was I stretching the concept when I listed Amex cards?" he asked.

"No, that works," Zhao answered. "Not much of a pyramid, but it's a pyramid, all right: the green card, the gold card, the platinum card. Now all the credit card companies are imitating the strategy." He shifted gears. "Hang on to that list and add to it when you can. Take a look at Swatch, the Swiss watchmakers, for example. See if you can build your list up to more than ten examples. But now, for today, let's talk about Multi-Component Profit."

Steve focused on Zhao.

"It's one thing to understand Multi-Component Profit, another to apply it. I've done the former; my friend Burton has done the latter. He captured the idea in reality."

"Fine," Steve said, a bit sardonically. "But what the heck is Multi-Component Profit in the first place?"

Zhao smiled indulgently. Leaning back in his chair, Zhao brought his fingertips together, arch-like, turned his eyes toward the ceiling, and quietly began to speak.

"Many businesses come in pieces. And all the pieces may not be equally profitable. In fact, in most cases, profitability is quite lumpy—sometimes high, sometimes low, sometimes non-existent.

"Think about Coca-Cola. One product, right? Yes—but several businesses. Coke has a grocery component, a restaurant component, a vending-machine component. Most of the profits flow from the restaurant and vending-machine sales."

Zhao saw Steve frown questioningly. "Steve," he continued, "how much do you pay for Coke from a vending machine—per ounce, let's say?"

Steve thought. "Let's see—seventy-five cents for a twelve-ounce can. That's about six or seven cents per ounce."

"And in a restaurant?"

"Probably ten to twelve cents an ounce."

"And what about at the grocery?"

"I get a two-liter bottle for a dollar nineteen. That's just around two cents an ounce." He shook his head. "Wow."

"Same product, several businesses," Zhao summed it up.

Steve frowned. "Just a minute. What's the difference between this model and Pyramid Profit?"

"What do you mean?" Zhao parried. "How are they *similar?*"

"Well, both involve taking advantage of the differing price sensitivities of differing groups of customers."

"Not necessarily," Zhao replied. "What customer category do you fall into for Coca-Cola?"

"I usually buy Coke from the vending machine in the office," Steve answered.

"Never anywhere else?"

"Well, I buy it in a restaurant once in a while. And last month, when I went to the Hamptons for a week, I bought a couple of cases at the supermarket... Oh, I see what you're saying. I actually buy Coke at *every* price point, depending on where I happen to be."

"That's right," Zhao nodded. "Same product, several businesses. Whereas the Barbie pyramid is really based on several very different products targeted at basically distinct customer sets."

"Okay, I get it."

"Good. Now think about a hotel," Zhao pressed on. It has lots of components. One is called 'a single room for one night,' another is called 'a one-day meeting for twenty people,' and yet another is called 'a three-day convention for three thousand people.' Think about the relative dollars compared to the relative costs. Same rooms, lots of ways to sell them.

"And think about a bookstore. It has a foot-traffic-in-the-store component, a book-group-member component, an online-website component, and a corporate purchasing component. Same books, lots of ways to sell them—each with its own profit picture.

"And that brings us to my old friend Burton. He was a perceptive, brilliant, and totally unassertive guy. We met back in my days with the economic research firm. He was a remarkably astute observer of organizational behavior who could have become a CEO—and a very effective one at that—if he'd had any stomach for corporate politics.

"But at age fifty-three, encouraged by me and his other friends, Burton did something very few CEOs have done. He wrote a great book. It dealt with the relationship between a company's organizational system and its profitability. Burton thought about the subject for fifteen years, then rented a cottage on Cape Cod and wrote the thing in eleven weeks.

"Burton was a lucky author. His publisher made a genuine effort to promote the book. As part of the publication process, Burton had a chance to speak to several groups of booksellers-owners of small, independent bookstores. A few of them became interested because they could see its application to them. As businesspeople, they were getting killed by the chain bookstores. They needed to learn about becoming more profitable—fast. Burton's book offered a message of hope.

"Some of the booksellers asked Burton to help them develop a new business strategy. At first, Burton declined—he already had more clients than he could handle. But one group, the Mid-Atlantic Booksellers Association, was very persistent. Eventually, Burton agreed to take a closer look at the book retailing business. And that led to a very unusual experience.

"You see, Burton was a serious student of Warren Buffett's investment methodology a decade and a half before Buffett became universally known. Studying Buffett led him to an examination of Coca-Cola's strategy—again, long before it became well known. So Burton understood the dramatic differences in profit potential among the various components of Coke's business. And after looking into book retailing, Burton saw the potential to recreate the same effect in the independent bookstore business."

"How so?"

"Burton recognized that the bookstore itself could be a base for building several new high-profit components: the corporate business, the book-group business, the personal-service business. After several months of working with the booksellers association, he developed a program to dramatically intensify the bookstores' outbound selling activities.

"It was simple stuff. He suggested having a couple of account managers call on corporate libraries and HR departments to promote the latest business books. Providing services to local book groups was next. And that was followed by promoting sales to high-purchase individuals. It was obvious, in a way. After all, the booksellers already knew that their best customers bought nearly $500 worth of books a year. But they'd never realized that these people represented a separate component of their business that they could consciously, deliberately target and grow. A simple but powerful insight.

"Burton's program was put into practice by about twenty of the more imaginative and energetic members of the association. The results were incredible. With little increase in labor costs (two account managers cost a total of $80,000), and no increase in assets, the existence of these independent bookstores was transformed. Bookstores that were barely surviving turned into obscenely profitable businesses. The numbers looked like this:

	Traditional Model ($MMs)	**Traditional + Outbound Model** ($MMs)
Revenue	$10.0	$12.0
Cost	9.9	11.0
Profit	0.1	1.0
Return On Sales	1%	8%
Assets	3.0	3.0
Return On Assets	3%	33%

"This happened over three years. A typical bookstore was able to develop two hundred company accounts (corporations, law firms, accountants), one to two hundred book groups, and over five hundred high-purchase individuals or families. The result was a huge increase in sales, much greater levels of customer satisfaction, and a greatly increased flow of information as to what customers were buying and wanted to buy.

"The funny thing was how the bookstore managers' thinking changed. These were bookish people who'd previously been resigned to eking out a living. Now they kept asking Burton, 'What's our next vending machine?'"

"'Seek and ye shall find?'" Steve asked.

"Yes, if you seek persistently enough. Burton helped them. He was unassertive but very tenacious. In the end, he not only helped them survive the greatest competitive test in their history, he made them rich. Believe me, a pretax profit of $1 million a year is a very big deal for a small business like a bookstore.

"It was especially poignant for these booksellers as they saw their colleagues around the country folding, one after another, when one of the superstores moved in across the street."

"What about Burton? I'll bet he made a pretty penny on the deal."

"Under normal circumstances, he *wouldn't* have. Burton was a little like Mozart—brilliant, creative, and penniless. He tended to give away his insights for nothing or next to nothing. It drove his wife and kids crazy, as you can imagine.

"But this story had a different ending, because of Carole Woodward."

"Who was she?"

"Carole owned one of the bookstores in the association. She was a fascinating woman with incredible drive and near-psychotic levels of energy. In some ways, she was a great bookstore manager—she loved her customers, loved her products, and loved the business. But strategy wasn't her strong suit. Luckily, she recognized in Burton the ability to provide what her business lacked—a smart business model based on a fresh style of thinking.

"Once Carole decided that Burton had what she needed, he was a goner. She was the person who made sure that Burton embarked on the bookstore project. There was no way he could resist her determination. It was a classic case of boulders to eggshells."

"Boulders to eggshells?"

"Oh, sorry—you haven't read *The Art of War* yet. That'll come later. But the point is that Carole organized the group and made it happen. Once the program was in place, Carole was also the one who would call

Burton every few months to tell him how they were doing. The success of the stores became a source of enormous satisfaction for him, like seeing a once-rock-strewn garden finally blossoming.

"Anyway, three years later, Carole organized a dinner for the twenty booksellers, all of whom were now clocking $1 million a year or better. At that dinner, she made an amazing thing happen. She announced that she was sending a hundred-thousand-dollar check to Burton, and that she fully expected each one of them to do the same. 'I know your numbers,' she said, 'I know you can afford it, and if you don't write those checks, I promise I'll make your life a living hell!'

"They folded in minutes. Over the next week, twenty separate registered letters containing hundred-thousand-dollar checks arrived in Burton's mailbox. You can imagine the atmosphere in the Burton household. It was like the greatest Christmas ever, four screaming kids and all."

Steve was stunned. "That never happens."

"Well, very, very rarely."

"What did Burton do?"

"He immediately retired. The investment income from his sudden windfall was a lot bigger than his pathetic salary."

"Did Burton ever write another book?"

"As a matter of fact, that was exactly what he set out to do the minute the ink was dry on his resignation. But the book was never finished."

"Why not?"

Zhao shrugged. "No pressure, no outcomes. Charles Dickens wrote — what? — thirty or forty novels, and big thick books they were, too. But most of his best stuff was written about twenty-four hours before deadline. So Burton, like most of us, couldn't be productive without someone depending on him."

"Too bad," Steve remarked.

"Not really. He deserved his retirement."

"So Burton discovered Multi-Component Profit and used it to retire rich and happy. Where else can the same profit model be applied?" Steve asked.

"Excellent question. In fact, that's your homework for this week. I want you to list three situations where Multi-Component Profit works. Not including soft drinks or bookstores, of course. And not including hotels — I gave that one away, too."

Steve thought three would be easy. *Hey, there are probably three divisions at Delmore that could apply this model — in fact, there are probably three divisions that are already applying it.* He was wrong, but he didn't know it at the time.

"There's also a reading assignment. A little book called *Obvious Adams*. It's an old story, originally published in *The Saturday Evening Post* in 1916."

"Published *where?*" Steve wondered.

"Never mind. The point is that most people would assume that the message of the book is outdated. If you're smart, you won't think so. Here it is—it'll be easier to borrow my copy than to try to find your own."

"By the way," Steve asked, "what's the picture for Multi-Component Profit?" he asked.

"Ah, the picture," Zhao said with a smile. He reached for his pad and his silver pen and paused, his hand poised in midair.

A half-minute passed. Then, with surprising speed, Zhao dashed off a diagram.

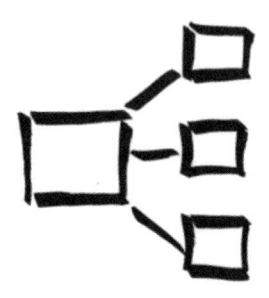

"The large box on the left," he explained, "is your base business. The smaller boxes on the right are your component businesses." For a moment, he gazed at the image thoughtfully, as if trying to envision the business components pouring themselves into the boxes. "So, Steve," he asked, "what's the idea behind this profit model?"

Steve thought a moment. "Different parts of a business can have wildly different profitability."

"And what else?"

Steve was stumped.

Zhao continued. "What about the customer?"

"Ah," Steve reflected. "The customer behaves very differently on different purchase occasions."

"Meaning what?" Zhao pressed.

"Different degrees of price sensitivity. Very different."

"You bet," Zhao agreed.

Steve started to rise from his chair, but Zhao stopped him. "What about your lunch with Frank?" he asked. "You were going to talk about

Customer Solution Profit and the telecom business."

"Oh, I almost forgot—we did talk about it." Steve shook his head. "I don't know—maybe the model won't work in telecom, at least not for Delmore."

"And why not?"

"According to Frank, the marketing people insist that the pressure from customers to keep prices down is so great that they just can't afford to expand what they offer to include complete solutions."

"Hmm. That's a bad sign," Zhao remarked.

"About the telecom industry, you mean?"

"No, about Delmore, Inc."

"What do you mean?"

"I mean that if Delmore's telecom division can't see how to develop Customer Solutions that customers would pay more for—and gladly—then Frank and his colleagues may not be in business a lot longer."

Steve's eyes grew wide. "Seriously? I mean, the business is still growing. And there should always be a market for well-made, inexpensive telecom equipment. Aren't you being a little alarmist?"

"One would hope so," Zhao replied. "It's very hard to keep making money, let alone to grow, once you've allowed yourself to be boxed into a no-profit zone. And it's remarkable how quickly a structure can crumble once cracks appear in the foundation." Zhao stood up. "Think about it, Steve," he said.

The lesson was over. Zhao returned the pad to its place in the desk drawer, and Steve left the office. Zhao's final words stuck in his mind. *A no-profit zone . . . how quickly a structure can crumble . . . think about it, Steve* . . . Was this just part of Zhao's profitability program, or was he sending some sort of message about Delmore? By the time he reached the subway, he'd made up his mind to call Frank—not on Monday morning, but that very afternoon. *Maybe it's time that somebody took a fresh look at Delmore's telecom business.* He shook his head. *I just wish it could be somebody smarter than me.*

4
Switchboard Profit

October 12. Steve arrived at the usual time to find Zhao leaning way back in his desk chair, eyes closed, as if asleep. Steve paused at the door and cleared his throat. Without moving, Zhao opened one eye and scrutinized Steve. After a moment of silence, Zhao swung forward, gave a cheerful "Welcome!" and waved Steve into the guest chair.

"I was just thinking about my favorite line from *Obvious Adams*," Zhao commented.

Steve grinned. He'd read the whole book. "And I bet I know what that line is, too," he declared.

"Oh, you do?" said Zhao playfully. "What is it, pray tell?"

"'There are no mountains in Holland,'" Steve intoned.

Zhao chortled and slapped the desk. "You got it!" he announced. "There's hope for you yet!" And both of them laughed.

"Of course," Zhao went on, more thoughtfully, "the obvious isn't always so obvious."

"What do you mean?" Steve asked.

"You have to know something about Holland to know that there *are* no mountains there," Zhao answered. "An awful lot of people seem to *assume* there are mountains without bothering to ask the question."

Steve laughed. "I know what you mean."

"Today," Zhao went on, "we'll talk about a profit model called Switchboard Profit."

"Switchboard Profit? I don't suppose that has something to do with old-fashioned telephone lines, does it?" Delmore's telecom business was still preying on his mind. He and Frank had spent the previous Sunday arguing about what needed to be done to arrest the revenue decline. They'd parted feeling no closer to a solution than when they'd started.

"No, it's not that kind of switchboard," Zhao replied. "Although the image isn't far wrong. The Switchboard happens to be one of my personal favorites. It has an elegance about it that few other profit models possess."

Steve smiled. Zhao seemed to talk about profit models as if they were old friends or great works of art. "Tell me about it," he urged.

"Last time, we talked about my friend Burton. He was a student of Coca-Cola. Well, around that same time, I was studying Michael Ovitz."

"The Hollywood agent?"

"That's the one. I tracked his career starting in the early eighties, just as he was beginning to be well known. It wasn't easy to study Ovitz then.

You had to read the entertainment press and talk to people in LA. But with enough persistence, you could piece together his story."

"How did it go?"

"Well, it was like this. Michael Ovitz started his career as a talent agent in television, where the practice of packaging talent was common. Because the margins in TV weren't large enough to absorb the inefficiencies of the typical Hollywood process for developing a movie project, talent agents would put together a package that included a screenwriter, stars, a director, and supporting actors, and bring the entire package to a studio to produce. The agent and his clients did well, of course, and the studio benefited from the arrangement because it offered a sort of one-stop-shopping for talent.

"Ovitz perfected the idea in the world of TV, then carried it over to film-making, where it was considerably more difficult to implement. But he did it."

"So a switchboard is another word for packaging talent?" Steve asked.

"No, no, no. The packaging concept was just the first step toward building a true switchboard. Packaging falls far short of creating the concentration of power that a switchboard requires."

"Okay, keep going."

"Step two," Zhao continued, "was to find a source of stories. In both TV and movies, good stories make the system go—they're the core around which everything is built. Realizing this, Ovitz knew he needed a great source of stories. So he befriended the leading literary agent in New York at the time, a fellow named Mort Janklow. It wasn't easy, by the way. Ovitz kept calling Janklow every week for a year before Janklow agreed to talk with him. But once Ovitz made the connection, it became a gold mine for him. The Janklow agency represented many of the country's top novelists, short story writers, and journalists, and it became Ovitz's source of stories. So now, with a good flow of stories, Ovitz had leverage with the talent. And by organizing the talent, he had leverage with the studios. Ovitz could bring a great story to a hot actor and a hot director and then bring all three to a studio hungry for movie ideas. It was a brilliant idea—and like many brilliant ideas, obvious in retrospect."

"So *that's* the switchboard?"

"No, not quite yet."

"There's a step three?"

"Yes."

"What is it?"

"You tell me." Suddenly, Zhao rose from his chair and left the office. Steve was alone.

A minute passed, then two. Steve realized that Zhao wouldn't be back soon. He was on his own. He started thinking, searching for the answer to Zhao's question—at first slowly and methodically, then furiously. He grabbed a yellow pad from a stack on Zhao's side table and started jotting down ideas, crossing them out, jotting new ones, rewriting, doing calculations, correcting, and recalculating.

Half an hour passed. Then an hour. As Steve continued to work, the outlines of a solution began to emerge. First dimly, then more and more clearly, he thought he understood the answer. His pen moved more slowly. The pieces were falling into place.

Suddenly Zhao returned. In his hand were six sheets of yellow paper from Zhao's own pad, covered with notes and figures in Zhao's dark, precise handwriting. He'd been calculating as well.

Steve stared. "I don't get it," he said. "Don't you already *know* the answer?"

Zhao lowered himself into his chair and dropped the small stack of pages on the desk. "Of course," he replied.

"Then, what—?"

"I spent the last hour recreating it from scratch," Zhao said quietly.

"But why?"

"Sometimes it's useful for a teacher to stand in exactly the same place as his student."

The two of them sat in silence, eyes locked.

"Well?" Zhao finally asked. "What answer did you come up with?"

"Critical mass," Steve said.

"Go on," said Zhao encouragingly.

"Well, here's how I see it," Steve continued. "Even if you have a source of stories, along with the persuasiveness and skill needed to put together a package of talent, you're only controlling two of the variables. There's a third variable—number."

"Meaning what?"

"Well, you could work your tail off putting packages together and still represent only three percent of the market."

Zhao smiled. "How interesting."

"I don't know a lot about Hollywood," Steve went on, "but I'm guessing there were probably ten or twelve good-sized studios at the time."

Zhao nodded. "Close enough."

"And probably several hundred stars, directors, and screenwriters that mattered."

"Also close enough."

"So if you're Michael Ovitz and you represent, say, a couple of dozen screen artists, the studios have lot of other options. They don't have to deal with you if they don't want to."

"Okay."

"But if you represent a couple of *hundred* artists, the studios' options start to narrow."

"Does that apply only to the studios?"

"No, that's the beauty of it. The more critical mass you build, the higher your probability of putting together a package that works. That, in turn, means that a star, a writer, or a director will be better off being represented by *you* rather than any other agent, because the odds of being part of a winning combination are so much higher."

"So?"

"So now the studios *have* to deal with you, and the stars *want* to deal with you."

"And what's the crossover point?"

Steve gestured toward his own stack of scribbled-on yellow pages. "That's tough. Obviously you don't have to control a hundred percent of the talent or anything like that, but how small a fraction will work? It's not three percent, it's not ten percent, but as best I can figure it, at somewhere around fifteen to twenty percent an upward spiral kicks in. The *perceived* probabilities go way up, and suddenly the talent and the deals all begin flowing in your direction."

Zhao nodded. "Good, good!" he agreed. "And how does the profit happen?"

Steve hadn't thought about that.

"See ya," Zhao said. And he was gone again.

This time, Zhao returned in just ten minutes. Steve was ready with a fresh pile of yellow pages.

"Let's say a star gets five million dollars for a picture," Steve began. "And let's say there are two big stars per picture—Meryl Streep and Robert Redford in the 1980s, or Tom Cruise and Nicole Kidman in the '90s. Figure the director gets a million and a half, and the writer gets half a million. On the original Hollywood model, the agent represents *one* star and gets a ten percent fee. That's $500 thousand. Here Ovitz represents a complete package and gets ten percent of $12 million, or $1.2 million. More than twice as much."

"Is that it?"

"Oh no, far from it."

Zhao sat up straight, staring at Steve. He just might have a great student on his hands.

"By representing a team rather than an individual, he has far greater bargaining power. He could raise that twelve million to fifteen million, or more. After all, the studio has nowhere else to go if it wants to get its hands on the biggest stars."

"And therefore—?"

"Therefore, the agent's fee would rise to one and a half million dollars, three times greater than in the traditional model."

"And that's it?"

"No, there's more. The biggest factor is that the probability of striking a deal goes way, way up. As the pool of talent you represent grows to two or three hundred, the chances of putting the 'right' talent together goes way up, and so does the probability that the studio *has* to deal with you. So your volume goes way up. The number of deals you can put together per unit of time will probably double or triple."

"Net result?"

"Profitability per unit of effort and unit of time is probably seven to ten times greater than in the traditional model."

"Wow!" Zhao's eyes were huge.

Steve sat back, grinning from ear to ear. Yes! He thought. *I've impressed the hell out of him!* For a moment, he soaked in the sensation of sheer, unadulterated triumph.

Suddenly, Zhao leaned forward and pushed his own small stack of yellow sheets across the desk toward Steve. Steve picked them up. They were densely covered with letters and numbers, but surprisingly clear and easy to decipher, and each was neatly numbered in the upper right hand corner. Steve began to read.

For the next few minutes he flipped through the sheets, his heart gradually sinking.

Here, he realized, was how he *should* have worked through the problem. From the initial facts and outline through the argumentation, the string of assumptions, the calculations, the analysis of pros and cons, to the options considered and rejected or selected and modified, here was a pathway of crystal-clear logic, focus, precision, and near-inevitability. It was nothing less than the mathematics of profitability.

Steve dropped the pages on the desk and looked at Zhao.

Zhao didn't smile. He knew how tough this moment was, especially for a potentially great student. Hadn't he experienced moments like this more than once in his own life?

"Don't let it get to you, Steve," he said quietly.

After fifteen seconds of silence, Steve spoke. "Months?" he asked.

Zhao said nothing. "Years?" Steve probed again.

Zhao took back his six carefully-inscribed sheets and dropped them in the wastepaper basket at his side.

"Forget about these. And forget about the top of the mountain. Focus on your single next step."

Steve sighed, glanced down at his hands for moment, then returned his eyes to Zhao's. He seemed to have regained his focus. "And what's that?"

"Name me three switchboards."

"Well, there's..."

"No, not now," Zhao interrupted. "Next week. Name me three switchboards, other than the ones we've talked about. And then name the three best *unexploited* opportunities to create a switchboard that you can think of. And for each one, a characterization of how the profit happens—because the profit mechanism made possible by the switchboard is not always the same."

Steve was taking notes furiously. It helped take his mind off the crushing disappointment of two minutes ago.

"By the way, Steve, how tall is Mount Everest?"

"Five or six miles, isn't it?"

"That's about right. It's 29,028 feet, to be precise. But when you're climbing Everest, you don't get to the summit directly. You start at the bottom." Zhao leaned forward. "You and I are already three thousand feet up."

Steve understood Zhao's point. He smiled. "But aren't the last few feet the toughest?"

Now Zhao smiled, too. "You don't know how right you are. But it's like starting a business. If you knew exactly how insanely tough it is, you'd never begin. So let's just stay focused on the first steps. The others will follow. Not automatically, but they'll follow."

Steve was reflective. His mood was slowly floating back up to the surface of reasonability. Finally he asked, "What about the picture?"

"Oh, yes."

Zhao seized his pen, paused, and considered. For a full minute, the whole room was absolutely still. Then, lightning-like, he marked the next page of the pad with a couple of dozen strokes.

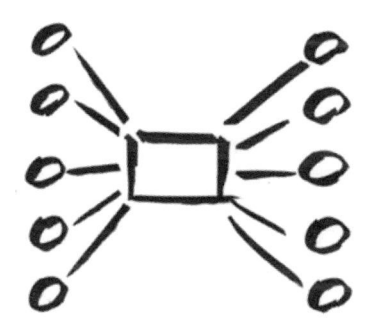

"There's your switchboard," Zhao observed. "But you didn't ask me about reading," he added.

"Yes, you're right."

"Two books. The first is about Ovitz—*Power to Burn* by Stephen Singular. Read chapter two and chapters six through ten."

"And the other book?"

"*Innumeracy* by John Allen Paulos. I want you to read chapter one, 'Examples and Principles.' But don't just read it. You should also solve every single math problem in it."

"Okay," Steve said, somewhat resignedly.

"And for every problem Paulos gives, I want you to invent and complete an additional problem of the same kind. So if Paulos asks you to measure the mass of Mt. Fuji, I want you to invent and answer another similar problem—to measure the volume of Lake Michigan, for example."

Steve looked puzzled and discouraged. Zhao's expression changed. His eyes softened, but he wasn't ready to fully relent.

"I see you don't know what I'm talking about. When you get the book, turn to page 25, which has the Fuji question. That'll give you a clue as to how to do the rest."

Feeling a little shell-shocked, Steve nodded his assent. This smelled like a lot of work—very hard work.

"You're right," Zhao nodded, "This will be very, very hard. So take it slow. You don't have to do it in a week—take four weeks."

A physical sense of relief swept through Steve. Zhao saw it, and quickly added, "Steve, this is critical stuff. It's not calculus or trigonometry, just arithmetic. But it's very important arithmetic. It's arithmetic that paves the way to the math of profits. Take it slow enough, see it as a series of puzzles, and you'll have fun with it. But start tonight."

"All right," Steve replied. Then he pointed toward Zhao's notes, just visible at the top of his wastepaper basket. "Can I have those?" he asked.

Zhao paused and considered. "If you do *Innumeracy* right, you can have them in four weeks."

"It's a deal."

Zhao smiled, fished the papers out of the trash and tucked them into his desk drawer. "See you in a month," he said, and Steve was gone.

This morning's session had been the longest yet. A little tired, Zhao turned his chair toward the great window in his office, with the harbor of New York spread out far below. Overhead was a mottled patchwork—a deep, bright blue sky overlaid with a shifting pattern of lighter and darker grays formed by many cloud layers, moving rapidly under the blows of a steady northeast wind, while the gray-green waters below were broken into a million drifting fragments of darkness and light. Zhao sat silently contemplating the scene, trying to imagine how a competent painter would see it . . . then how a painter of genius would see it. And recreate it on canvas.

Zhao sighed. There was so much he would like to be able to do that he would never do, even if he lived to be a hundred and twenty years old. *A painter of genius!* He thought. *What I'd give to simply be a teacher of genius . . . even for a week, even for a day.* For a moment, he sat slumped in his chair, as though drained of energy by the mere thought of how far he had yet to travel. Then he sat up, shrugged, and took a deep breath. *No point in becoming as depressed as Steve was five minutes ago,* Zhao thought. He reached for the telephone on his desk.

5
Time Profit

November 9. Four weeks had passed since Zhao's and Steve's last meeting. A foretaste of winter was in the New York air. Steve arrived at Zhao's office ten minutes early. He'd enjoyed having three Saturday mornings to sleep in, but riding up in the elevator, he suddenly realized that he'd missed these meetings, too . . . and that he'd even missed Zhao himself. He strolled down the silent hall toward Zhao's familiar office.

Zhao's broad smile said that he'd missed Steve, too. "Welcome back," he exclaimed.

"Good to be back," Steve replied, and they shook hands warmly. "I have some news for you," Steve said as he took his chair.

"About Delmore, I suppose?"

"That's right. I've been thinking a lot about our last class session—about the Switchboard pattern. Ovitz created a Switchboard by connecting service suppliers—actors, writers, directors—with the movie production companies that needed their services. Seems to me it could work with products just as well as with services."

Zhao nodded slightly. "With some kinds of products, certainly."

"And why not with telecommunications equipment?"

Zhao smiled. "I see what you're getting at."

"Why couldn't some company create a kind of telecom Switchboard by offering equipment, software, services—the whole nine yards—from every supplier, expertly mixed and matched for customized needs?"

"I don't know—why not?"

"I think they *could*," Steve replied. He was starting to talk a little faster than usual. "The profit would come from selling the equipment itself as well as from having inside knowledge of everybody's products, not just those of a single supplier. And the company that moved first could really make it work by signing deals to represent all the best manufacturers, consultants, and software makers. Of course, you'd need top-flight experts to work with the customers, to make sure that the systems you put together were absolutely the best. And you'd have to invest the time in studying each customer's business instead of trying to sell cookie-cutter solutions—a little like the Customer Solutions model. But the time invested up front could really pay off on the back end, with contracts to service and expand and upgrade the equipment continually. It could work—it really could!"

Zhao looked thoughtful. "What if this company you're describing also happened to be a manufacturer of telecom equipment?"

"So much the better!" Steve declared.

"How so?"

"Well, they'd make manufacturer's profits on the equipment they supplied directly, wouldn't they? So there'd be even better margins on those sales than on all the others."

"And would that present any risks?"

Steve paused. He hadn't considered that before. "Well," he finally replied, "I guess there's a risk that the company would want to push their own products rather than making objective choices in the best interest of the customer."

"Perhaps so," Zhao agreed.

"But they'd just have to resist that temptation," Steve went on. "That would be the price of admission to the Switchboard game."

"You're right about that," said Zhao.

Steve recovered his enthusiasm. "Frank and I have been working on the concept for the past two weeks," he announced, a touch of pride in his voice. "We're going to present it to the management team at DelCom on Monday afternoon. Isn't that something?"

Zhao's face was almost expressionless. "Yes, that's quite something," he answered. "I'll be very interested to hear how your presentation is received."

"I'll tell you all about it next week."

"Something to look forward to," Zhao remarked. "But meanwhile, how did you enjoy *Innumeracy*?"

Steve chuckled. "*Enjoy* might not be the right word," he answered. "But it was . . . interesting."

"How did you handle the puzzles in the chapter?" Zhao asked. "The Mount Fuji exercise, for example."

Steve shook his head. "Geez," he responded, "That was a weird question. It took me quite a while to come up with even an approximate answer."

Zhao nodded. "That figures," he said. "Of course, what matters isn't so much the correctness of your answer as the method you devised for calculating it. How did you do it?"

Steve pulled a sheaf of yellow lined pages covered with scribblings from his pocket. "Well, the question was, 'How long would it take to cart Mount Fuji away with dump trucks, one truckload at a time?' So the basic issue was, 'How much is the volume of dirt and rocks that make up a mountain that size?' Not the kind of question they asked in tenth-grade geometry—or in my accounting class in college, for that matter."

Zhao smiled. "No. But then, none of the interesting questions are."

"So I looked up the height of Mount Fuji—it was something over 12,000 feet, but I just used 12,000 as an easy number to work with."

"Good decision. Getting the order of magnitude right is what matters, not the details."

"Then, I figured that Fuji was basically shaped like a cone. Everybody's seen pictures of it, in travel books or in Japanese prints, and it's pretty symmetrical. So I worked from that assumption, and I found the formula for the volume of a cone in an old math textbook."

"What is it?"

"Actually, I don't remember—something with *pi* in it. But I know where to find it if I need it again."

Zhao nodded approvingly. "Good, good."

Steve walked Zhao through the rest of his calculations. He'd had to call an old high school buddy who worked for a construction company to get the volume of an average dump truck. Otherwise, solving the problem had turned out to be surprisingly easy—a matter of multiplying and dividing—though time-consuming.

"So what did you learn from all this, Steve?" Zhao finally asked.

"Aside from the fact that it would take 8,000 some-odd years to move Mount Fuji by truck?"

"Yes, aside from that."

Steve thought. "I guess I learned that even weird numerical problems can usually be solved by using some information that's generally available and a little common sense."

"Not a bad lesson to learn," said Zhao. Being fast with numbers is important. But there's a little more to *Innumeracy* than that. The key is to *use* the numbers to ask and answer critical questions. Suppose you *had* to move Mount Fuji for some reason. Would dump trucks be a practical means? Are there enough trucks and drivers in Japan to do the job? How much would it cost? Where could you put the dirt? Without too much difficulty, you could figure out the answers to all these questions and more with the same basic information you already have.

"Now transport these kinds of questions to a business setting. How many people really ask the right questions about a business plan, a new product launch, a major investment, a marketing campaign, an HR program?

"It's surprising how many people in business aren't used to thinking this way. Very often you can work out fewer than seven calculations that will blow up an impressive-looking but fatally flawed business plan. I know—I've seen it done, and I've done it a few times myself." Zhao shook his head. "It *ought* to be done more often.

"By the way, there's a faster way to solve the Mt. Fuji puzzle. Maybe I'll show you some time. Meanwhile, keep thinking about *Innumeracy*, Steve, and look for ways to apply the principles. Being able to take the measure of the world is one of the most crucial skills we can develop.

"Which brings me to one of my favorite number-crunchers—a woman named Terry Allen.

"Terry started working for Waterstone Brothers straight out of college," Zhao continued. He leaned back in his chair and gazed at the ceiling thoughtfully, wanting to call up the story in all its details. "Have you heard of them?"

"An investment bank, right?"

"That's right. A small but very successful boutique firm peopled by brilliantly innovative folks—rocket scientists, as they're called. Terry fit in great from day one. She was a maniac with an enormous appetite for hard labor and a great deal of self-confidence.

"Terry spent her first year at Waterstone's doing basic number-crunching on their current deals. She was very good at it. She also found it supremely boring. She wound up doing the work in half the time by setting up all sorts of clever systems for herself, from smart files to spreadsheet subroutines.

"As a result, she had a lot of time to observe the place, learn the investment business, and try to figure out how the profit was made. She also pushed hard to get reassigned.

"Eventually, she was assigned to a group that worked on innovations in financial instruments.

"They were a small team, but very good. They'd come up with a great little innovation every ten months or so. Terry loved it. She pitched in and was terrific at it—smart and creative.

"But as Terry watched how the game was played, she couldn't help noticing how the big investment banking houses copied Waterstone's innovations, usually nine to twelve months after they were introduced. It irked her to see other companies riding on the coattails of her team's inventiveness. She went to Herb Waterstone, one of the three brothers who'd founded the firm. 'Can't we stop these guys?' she challenged. 'Can't we sue them or something?'

"Herb shrugged. 'Look, Terry,' he explained, 'Disney has copyrights, Merck has patents, but we have nothing. You can't copyright or patent a financial instrument or a financial service innovation. We play by jungle rules.'

"'So why do we do it?' Terry asked.

"'Because,' Herb answered, 'we make a ton of money before the imitation starts, and sometimes it helps us get a new long-term client or two.'

"Terry went away from this conversation feeling disturbed. 'There's got to be a way to beat this,' she thought.

"A few weeks later she was back in Waterstone's office. She outlined a plan. Waterstone liked it. She called in her team, and they organized to try it. The first time through the process, everybody went a little crazy. The second time, it ran much better. The third time, it was smooth as glass."

"What did they do?" Steve asked.

"Well, first of all, Terry figured out that Waterstone's made money the same way Intel makes money." Zhao grabbed his legal pad and drew a picture. Four strokes only and four labels.

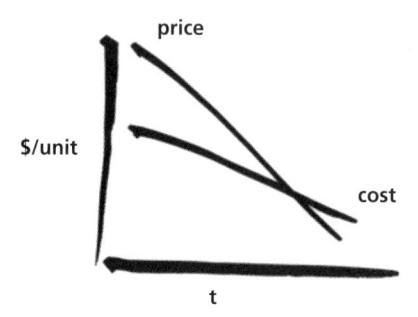

Steve studied the drawing, and he thought about what he knew about the microchip business. "Meaning that Intel invents a new chip and makes money by being the first to market?"

Zhao nodded. "Basically right," he agreed. "The main difference was that Intel usually had two to three years to profit from their innovations, while Waterstone's had only six to nine months. So Terry asserted that they needed instant diffusion—a faster way to squeeze out the juice before everybody else learned the secret. She helped design a neat system to accomplish this.

"Two weeks before announcing a new product, Waterstone's would send out a letter to two hundred clients letting them know it was on the way. A week in advance, they called them on the phone, saying, 'Our new product will be available next Monday.'

"Thursday evening before the launch, they'd start a training session on the new product for everybody in the company—a crash course covering every detail. The class continued on Friday morning. Any unanswered questions raised by the participants had to be researched on Friday afternoon. Saturday morning they'd be at it again. They kept working through the weekend until the entire firm was ready to explain the new product in their sleep. "The client calls started coming in on Monday morning. By the end of the week, they'd have fifty or sixty inquiries. Within two weeks, the number would be up to a hundred.

"By the third time through this process, they had the system fully tuned. It busted the bank. In the past, they'd made $30 million in revenue and $15 million in profit on a typical new instrument. With the new 'instant diffusion' system, the numbers went to $100 million in revenue and $70 million in profit."

"Terry was pretty smart," Steve observed.

"More important, she was persistent. Stubborn, in fact."

"Why? Did Waterstone's fight her system?"

"Not at all, they loved it."

"Was it the clients or the competition?"

"No."

"Then what was the problem?"

"Tedium."

"Tedium?"

"Yes. Tedium is the greatest single challenge for a business that's built on innovation. It may have been said best by Paul Cook, the President of Raychem Corporation."

Zhao slid open a desk drawer and extracted a thin, stapled document. He folded back the first couple of pages and drew a big circle with his marker around two paragraphs. He tossed the document to Steve.

"Steve, these hundred and fifty words are worth more than reading most whole books. This is where the money is."

Steve read:

> "What separates the winners and losers in innovation is who masters the *drudgery*. The creative process usually starts with a brilliant idea. Next you determine whether, if the brilliant idea worked, it would be worth doing from a business standpoint. That's the exhilarating part. It may be the most stimulating intellectually, but it's also the easiest.
>
> "Then comes the real work — reducing the idea to practice. That's the *drudgery* part of innovation, and that's where people need the most pressure and encouragement. You

can draw a chart of how the original excitement of a new idea creates all kinds of energy, but then people go into the pits for a long time as they try to turn that idea into products that can be manufactured. That's when you use the phone and the fax machine. That's when you have review meetings between the technical people and senior management. That's when, as CEO, you show the entire organization that you are just as interested in new product and process development as you are in manufacturing costs, sales, or quality."

When Steve finished reading, Zhao continued. "The amazing thing was that Terry Allen, who I thought was the most easily bored person in the world, ironed out the details, personally talked to all the people involved, and stuck with her system despite all the inevitable screw-ups of the first two go-rounds."

"She should have gotten a big bonus."

"She did."

"Is there anybody else who learned from Intel's Time Profit model and applied it so well?"

"Very, very few."

"How about in semiconductors?"

"I can't think of a single large-scale example in the whole $150 billion semiconductor industry."

"That's surprising."

"It's a paradox. They copy each others' chips, but not each others' business models."

"Shouldn't that change in the next five years?" Steve wondered.

"I think so."

"And if it does, then Intel will have to come up with something different."

"I think they will. I think they've already started."

Zhao paused.

"For next week . . ."

"I know, I know," said Steve, "give me five examples of the Time Profit model."

"Exactly," Zhao grinned.

"Suppose I can't find them?"

"Then think of where the Time Profit model *should* be applied."

"Fair enough. And what about my reading assignment? Didn't Andy Grove write a book?"

Zhao laughed. "Hold on, who's the teacher here?" he protested. "Yes, he wrote several. The most famous one was *Only the Paranoid Survive*, and it's well worth reading. But that's not your assignment. Take this interview with Paul Cook"—he pushed the pages toward Steve—"and read it all. That's enough for one week. See you next Saturday. Oh, and good luck with your telecom presentation."

Zhao turned around in his chair, opened a door in the credenza behind his desk, pulled out a stack of files, and began to thumb through them, looking for something. For a long moment, Steve didn't move. Then Steve cleared his throat.

Zhao looked at Steve over his shoulder. "Is there something else?" he asked.

"Er, last time—" he paused.

"What is it?" Zhao asked, a little impatiently.

"Your notes about Switchboard Profit—remember? You said I could have them if I did the *Innumeracy* problems—?"

Zhao frowned, then laughed. "Oh, right," he said. "Where are those?" He found the pages in a desk drawer and tossed them over to Steve, who eagerly gathered them up. "But Steve," he said, "don't spend too much time on those. We've got a lot more to cover. And you've got to learn how to solve these problems in your own way, not my way."

Steve was already halfway out the door. "I know that," he replied. "But an art student might want to copy a Picasso or two, even if he doesn't plan to paint that way his whole life." The door slammed shut behind him.

For an instant, Zhao was startled. Then he laughed out loud. "Copy, yes," he thought. "But Picasso, no."

6
Blockbuster Profit

November 16. Zhao nodded Steve into his usual chair. "So?" he asked.

"So, what?" Steve replied.

"So, how did your telecom Switchboard idea go over?"

Steve flushed a little. He'd spent most of the week trying to forget about Monday afternoon's meeting.

"Not very well, I take it?" said Zhao.

Steve was indignant. "I don't think they even got it!" he replied.

"How so?" Zhao asked.

Steve shook his head. "The questions they asked! The comments they made! Talk about narrow-minded. Paul Kozlowski—he's the president of the division—he was the worst. 'Why would we want to get into the retail business?' he kept asking me. 'Why should we compete with our own dealers? What will happen to them?' It was like he didn't see the benefits of *owning* the business, instead of just being another supplier."

"And how did you respond to his questions?" Zhao asked.

Steve shrugged. "I don't even know," he answered. "Frank and I were just taken aback. Who *cares* about the dealers, when you have the opportunity to take the business to a whole new level? And meanwhile Delmore's stock price keeps going down."

"Another two points in the last week," Zhao agreed.

Zhao was silent for a moment. Then he quietly commented, "You might want to think about Kozlowski's questions a little more, Steve. They strike me as quite interesting and *à propos*."

Steve groaned. "You, too?"

Zhao nodded. "Yes. And they're just two of the many questions that need to be taken seriously before a profit model shift can take place."

"But don't you think a Switchboard could work in the telecom business?"

"It probably could," Zhao answered. "But you wouldn't want to start developing one by ticking off the dealers who provide one hundred percent of your current revenue base."

"Hmm. When you put it that way, I guess not," Steve admitted.

"Furthermore," Zhao went on, "why would the *customers* want to turn to DelCom to be the supplier of all their telecom needs?"

"Well," Steve replied, "if we had access to all the best equipment from the best suppliers, as well as the expertise to put it all together . . ."

Zhao shook his head. "And what prevents a big customer—a Fortune

500 company, say—from putting together those same advantages on its own? Or from hiring a consulting firm to do it for them—someone whose independence isn't compromised by being a subsidiary of Delmore, Inc?"

Steve flushed again. "Nothing, I suppose. But if DelCom moved fast to claim the high ground in the industry, couldn't we become the supplier of choice?"

"Maybe," Zhao answered. "Ovitz leveraged unique personal qualities and connections to make his Switchboard the preeminent source of movie talent. Does DelCom have the same kind of unique qualities and connections in telecom?"

"Well, we have excellent technical capabilities," Steve replied. "Our gear is ranked with the best in the industry."

"So much so that everyone would immediately name DelCom as the most prestigious and powerful brand name in the business?"

"Not quite *that* good," Steve admitted. "There are other manufacturers on a par with us."

"And do you have a monopoly, or a near-monopoly, on the best minds in telecommunications research?"

Steve shook his head. "No, not at all."

"So is DelCom in a position to take over the marketplace just because it wants to?"

Steve was silent. "Maybe not," he finally conceded.

"Did the DelCom team kill your idea?" Zhao asked.

"Not in so many words. They said they'd study it. But the atmosphere wasn't very positive." He sighed.

Zhao let the silence linger for a moment. "Any lessons to be learned from this episode?" he finally asked.

"I guess I need to work my plans through a little better before proposing them," Steve said. His expression was sheepish.

"I think that's fair," Zhao said gently. "And consider them from the point of view of the people you need to work with," he added. "Most business people bring a lot of history to the decisions they make. It's not very realistic to expect them to jettison it all just because a bright young man comes along with a good idea."

"Point taken," Steve nodded.

"So let's move on for now," Zhao said. He reached into his desk drawer, grabbed the familiar yellow pad (already noticeably thinner than when they'd first met), wrote two words, and tossed the pad to Steve. Steve read aloud: "Marc Geron."

"No," Zhao corrected, "with a soft g. It's like the g in the French word *gendarme*, or as if it were written *zh*—like my name."

"Geron," Steve repeated, pronouncing it *Zheron*. "Who is he?"

"He's the man who taught me about Blockbuster Profit."

Steve waited. He was beginning to learn the uses of silence from Zhao.

Zhao noticed. He was encouraged, but made no comment. In a minute, he continued.

"Marc ran U.S. manufacturing for a Swiss-based pharmaceutical company. It was a mess. He asked me to help. We worked on a couple of truly great projects together, and we became friends as a result.

"Marc had a passion for knowledge—real knowledge—and for profitability. His aim was always simple: it was to build the single most profitable operation in his field. Blockbuster Profit was his third model. He didn't invent it—few of us ever invent a profit model—but he did perfect it."

"What were his first two models?"

"Quality, and Field Force Morale."

"Say again?"

"Just listen. When Marc and I started looking at his manufacturing operation, neither of us knew what we were doing. We knew it was in trouble, but we couldn't tell how to fix it. We wrestled with it for five months. The answer we found was Quality—specifically, what you might call upstream thinking.

"To describe it in slightly oversimplified terms, Marc and I were dealing with a twenty-seven-step manufacturing process. After studying it exhaustively, we realized that if we could prevent problems in steps one and two, we'd save tons of money in steps eight, nine, ten, and so on. The effects were huge.

"Geron turned around manufacturing in the U.S. Later, he did the same in the UK, then in France.

"In France, he was also given responsibility for the salesforce. He did all right, but he wasn't really satisfied. Then he was assigned to the U.S. to solve the salesforce puzzle there. That led to our second opportunity to work together.

"Again, it took us several months to figure out what was wrong and how to fix it. But we got it. This time, the model was Field Force Morale.

"We did a pretty neat survey of the salesforce. It took us two months to put it together. We found almost all the problems. Marc then fired people, reorganized those who remained into specialty groups, gave them great information they could use to make better decisions, and most important changed the compensation plan from fifteen percent variable to fifty percent variable."

Steve interrupted. "Meaning, a lot bigger payday for the best salespeople, a lot less for the worst?"

"That's right. It was risky, but it worked. We surveyed again a year later, and the results were extraordinary. The *esprit de corps* that the new compensation scheme helped create led to huge sales increases. Marc was a company hero for the second time over.

"During Marc's U.S. salesforce days, he spent a lot of time observing and learning the company's research and development organization. He was puzzled by how they operated. He thought it made no sense. At any given time, there'd be dozens of projects under way. They were plagued by countless delays. There was no shaping of the information around an individual project molecule, no building of an aura around it.

"Marc started reading reams of literature on product development, on how to do it well. He was disappointed by what he read. He and I started talking about it and puzzling it through. Little by little, we began to figure out what it took to create huge new products—blockbusters.

"This was in the mid-1980s. Over three years, Marc and I focused our study on three companies: Merck, Disney, and Glaxo. One had built a blockbuster machine, the other two were in the process of doing so.

"Finally, Marc felt ready to tackle the challenge of building his own blockbuster model. When there was an opening to run Agri-Chem, his company's herbicide and pesticide division, Marc asked for it. He politicked, lobbied, and cajoled for two months. The Swiss finally caved. They were afraid of losing him.

"Once again, Marc moved his family, this time to Memphis. And he and I were collaborating for a third time.

"The biggest change in Marc over his fifteen years of manufacturing and salesforce repair jobs was the growth in his confidence. Without that, I don't know whether he could have pulled off what he did at Agri-Chem.

"When Marc took over, Agri-Chem was doing okay financially, but its new product pipeline was a disaster. Worse, there was no method in place for thinking about R&D, about *how* to manage R&D activity, about how to tell the difference between high-profit R&D and anti-profit R&D."

"Anti-profit?"

"Sure, most R&D is anti-profit."

"Why? Because there's no telling which project will work and which one won't?"

"No, I'm not talking about the uncertainty. It's inevitable that not every R&D project will hit the target. R&D is anti-profit when it has no clear target, the *wrong* target—for example, a market where customers won't pay for what you've developed—or a *trivial* target, where the total profit return is a fraction of the total investment.

"Marc set to work to change all this. He was not greeted warmly, but that didn't bother him. He was a great line-drawer, and in six weeks the place was his."

"A line-drawer?"

"Yes. He would assert himself in numerous symbolic ways. He'd change the time or place of a meeting, change the list of attendees, require reports. Altogether it amounted to a thorough, ongoing campaign to define who was the boss.

"Once that was established, everything became more efficient. He had to ask for something only once. Soon his people learned to anticipate what Marc wanted, so he didn't have to ask at all.

"Then, of course, came the hard part—figuring out what to do. Marc had an advantage, because he'd spent so much time nosing about the R&D organization in the pharmaceutical company. He suspected that Agri-Chem's R&D profit model might be similar.

"He was right. But then he had to figure out how to apply it. He studied every project, read every market research report. He spent entire weekends reading the science, learning all there was to know about bugs and weeds and what it took to kill them—safely. He became a terror at R&D review meetings, asking questions that were not only pointed but supremely well-informed.

"But none of this was enough. Marc found that he was getting sucked into an internal vortex. He realized that he wouldn't get really good answers, or at least clues to the answers, without going outside the organization. So he started hitting the road, talking to reps, to customers, to the customers' consultants and advisors.

"Now his questions became even more ferocious and more targeted. Gradually, it became clear to Marc and then to everyone in the organization that all of Agri-Chem's profit was in a few blockbuster products. Yet the blockbusters were getting very little of the right kinds of R&D attention.

"Marc changed that quickly, starting with the entire tenor of the project discussions. Projects of trivial value began to get no airtime. Soon they died of neglect.

"By contrast, the potential big winners got a tremendous amount of workover, discussion, and debate. The attention focused on them was so forceful that the dialogue often spilled over into the hallways, into after-hours, into the agenda of other management meetings. Everyone got focused on the new key questions: *How can we increase the feasibility level of the big projects? How can we accelerate their development? Can we parallel-process? Can we get more studies done to improve their positioning? What will it take to hit a home run?*

"Within ten months, the place was buzzing. Deadlines and milestones, which had once been meaningless, became a very big deal. People paid attention. They knew Marc was watching, and they knew you couldn't fool him.

"So far, so good. But Marc was worried. He knew that you could create focus on the most important projects, but that you couldn't remove all the uncertainty. The big bets could still go bust.

"So Marc now went into total risk-management mode. He started doing role-plays for the FDA approval process, getting tough but actionable opinions from external scientific advisors, and challenging the organization to identify super-high-value projects that weren't in their portfolio but should be.

"I remember Marc telling me that this R&D turnaround was the toughest management job he ever had, because the cycle was so long. But he kept at it. His second and third years were tough, because of past mismanagement. He had to work very hard to pare expenses in a way that didn't undermine the long-term potential of the business. He was a real steward, a real fiduciary.

"In year four, the situation started to turn. The first new product of Marc's regime was launched, and it produced good numbers. It wasn't a blockbuster, but it breathed new financial life into the division.

"The second product was a disaster. It was a good product, but two competitors came out at the same time and swamped it, outspending Marc ten to one. Marc reacted aggressively. He pulled back on large marketing expenditures and focused on two specialty segments, pushing hard to win there and husbanding resources to fight the big battle another day.

"The third product arrived in Marc's fifth year, and it was the big one. Marc was very politically savvy. He'd set management's expectations at a very low level, especially after the difficulties with the second product. But this one beat the forecasts handily, month after month after month.

"And Marc was ready. He always had a contingency plan for everything. He started plowing the profits back into R&D, to feed the other potential blockbusters he had been lining up over the last three years. He relied heavily on outside research organizations to avoid building fixed costs. He finally had the system tuned to where he wanted it to be.

"Perhaps most crucially, he'd also built the organization's self-confidence."

"Self-confidence?" asked Steve.

"Yes. The Blockbuster model is a mind game. It takes huge confidence to aim high, to deliberately set out to build the next great blockbuster. When Marc got there, the dominant mood in the organization was *We can't.* By his sixth year, the assumption was reversed to not only *We can* but to *We probably will.*"

Zhao paused. He realized he'd been talking a long time.

"That's quite a story," Steve said. "Did Marc get another promotion?"

"He did. He had a chance to go back to Switzerland to be a real bigwig. But he turned it down. It led to a very funny outcome."

"How so?"

"Well, by this time, Marc was really into the Blockbuster model. Because of his first three successes, he now had a river of cash to work with. And he'd developed a deep familiarity with the science. Even though he didn't need to any longer, he'd spend weeks poring through the literature, reading the most recent articles on advances in crop protection, terrorizing his organization with a vigorous stream of new ideas.

"He decided he would push the Blockbuster model even further. He studied Merck. He studied Disney. He developed his own ideas."

"Such as?"

"Such as insisting that Agri-Chem develop an imaginary portfolio of the top fifteen blockbuster opportunities in their markets, whether or not they had a corresponding product. It took six months, but he got them to create that list."

"And?"

"Well, they had actual projects for only seven of those ideas. So Marc pushed them to search for *all* of the others, either through licensing or internal discovery. In two more years, he had one research molecule directed at each of the fifteen. Or, I should say, at least one."

"At least one?"

"Yes. Marc knew, like everybody else, that the risks in the R&D game were quite high. But he went beyond the others to do something about it. He insisted that each of his lead projects have at least one back-up compound, sometimes two. That way, if the lead failed, they would learn from it for the next one, rather than suffering a total write-off."

"A real blockbuster management system, then?" said Steve, a touch of wonder in his voice.

"Exactly so."

"Wow! I would have liked to work for this guy."

"You certainly would have. I worked with him for over a decade, and I learned more from him than from any other manager."

"He wound up running the whole company, of course," Steve ventured.

Zhao burst out laughing. "Of course not!" he roared.

Steve's eyes were round. "What? With that record?"

"That's the problem—Marc was *too* successful. Don't you see? He angered the Swiss. He was creating incredible earnings growth and becoming too much of a standout. He was always pushing the model to the next level, to a more contained and more managed level of risk, to a higher level of technological sophistication. Every other division of the company looked a little lackluster by comparison. Do you think that's a way to make friends? No way!

"By year seven, as Marc continued to immerse himself in the science, it was clear to him that Agri-Chem would have to become a major force in biotechnology if they were to continue their growth in intellectual leadership in their field. He started pushing that theme with his bosses."

"What did he want to do about it?"

"He wanted to make an acquisition, or two, or three. He wanted a research deal with a major university or two. He wanted to hire two or three standout talents. But the harder he pushed, the more they resisted."

"That's crazy!"

"Not as crazy as it got."

"What do you mean?"

"In the end, they fired him."

"What! How could they?"

"Easy. It was their company. They owned the marbles."

"That's outrageous."

Zhao looked sober. "Steve, it happens all the time." The two men fell silent for a long moment.

Finally, Steve asked, "What did Marc do?"

"What could he do? He smiled, and he cleaned out his office."

"And today?"

"He's having a wonderful time. He teaches strategy in Florida. The students either hate him or adore him—often both. He's still a real challenger. And he does a lot of deep-sea fishing—it's a passion for him."

Steve had been jotting notes about Marc's story, but his pen had lagged Zhao's narrative. After Zhao fell silent, Steve continued to scribble furiously for a couple of minutes. Finally he'd caught up, and he put down his pen.

"So what do you think?" Zhao asked.

Steve shook his head. "It's another paradox. A story of human foolishness—like so many of your stories."

Zhao pondered this. "Maybe so," he finally conceded. "But it's easy for us to see the mistakes, at a distance and with hindsight—not so easy on the ground with events unfolding and emotions running high."

Steve grunted. "I suppose." He didn't sound convinced. "What's my reading assignment?"

"Read A *Technique for Producing Ideas* by James Webb Young. That's where Geron learned front-end loading."

"Front-end loading?"

"Yes. It's the opposite of cramming for an exam, or writing the term paper in the last forty-eight hours."

"Meaning—?"

"You put the cramming up front. You squeeze the maximum reading into the first forty-eight hours rather than the last. You practice total immersion, early. Read as much as you can as fast as you can, read till you get a headache, and keep reading. And you do all this at the *beginning* of the project.

"Here's what happens. You build a structure of knowledge that's incomplete but very powerful. Why? Because every new fact or idea or hypothesis you run into later gets integrated into an evolving structure that keeps getting stronger over time."

"Front-end loading," Steve mused.

"Young's *Technique* is very short. So please also read *Einstein's Dreams* by Alan Lightman. It can open your mind, if you let it. Let it."

Steve smiled, and left.

Zhao sighed and went to the window. He gazed down at the Brownian bustle of Saturday morning strollers, joggers, and shoppers in the street forty-four floors below. He wondered whether he was getting anywhere. Steve was very bright, and Zhao genuinely liked him. But he was also young and headstrong, as his misadventure with DelCom had demonstrated. He had so much to learn about how to work with and through people, about how to turn intellectual understanding into practical knowledge. Were Zhao's lessons conveying any of the pith of the business life, or only its surface?

These stories are essential, Zhao reflected, *but they're so after-the-fact, so cut-and-dried, so pat. Is there any way to make someone like Steve really understand how to react like a Marc Geron—other than to throw him into the pool and see whether he swims? Instead of which I'm telling him stories about the world's greatest swimmers . . . oh, they're entertaining, no doubt. But are they anything more than that?*

Zhao suddenly realized that someone had been knocking on his door. "Come in!" he called.

It was Frances. "Good morning, David! I'm just here for an hour or two—got to print out the latest draft of that report on the structure of the chemical industry. And don't forget your three o'clock meeting."

Zhao almost *had* forgotten. It was a meeting with a good friend from three blocks away, an easy one to reschedule. "Cancel it, please, Frances."

Instead, Zhao would spend the afternoon rethinking his plan for the next fourteen weeks. *How can I design Steve's experience so as to unlock all that he's capable of?* He thought about Ezra Pound, one of his favorite writers, and he smiled: "Make it new," Pound used to say. *How do I do that for Steve?* How do I make it new? He returned to his chair, grabbed a fresh legal pad, and swiftly began to write.

7
Profit-Multiplier Model

November 23. "Any more fallout from your telecom proposal?" Zhao asked Steve when he arrived the following Saturday.

"Not too much, no," Steve replied.

Zhao raised an eyebrow but said nothing.

"I've gotten some interesting reactions from people, that's all," Steve added.

"Such as?"

"Frank says that a couple of his colleagues in the division thanked him for raising the issues, even though our idea got shot down. And my boss—Cathy Hughes, the VP of strategic planning—asked me not to push any ideas of my own without running them by her first."

"Not surprising."

"No. But then she asked me to give her the backup on the Switchboard concept, and when she mentioned it in our staff meeting. It sounded as though she actually liked the idea."

"—Just didn't like the way you handled it," Zhao concluded.

"That's about it."

"Anything else?"

"Cathy's assigned me to head a team looking at a building supplies company we bought two years ago. She used the same term you use, profit model. She said she thinks their profit model may be running out of gas."

"That was the Devereau acquisition, right?" Zhao asked.

"Right, Devereau Industries. Now called Delmore Supply. Insulation, air filters, furnace linings, door and window screens, stuff like that. A very cyclical business. It's another one of our companies that's been hit by the current slowdown. But Cathy and the top brass are worried that there's more to it than that."

"Any comparison to the telecom business?"

Steve thought for a moment. "Could be. Like telecom, it's an almost commoditized industry. One or two companies have broken out of the pack with meaningful differentiation of their products, but most are still competing on price. And when building falls off, they're left scrambling for crumbs."

"I'll be curious as to what solutions you come up with, Steve."

"Any ideas to suggest?" Steve asked with a sly grin.

"I think I'll let you earn your salary on this one, Steve. But we can talk about *your* ideas if you like."

"Fair enough. I'll keep you posted."

"So what about the Blockbuster model from last time?" Zhao asked.

"It's a really exciting one," Steve beamed. "Here's my list." He handed Zhao a sheet from a yellow legal pad and waited, wearing a look of proud expectation.

Zhao took the list. It had twelve entries. He studied it carefully. Without lifting his eyes from the page, he reached inside his jacket pocket and pulled out his fountain pen. Then he methodically crossed out entries 4, 5, 6, 7, 8, 10, and 12. At the bottom of the page, he carefully printed the words "Do Over" and handed it back to Steve.

Zhao leaned back in his chair and, in a conversational tone, asked, "What do you think a Profit-Multiplier model is?"

Steve was still staring at the page in his hand. His face was a little red. Zhao reached over, gently grabbed the page, turned it over, and handed it back. Steve opened his mouth as if to speak, shut it, opened it again, and finally chose silence. Shaking his head, he folded the page and tucked it into his shirt pocket.

Zhao asked again, "What do you think a Profit-Multiplier model might be?"

"Taking a profit and doubling it?"

"Yes, but how?"

Steve sat back and began thinking. Seconds went by in silence. Steve's eyes searched the corners of the room, as though an answer might be lurking there. A minute passed. Then two. Finally, Steve burst out, "Any way you can!"

Zhao's laugh was open, expansive. It dissolved the tension that had filled the room.

"Very good. You're not even wrong! But the fact is, you don't have to stop at doubling your profit. You can multiply it several times over. Now give me an example."

Steve recoiled. He liked it better when Zhao spent more time telling stories than asking questions.

"I can't think of one."

Zhao saw that Steve was still shaken by the crossed-out lines on his homework. He decided to change his approach.

"Steve, what does Honda make?" he asked very quietly, almost gently.

"Cars."

"And?"

"Motorcycles."

"And?"

Steve thought. He remembered a commercial, vaguely.

"Lawnmowers."

"And?"

Steve thought. Remembered something else, even more vaguely. "Outboard motors for boats—?"

"Yes. And?"

Steve had run out of ideas. "Industrial motors?"

"Do you know, or are you just guessing?"

Steve laughed. "Just guessing."

"Well, you're right."

A small light went on. "So," Steve said, "Profit-Multiplier is taking one skill and making money from it five or six times."

"Well, it could be a skill, or it could be something else. What else?"

Steve thought. More long seconds passed. Nothing in particular occurred to him. He was feeling mildly irritated. *Why doesn't Zhao just tell me what I need to know, like other teachers? What a character!*

Suddenly, Steve's frown exploded into a laugh. "I know!—a character—like a Disney character!"

Zhao nodded. "Sure. Or a bunch of characters—the Muppets, say—or a great story, or a valuable piece of information."

"So you take a character, or a story, or a skill, or any other asset, and iterate it, reuse it, and give it a different form."

"That's right. And how does the profit happen?"

"Well . . . lower R&D or development cost. You don't have to reinvent the wheel every time you use it."

"And what else?"

Steve frowned again, not with irritation this time but with the effort of thought. More silence.

Zhao gave Steve a nudge. "What's important in R&D or development, Steve?"

"Like I said, the cost."

"Yes, but what else?"

"Well, the odds of success are important. We talked about it last time. Most R&D projects don't produce anything of value. If you could improve the odds—"

"Exactly," Zhao interrupted. "And what happens to the odds of success for a Honda, or a Disney, or a Henson Productions, or a Bloomberg?"

"They have to go up. Probably way up."

"Indeed they do," Zhao nodded. He was looking pleased.

"It's a little like Multi-Component profit, isn't it?" Steve observed.

"Is it?" Zhao fired back.

"Well, sure. Both involve taking the same basic idea and recycling it in many forms."

"Maybe," Zhao said. "But they're not the same thing. Remember the bookstore business we talked about, or the hotel business. How many different products were they selling?"

Steve thought. "I guess they were really selling the same product, only in various packages."

"Right," Zhao agreed. "What about Disney? Is *The Lion King* on Broadway the same product as *The Lion King* on DVD or a Lion King lunch box or video game or theme park attraction?"

Steve saw the point. "No—they're all different products spun off from the same original asset."

"You've got it. Now, can this profit model work in every business?"

"No." Steve answered quickly.

"Are you *sure*?" Zhao asked.

As soon as Zhao asked the question, Steve realized he wasn't at all sure. "Can I think about it?"

"Yes. Make a list of the *best* examples you can think of for the Profit-Multiplier model, but then think again about whether *every* business has the opportunity to work this way. And if not, why not. That's enough for today. I'll see you in two weeks—we'll take the Thanksgiving weekend off."

"All right. Is there a drawing for the Profit-Multiplier model?"

"Of course." Zhao grabbed his pad and sketched eight boxes connected by seven lines. He handed the sketch to Steve.

Other forms of realization

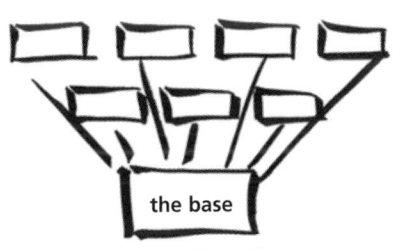

the base

skill, asset, intellectual property

"One more thing," Zhao said. "Did you read *Einstein's Dreams*?"

Steve's reply was enthusiastic. "I sure did. Great book!"

"You see the relevance, I suppose?"

Steve flushed a little. "Not really," he admitted.

"Well, what is the book about?"

"It's about all the different kinds of time that could exist in the universe—backward time, time as a loop, multiple-track time, and so on and so forth."

"And isn't there a connection to what we've spoken about today?"

Steve considered the question. Then, tentatively, "Well, the Profit-Multiplier model is about variations on a theme—finding alternative ways of mining value from the same asset. Is that the connection?"

"You're close," Zhao replied. "Remember what I said about letting *Einstein's Dreams* open your mind? That's the point. And it relates not just to the Profit-Multiplier model but to all the profit models. Many people see only one way of making a profit—the one they grew up with, usually, or the one that's been written up in the most recent issue of *Fortune* magazine. Just as they can imagine only one kind of time. Reality is much more complicated and promising than our limited imaginations often let us recognize."

The two men lapsed into silence. Finally, Steve asked, "Is there a reading assignment for next time?"

"*Asimov on Astronomy*, chapter eight."

Steve left. Zhao sat for a time, reflecting on that day's session. I wonder how well I'm getting through to him, he thought. Or rather, how well he's getting through to the world beyond. Steve is smart, no doubt about that. But is his mind open enough to perceive the alternate universe waiting around the next street corner?

The next few weeks would tell a lot.

8
Entrepreneurial Profit

December 7. Steve had forgotten to set his alarm clock. He'd awakened half an hour late with an unusually vivid dream crowding his consciousness. He'd been working at a desk on a high floor in a tall office tower, not unlike the midtown building he actually worked in—or Zhao's downtown building, for that matter. Suddenly he'd found himself outside, looking up at the building, which now appeared to be a thick-walled, moated castle like something out of the middle ages. As he looked, huge cracks appeared in the castle's foundation, and stones from the high turrets began to topple into the moat, sending cascades of water into the air, engulfing him . . .

Steve awoke with a start. Seeing the time, he gulped a cup of coffee, threw on his clothes, and raced for the subway. When he finally walked into the office seven minutes late, Zhao waved Steve into his usual seat across the desk and, with no preamble, launched into a story.

"I met my friend Jack Sanders for lunch last Tuesday," Zhao said. "Jack is the cheapest guy in the world. He's now on his fourth venture. He sold his first three for a fortune. Two are doing well, and he regrets having sold them. The third one's in trouble, thanks entirely to mediocre, 'imaginationless' management. Jack is in discussions to buy it back. He thinks he can fix it in under ten months."

Steve settled into his chair and tried to focus on Zhao's story. "That's a pretty precise estimate."

"Jack's a pretty precise guy. He has more detailed knowledge of where all his nickels are than most people have of their twenty-dollar bills."

Steve grinned. "So who paid for lunch?"

Zhao did not grin back. "It was Jack's turn."

Steve caught the funny tone in Zhao's reply. "But—?" he suggested.

"But he said he'd flip for it. Double or nothing. Anything to avoid an expense."

"And what happened?"

"He won. It was amazing—Jack was so very, very happy."

"What else does Jack do besides being very cheap?"

"The most important thing about Jack is that he preaches frugality the way missionaries preach their faith: with zeal, passion, and absolute commitment. He creates a psychology of saving that is absolute and universal. And he makes himself into an example."

Steve realized that this was more than small talk—that today's lesson had already begun. He started scratching notes on a pad. "How so?" he asked.

"Two dozen ways. For example, when he travels, he always flies coach, and he always stays in the cheapest hotel that observes *basic* principles of cleanliness.

"Jack also saves money by challenging the necessity for most trips. He likes to ask questions like, 'Why can't we make a deal using the phone and the fax machine?' He's only right forty percent of the time, but that's enough to make a huge difference. The productivity hit is huge. It saves a lot of dollars, but, more important, it frees up thousands of fresh-for-fighting hours that his troops have available to apply to the tasks that matter."

Zhao paused. Steve remarked, "Sounds smart and tough."

Zhao went on: "He's also a great believer in communication, but communication on the cheap. His typical off-site meeting is held at a high school gym. It starts early, ends late, and features a high-fiber agenda, each item focused on customers, or reducing costs, or selling more. He sets expectations very clearly."

"What else does he do?"

"Well, you've heard enough about him. *You* tell *me*."

Steve felt as if he'd suddenly been thwacked with a big, flat stick. *All right, I'm game.* He thought for a minute. "He must be hell on suppliers," he finally said.

"Tough, yes. 'Hell,' no. Jack wants rock bottom prices, but also creativity and new ideas for better ways of doing things. So he's intense with suppliers, but he doesn't beat them up. He persuades with passion, making suppliers understand how they'll benefit if Jack can keep on growing twice as fast as the rest of his industry. And Jack's habit of planning in advance and being hyper-organized saves the suppliers a tremendous amount of headaches and money. So for most of them, he's a very tough yet very profitable customer."

Zhao paused. "So what else does he do, Steve?"

Steve thought furiously.

"He delays capital expenditures, and he asks hard questions about every major expense."

Zhao considered this. "The questions he asks are hard but always very well informed. And he doesn't ask about *major* expenses only. What else?"

Steve thought.

"He holds contests among his people to test the frontiers of great performance."

"Yes, good. More?"

"He throws parties to celebrate star performers."
"Right. What else?"
"And he copies shamelessly from competitors."
"Yes, shamelessly. Is that all?"
"Isn't that enough?"
"Well, yes. But not for Jack."

Steve thought more. "I bet Jack experiments a lot," he ventured.

Zhao's eyes widened, almost imperceptibly. He rose one notch in his seat. "Yes, he does. And what does he do with the results?"

"Well, when he fails, he cuts back quickly."

"And when the experiment works?"

"He pours it on."

"How do you think the people in his little company *feel*?"

Jack considered. "He must drive them crazy at times," he finally commented.

"Sure," Zhao agreed. "And a few people who can't handle the pressure leave. But what about those who stay?"

"Most of the time, I imagine they feel . . . excited, engaged. At least they know they're not wasting their time or their energy."

"Right!" Zhao thumped the desk with his fist. "Plus, winning is more fun than losing. And more fun than being bored."

"Where did Jack learn all this?" Steve wondered.

"Half from his father, who was an excellent but unambitious businessman. The other half he learned by assiduously studying Sam Walton. But there are other models, of course. Jack reminds me of Soichiro Honda: He raised hell, drove his company hard, and created a tremendous amount of fun in the process."

Zhao and Steve paused, savoring the story.

"Okay," Steve was the first to break the silence. "What's the profit model for today?"

"We just did it."

Steve started. "We did it? What is it?"

"You tell me."

Steve thought about Jack, about Sam Walton, about frugality squared, about clear communication, about speed, experimentation, and fun. "Smells like what people call entrepreneurship."

"That's right," Zhao affirmed. "The strongest force in business. One that, among other things, totally aligns an organization behind rational, common-sense, profit-seeking activity, rather than all the extraneous nonsense that only large organizations can afford or tolerate. It's a simple mindset, one that says, 'We can't *afford* to operate any other way.' That's the source of a hell of a lot of profit.

"The hardest thing in business is to keep the entrepreneurial spirit alive and flourishing in the wake of continued success." Zhao paused. "Not unlike the drudgery of innovation, in a way."

"So," Steve commented, "I guess this must be the Entrepreneurial Profit model."

"Yes, exactly. Have you ever experienced it directly?"

"No."

"Of course not. Delmore is a large organization, one with enough cash flow from legacy successes to subsidize all sorts of non-entrepreneurial behavior."

"Like having a strategic planning department," Steve remarked wryly. "We like to think that's a *good* thing. You make it sound like the curse of success."

"It can be — or rather, it can be *one* of the curses of success," Zhao corrected him. "I have a feeling Colonel Delahanty would have understood that."

"Who?"

"You never heard of Cyrus Delahanty? — the founder of Delmore?"

"Not really," Steve admitted.

Zhao shook his head. "Look him up some time. Not one of the greatest business figures of his day, but a rather typical one. Did all kinds of things to make a living during the 1880s and 1890s — repaired bicycles, built chimney covers, manufactured barbed wire. Finally hitched his wagon to the automobile business. Started making acetylene lamps, bumpers, and other auto parts. Branched out into aircraft parts during World War One. By 1925, Delmore was a major supplier to Ford. It all started out of Delahanty's barn in Indiana."

Now, Steve thought, *seventy-five years later, Delahanty's barn has turned into a moated castle . . . with cracks in the foundation.* "I will look him up," Steve promised. "Is there a picture for Entrepreneurial Profit?"

"Not really. Sometimes a story is better than a picture."

"Anything I should read?"

"*Made in America*, by Sam Walton with John Huey. It's the best learning on Entrepreneurial Profit that I've ever encountered — by far. It also has two other profit models buried in it. But more on that later, when we get to it. You don't have to read the whole book now, just the first five chapters, a hundred pages or so."

The meeting seemed to be winding down. "Is that all?" Steve asked.

"Not quite. What did you think about *Asimov on Astronomy?*"

Steve thought. "Interesting book — good writer."

"Yes, and — ?"

"And a great head for numbers."

"That's true," Zhao said. "But there's a point here that goes beyond the *Innumeracy* idea. Did you see how Asimov uses the numbers as the basis for a story?"

"I'm not sure what you mean," Steve replied.

"Remember what he points out about the relative distances of planets from the sun, and what this tells us about the nature of the Tenth Planet?"

"Oh, yes. I recall the phrase 'utter isolation.'"

"Exactly. If there is a Tenth Planet in our solar system, it is almost certainly farther from the ninth planet, Pluto, than the Earth is. It would come within two and a half billion miles of Pluto only once every 2,700 years. Think of the loneliness of that."

"It's like science fiction," Steve commented.

"Yes, but it's strictly fact-based. It's one thing to play with the numbers. It's another to sense what the numbers tell you about relationships, connections, cause-and-effect."

"I'm still trying to get comfortable with the numbers themselves," Steve remarked ruefully. "I really don't understand how you do it."

"How I do what?" Zhao asked.

"How you calculate so fast—without a calculator."

Zhao broke into a broad grin. "Easy. I cheat!"

"Cheat?"

"Sure. I simplify, I take shortcuts."

"But how?"

"Easy. First, I do a very rough cut, very fast. Then I decide whether it's worth refining. Want to see?"

"Absolutely."

"Okay, let's go back to Mount Fuji. If you just let yourself estimate, you can do the Fuji problem in thirty seconds, all in your head. Listen.

"Imagine Fuji is a mile high. That's wrong, but it *doesn't matter*. We'll fix that later. Now imagine that it's a cone inside a box one mile on each side. To figure the volume of the box, instead of 5,280 feet on a side, use five thousand. So the volume is five thousand, cubed. How much is that, Steve?"

Steve figured. Five times five times five is 125. A thousand times a thousand times a thousand is a billion. "125 billion," he answered.

"Okay. If Fuji fills about half of the cube, that would give us about 60 billion cubic feet, right?"

"Right."

"Now divide that by about 2,000 cubic feet for each truck."

"That gives us 30 million truckloads."

"Figure each one takes an hour. So divide 30 million hours by 24 hours per day."

That took Steve a few seconds. "Umm, one and a quarter . . . it comes to 1.25 million days."

"And divide that by 365 days per year. Call it four hundred, that's easier."

"That makes around three thousand years."

"Great. Now you can go back and refine the figuring if you need to. Fuji is more like two miles high, for one thing, so the volume actually quadruples. Think of it this way. If the cube measures ten thousand feet to a side, then the volume is 10K times 10K times 10K, which comes to one trillion. Half of that is 500 billion. Which is four times 125 billion. Do you follow me?"

"Barely," Steve admitted.

"Anyway, the result is far from exact. But at least you know the order of magnitude you're dealing with. The answer is more like ten thousand years than five hundred years or ten million years. And you did it in thirty seconds flat."

Steve was impressed.

"Steve," Zhao pressed on, "*always* play the arithmetic. It'll be the strongest ally you have in the room. It'll be your truth tester and your opportunity detector."

Steve was starting to feel a little better. *I might be able to do this*, he was thinking. "Any way to practice this?"

"Sure. *Innumeracy* is full of examples. So is Asimov. You already read chapter eight. Now read chapter nine.

"But the real answer, Steve, is that you can do this by yourself any time you want. Any time you read an article in *Business Week*, play with the numbers—the extrapolations, the projections, the implications. Same with *The Wall Street Journal*, or *Fortune*, or *Forbes*. To say nothing of the reports that cross your desk. You must see a lot of the numbers related to Delmore's businesses, right?"

"Sure."

"Don't take them at face value. Peel the top layers off them and figure out what they tell you.

"You'll read and think much more critically when you get into the habit of rubbing two numbers together. The *habit*. And it is a habit—a silly little, wonderful habit.

"It'll get you a lot closer to winning. It'll help you make slightly better decisions every day. And once a month, it'll keep you from making a mega-mistake."

Zhao suddenly stopped talking. He seemed to realize he'd been on a soapbox—one of his favorite soapboxes, in fact. He paused. Then, more gently, he asked Steve, "Get all that?"

Steve smiled. "I got it."

"Good. I'll see you next week."

9
Specialist Profit

December 14. "You look glum," Zhao commented as Steve walked in.
"And I bet you know why," Steve replied.
"I can guess." Zhao had seen that week's headlines:

DELMORE WILL CUT WORKFORCE BY 16,000
Expected $1.1 Billion Loss Spurs Layoffs, Sales of Businesses

"They're already cutting back on staff positions," Steve commented. "Cathy told me my job is okay for now. But three people in my department are being let go. And so are some of the people I've worked with in the chemical and pharmaceutical divisions. They haven't decided yet which companies to sell."

"Those are tough choices to make," Zhao remarked. "The businesses you can get good money for are usually the ones you don't want to sell."

"What worries me," Steve said, "is that lots of folks at Delmore are starting to *hope* their divisions will get sold. They're saying, 'At least we'll have a fighting chance if someone buys us who knows what to do with us.'"

"So the pressure on you and Cathy and the rest of the planning group is that much greater."

"I'll say," Steve agreed.

"Any bright ideas on the building supplies business?"

"Not yet . . . but we'll talk about it soon," Steve replied. "Meanwhile, please teach me something new. I could use a little distraction."

"Okay," Zhao said. "Let's start with a story." He leaned back in his chair. "When my son was growing up," Zhao began, "we'd always go to the Museum of Science in Cambridge, Massachusetts, especially on Saturday afternoons when it was raining. We'd always go to the Omni Theater for their latest show on sharks, or earthquakes, or volcanoes.

"My favorite spot in the museum was the math wall in the math room, where there were short biographies of major mathematicians, from Ptolemy to Fermat to Neumann. My favorite panel was the one on Hilbert. Hilbert's strategy for learning was extraordinarily simple: sequential specialization. He would focus on one discipline for months until he approached mastery. Then he moved to the next. Then the next. It was a tight series of S-curves."

Zhao took out his pen and penned seven quick strokes on the next page of his yellow pad.

Learning

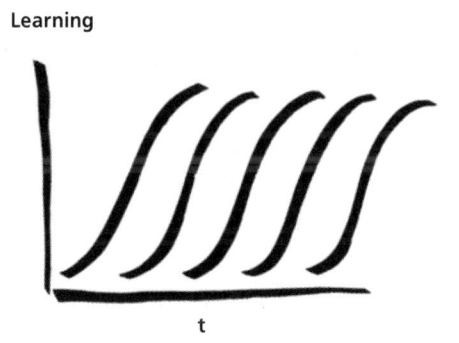

[Figure: five learning curves rising along a t-axis]

t

"Think of algebra, trigonometry, calculus, topology, and so on. Think about '*really* knowing' versus just 'knowing,' and you have the essence of Hilbert's strategy.

"That's also the secret behind EDS's extraordinary value growth from 1962 to 1995. In building its systems integration business, EDS did not learn everything at once. It chose a segment — health care, for example, or banking or manufacturing — and learned it exquisitely well, until it really knew the customers' processes and costs as well as its own cost of providing services. And it knew those numbers not in general, but specifically, for a particular manufacturer, or a bank, or a hospital. It was Hilbert's sequential specialization applied to systems integration.

"The economic results were fantastic. Several years ago, in the early 90s, EDS's margins were thirteen to fifteen percent, while IBM was just breaking even.

"Nor is EDS the only example of specialization profit. In the world of business forms, Wallace achieved the same extraordinary level of profitability in the telecommunications sector. While other competitors served a half dozen segments from health care to financial services, government, manufacturing, transportation, and so on, Wallace focused on telecom. They knew the processes and structures of telecom operations inside out. They knew how contracts were structured, how processes worked, where the greatest value could be added. They earned margins unheard-of in the business forms world."

Steve listened, fascinated. But then Zhao flipped a switch.

"Okay, Steve. Now tell me *why* they were so profitable."

Steve was almost caught by surprise, but not quite. The last few weeks had half-prepared him to expect a tough question at a surprise moment in the flow.

His mind shifted into high gear. "Well," he began, "their better knowledge of the customer's system gave them a cost advantage in delivering their products and services."

"*Cuanto?*" Zhao asked.

"Excuse me?"

"I'm sorry—that's an expression I like to use. It just means, how much?"

Steve thought about it. "At least five to six percent."

"Could it be higher?"

"Yes."

"*Cuanto?*" Zhao asked again, this time with a small, wry smile.

"Seven to ten percent?"

"What about higher than that?"

"Hmm . . . I doubt it."

"Okay. What else?"

"They might have a price premium."

"Big?"

"I doubt it."

"*Cuanto?*"

"Three to five percent."

"What else?"

Steve pondered. "Reputation within the segment. As in, 'These are the guys who really know our business.'"

"So what? What does that *translate* to?"

Steve sifted through the economic variables that mattered to profitability. "Well, they'd have a shorter selling cycle."

"Therefore what?"

"Therefore, higher average utilization in the business compared to the non-specialist."

"Anything else?"

Steve was stumped, but he kept at it. "They could attract better talent."

"Therefore, what?"

"Therefore, better quality, better cost, better ability to sell follow-on business."

Zhao was relentless. "Therefore what?"

"Therefore, better pricing and better utilization."

"All right." Zhao paused. Was he satisfied, finally? Not quite. "Have we explained the entire fifteen percent differential?"

Steve thought for a moment. "Close, but not really," he admitted. "There must be something else."

"There is," Zhao confirmed. "The specialists also tend to manage pricing better by building menus. They know delivery costs so well that they can price *á la carte* and do it accurately. They never say 'No' to the customer, but they do tell the customer how much it will cost. Whether it's EDS, or Wallace, or Hewlett-Packard in its Global Account Management program, the menu of services and its pricing algorithms are critical to the difference between breakeven and fifteen percent profitability. *Now*, is there anything else?"

Steve kept exploring the question in his own mind. A new thought came to him. "If you invent something—a solution to a problem—and you are well known as a specialist, you can sell that same solution over and over, five, ten, fifteen times or more."

Zhao's heart leaped for joy, but his face and manner remained completely impassive. Quietly, he put the next question. "And what might the margins on that be?"

"Sixty to seventy percent?"

"That high?"

Steve stood his ground. "Yes, that high."

"Why?"

"Because most of the cost is in the development of the solution, the idea. If you can replicate it and price to market, the operating cost can be quite low."

"So just a few of those would have a huge impact on the bottom line?"

"Huge, and . . ."

"And—?"

"And the probability of coming up with those solutions, those ideas, is much higher for the specialist than the generalist."

"So there's a volume effect?"

"Yes. The specialist might come up with several solutions a year. The generalist might develop one, or none."

"What else?"

Steve wanted to ask, "Isn't that enough?" But he knew better. He kept pushing his thinking. "The specialist not only has something to replicate, but can test it sooner, and sell it sooner, because of connections into the industry, into customer companies, into specific decision-makers."

"So they're wired?"

"Precisely."

Zhao chuckled. "Hey, wait a second, that's my line. You should be inventing the answers."

Steve grinned. "Sorry about that."

"You're forgiven. So, we have EDS, Wallace, HP in its Global Account Management program in the early 90s. We have ABB."

"Huh?"

"ABB, a great European engineering firm. That's your reading assignment. Get a copy of *The Profit Zone* and read chapter twelve. It's all about creating the circumstances for specialization profit in the world of engineering and then exploiting the opportunity to its maximum extent.

"Are there any other examples we've left out?"

Steve was quick on the trigger.

"Great antitrust lawyers, like the guys here at Storm & Fellows. Cardiologists and engineers. The best minds in law, medicine, the whole world of the professions."

"That's right. Actually, ABB is the application of that principle to engineering on a very large scale. Any others?"

Steve kept flipping through his memory files. He wondered whether he could preempt Zhao and do this week's assignment on the spot. "Professors in schools. Category-focused retailers. Specialized construction companies."

"All good thoughts. And what are the common elements cutting through all of them?"

Steve ticked them off on his fingers. "Number one, lower cost through better knowledge. Number two, better price through reputation or through the unique design of their offering. Number three, shorter selling cycle. Number four, more rapid and universal penetration because of the wired effect. Number five, windfall profits because of the replication of high-value, high-margin answers throughout the marketplace."

This time, it was Zhao who was taking notes. He liked the crisp, clean answers Steve was giving. He was hoping that Steve would continue.

Steve did.

"Add all these up, and the *difference* in profitability between generalist and specialist will be ten to fifteen points of margin. When generalists break even, specialists make fifteen percent. When generalists make ten percent, specialists can make twenty-five percent."

Zhao was satisfied beyond measure. He was so sorry that he couldn't show it more openly. "Now that you've done your homework on the spot, in advance, what will you do this week?" he asked.

Steve cast about for an answer and tripped over a great idea. "I know—I'll spend the time going back over the last nine lessons, going through the drudgery of reviewing the ideas to see if I can internalize them, to be able to summon them semi-automatically."

Zhao was stunned. This was an unexpected level of strategic maturity. He responded quickly. "Keep in mind something that a brilliant Japanese translator once told me."

"And that is?"

"There are four levels to learning: Awareness. Awkwardness. Application. Assimilation."

Steve loved it. But the wheels in his head were still spinning. "Actually, there's a fifth," he said.

"What's that?"

"Art."

Zhao smiled. "One day, yes. If you can get to Assimilation, I'll be happy."

"I'll get there—I hope."

"I'm beginning to suspect you might. Meanwhile, try to stay focused at Delmore."

"It won't be easy."

"I know."

"Everybody is beginning to look for life rafts."

"Including you?"

"I've thought about it. But you know, I still think there's something worth salvaging there."

"Oh, I *know* there is," Zhao responded, with surprising vehemence.

"You *know* it?" Steve echoed.

"I told you that I've followed the company," Zhao said. "It has talented technical people poised to create value in a dozen different industries that should do well over the next twenty years. The problem is—"

"The problem is getting that far," Steve interrupted.

Zhao nodded, but he added, "Getting that far, and figuring out where the profits are going to be in each of its businesses. The answers vary. Figuring each of the answers out is what people like you had better be doing."

"We're trying," Steve answered.

"Keep trying."

10
Installed Base Profit

December 21. "Think about cameras," Zhao started without introduction. "Especially Polaroids. Think about razor blades. Think about personal copiers."

"I'm thinking," Steve joked.

"Good. Now think about two buckets. In one bucket, you have the equipment, in the other you have the consumables."

Steve shut his eyes and grimaced as if concentrating intensely. "Got it."

"Got what?"

"The two buckets."

"Okay. Now, what's important about them?"

Steve dropped his flip mindset and started thinking in earnest. He looked to Zhao for a clue. "Profit margins?"

"A-h-h-h."

Steve thought some more. "Low and high."

Zhao rolled his eyes, as if saying "give me a break."

"Very low and very high?" Steve ventured.

Zhao grunted in assent. "Estimate?"

"Maybe two to five percent on the hardware, maybe ten to fifteen percent on the consumables."

"Good."

Zhao grabbed his pad and pen and quickly drew eight strokes. He labeled the diagram "Relative Profitability" and tossed it across the desk to Steve. "You fill in the rest," he suggested.

Relative Profitability

[Bar chart with y-axis labeled "%", showing a small bar labeled "HW" and a tall bar labeled "C"]

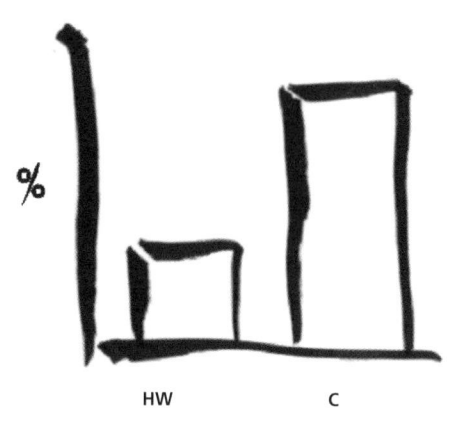

Steve took Zhao's pen, thought, and wrote. He labeled the shorter column "HW" and the taller column "C".

"Good," said Zhao. "Now, anything else?"

Steve was irritated at himself. He should have been thinking ahead to the next step. Stumped, he looked at Zhao again, who stared back, impassive.

Steve felt stuck, but he forced—no, induced—himself to relax. He turned away from Zhao and stared at the Statue of Liberty in the blinding noon sun for a long, long moment. Finally, something triggered the idea: "Demand volatility?"

"Ah, yes."

Steve brightened. "Very high and very low. Driven by very different factors. New demand and continuing demand. In fact, the bigger the installed base, the bigger the difference."

"Good. What else?"

Again that sinking feeling of standing face to face with the wall he had just run into. "How about a clue?"

"Umm . . . customer price sensitivity," Zhao tried.

Steve leaped at it.

"Got it. High on initial purchase, much lower on consumables."

"Why?"

"Much lower ticket item. Much, much lower."

"Anything else?"

Steve thought hard. This last answer had given him confidence. "Power!" he shouted.

"What about it?"

"It has shifted."

"How?"

"In the original sale, the buyer had it . . . lots of choices. In the after-sale, the seller has it because the buyer is locked into the seller's consumables."

"Thank you."

"One more thing," Steve volunteered.

"Oh?"

"The seller can screw it up."

"How?"

"Two ways. One is pricing too high. The buyer gets so upset that he switches brands or drops the product altogether. The goose gets killed."

"And the other way?"

"The seller doesn't work to make it easy for the customer to buy."

"How do you mean?"

"Early notice. Reminders. Multiple units per follow-on sale. Moving from passive receipt of installed-base profit to stimulating usage and growth."

Zhao paused. "Not a very powerful point, but good evidence of a willingness to think another step or two." He paused. "I like it. We're done for today."

Steve took a deep breath. It hadn't been a long session, but it had felt strenuous, like an intense aerobic workout. Parts of his mind were working harder than they had in years . . . or ever.

"I just thought of something," he abruptly remarked.

"What's that?" Zhao asked.

"A big chunk of our building supplies business is built on Installed Base Profit."

Zhao looked a little surprised. "Really? Say more."

"Filters for central air conditioning units and heaters. Linings for furnaces, flues, and chimneys. Door and window screens. People tend to buy what they bought the time before, or whatever came with the unit when they purchased the house or the appliance. But we've treated it as a passive business—no real effort to keep those customers or upgrade them."

"Would it be possible to upgrade them?" Zhao wondered.

"I'm not sure." Steve sat up straight. "Wait, I think it could be. Just yesterday I was reading a report about some of the new products we've been bringing out. Non-allergenic air filters. Eco-friendly supplies for heaters and furnaces. Screens and insulating materials that cut heating and cooling costs as soon as you install them and also reduce indoor air pollution."

"Have you been marketing these products aggressively?"

Steve shook his head. "Not really. We let our dealer network know what's available. Then it's up to them to move the stuff. Most people still buy the traditional supplies, at one third the price." A strange look crossed his face. "You know what, there might be the makings of something here."

"A Pyramid?"

"Yes, I think so." Steve looked excited. "I mean, I've got a lot of work to do to figure it out. But I think we've got a bunch of haphazard product lines that we've never really developed in any logical fashion . . . but which we could organize for maximum profit with a little thought. It might work—it just might."

Zhao nodded. "Dig into it before you make any decisions. Remember, let the customers guide you. They're the ones who'll decide what they're willing to pay for, and how much."

"Right, I get it," Steve agreed. He rose to his feet, looking eager to leave and get back to work. "Oh, is there any reading assignment?" he asked.

Zhao regarded Steve quizzically. The fact was, Steve had caught him unprepared. He hadn't thought through what the right next reading would be. But with a week off for the holidays, he had to give Steve something meaty to chew on. After a moment's thought, Zhao recovered.

"Read *Made in America* again. This time the whole book. And bring me a list of all the key points you missed on the first reading."

Steve nodded. "Same time in two weeks?"

"No. Next time we'll meet at two. After lunch. Meanwhile, Happy New Year to you."

"Same to you."

Steve left. Zhao breathed a sigh of relief. *That was a close one*, he thought to himself. And then he laughed. *If only Steve knew! But it's a good thing he doesn't — for both of us.*

11
De Facto Standard Profit

January 4. Big, soft flakes were drifting past Zhao's office window as Steve walked in. It was the first snowfall of the season.

Steve tossed his wet jacket onto the coat rack by Zhao's door, dropped into his usual chair, and sat drumming his fingers on the arm rest and staring into space.

"What's the matter?" Zhao asked.

"Did you hear the NetCom announcement yesterday?"

NetCom was one of the fastest-growing telecom companies, a burgeoning rival to DelCom. "No. I was flying back from Madrid. What's up?"

"They've launched a telecom Switchboard. All the major players have signed up as suppliers. Including Delmore!" Steve uttered a single mirthless laugh.

"Is that all?" Zhao asked. "The way you looked, I thought you'd had your apartment broken into or something!"

"'Is that all?'" Steve repeated. "Isn't that enough? Frank and I knew the idea would work, we *knew* it, and if Delmore had gotten started when we proposed it, we might have beaten NetCom to the punch. Now it's too late. What's the matter with those guys? I just don't get it."

Zhao shook his head. "Relax, Steve. Number one, you don't know whether NetCom's project will work or not. Number two, even if it does, that doesn't necessarily kill Delmore's chances of getting into the same business down the road."

"But by then—" Steve interrupted.

Zhao ignored him. "And number three," he spread his hands, "so what? There are lots of other businesses to get into. The real key is for both you and Delmore to learn from a missed opportunity."

Steve seemed to calm down a little. "I suppose you're right," he conceded. "But it's so frustrating to feel like we *had* the idea and just couldn't make it happen."

Zhao chuckled. "If you're going to let that upset you, Steve, all I can say is be prepared to be upset a *lot*."

Steve didn't laugh. "Okay, I'm impatient," he said. "That's how I am. Isn't that normal? Isn't it *good* to be driven?"

"Sure it is," Zhao replied. "But I've traveled around the sun a few more times than you have. I still care . . . a lot. But I've learned not to take setbacks too personally. Otherwise you burn up a lot of energy in irritation and anger, which tends to lead to further mistakes.

"Instead, I recommend you look ahead."

Steve sighed. "All right," he agreed. "New year, new opportunities. What have you got for me today?"

Zhao jumped into action. "Are you familiar with the mini-computer industry, Steve?"

"Just vaguely."

"In its day, it was a wonderful example—perhaps the ultimate example—of the Installed Base profit model. Customers were locked into proprietary systems, paying high prices for years. Its success was also its demise, because of the incredible anger it created in the customer base."

"You mean because of the high prices?"

"No, not really. That was the surface reason everyone assumed, but the real reason was the high costs generated by incompatibility."

"I thought you said that costs weren't the main issue."

"Not direct financial costs. It was the other costs, in time, energy, and irritation, that had the most profound impact."

"I get it."

"The resulting landscape led to the opportunity to create a standard. Which produced our next profit model—De Facto Standard Profit."

"So creating the de facto standard created extraordinary profitability."

"Not exactly," Zhao demurred.

"What do you mean?"

"Well, think about it. Does creating the standard create profitability directly?"

Steve paused. He'd learned to be cautious in answering Zhao's questions. He was tired of thinking hard, but he was also getting used to it.

Zhao pressed on. "Think about Microsoft. Where does Microsoft make its money?"

"In the upgrades."

"Yes, that's part of it," Zhao agreed.

"And in the applications."

"Yes. And . . . ?"

Steve was stumped. He knew that Zhao was searching for something, that it was reasonable, and that Steve couldn't think what it was. "There are probably some unquantifiable factors," he ventured, even as he thought, *Boy, that probably sounds lame.*

Zhao arched his eyebrows in surprise. "You're on the right track," he remarked.

Steve continued to sort through possible answers quickly. He remembered his favorite quote from the late chairman and CEO of Coke, Roberto Goizueta: "You can think through a problem so hard you develop a sweat." He was feeling that way now.

He tried simulation. He imagined himself in Microsoft's position in the world of Windows 3.0, 95, 97, 98, and NT, or in Oracle's in the world of Oracle 5.0, 6.0, 7.0, 7.1, 7.2, 7.3.

It came to him in an unexpected leap. "Plannability."

Zhao made no response, just listened harder.

"Surprises cost money," Steve went on. "They cause you to react, respond, scramble. The owners of the de facto standard can plan and can shape the next stage of the industry's unfolding landscape, because it's their business plan that drives it."

Zhao let a half-smile escape. He wanted to stop there and not ask the next question, but he knew he had to. He called forth the image of Phil Areeda, the great Harvard Law School contracts professor, who was better than anyone in driving and leading the student further, always to the next question, always one level deeper. *Phil Areeda at Harvard Law School . . . John Bishop at Harvard Business School . . .* there are so few like them, he thought.

"What else?" Zhao asked.

Steve was shocked. *He's pressing for more? How can this be?* But Steve was getting used to reverses. He sprang back into hard-thinking mode, jumping back into his Microsoft or Oracle simulation, trying to imagine the next factor.

More than ten minutes went by.

Zhao, totally immobile, was staring out the window at the glass walls of 60 Wall Street, their next-door neighbor.

Finally, Steve spoke. "Your customers do your marketing for you and reduce your marketing expenses."

Zhao turned slowly towards Steve and smiled broadly. "Example?" he asked.

"Well, last week the newspaper described a major accounting firm pulling out its Lotus products and replacing them with Microsoft's, because of requests and pressure from customers who had standardized on Microsoft."

"And how much is that worth?"

Steve was about to say "a lot," but he didn't want to settle for that. He tried to imagine what percentage sales and marketing costs were of sales. Finally, he replied, "It saves you sales and marketing costs of twenty to thirty percent on *that* sale, because the customer does it for you."

"And what percentage of sales might this affect?"

"Maybe a quarter or a fifth."

"For a total of . . . ?"

"A quarter or a fifth of sales, at a savings of twenty to thirty percent, so a range of four percent at the low end to nearly eight percent at the high end."

"Big number."

"Huge," Steve agreed. "As long as it lasts."

"And what's the longest-running standards business?"

"IBM mainframe?"

"And that has lasted how long?"

Steve tried to remember. "Twenty-five years? Thirty? I'm not really sure."

Zhao had the answer. "From 1964, the introduction of the IBM 360, to today. More than thirty-five years."

"A hell of a ride."

"And not likely to be repeated in the future. Today, you have to do more jumping from one lily pad to the next."

Zhao was very happy. He hadn't expected to get this far halfway through the lessons cycle. "No homework this week. None, I mean it."

"What about reading?"

"No reading either. No, wait." Zhao remembered suddenly what next week's topic would be.

"Here, have some fun." He pulled out two books from his shelf. Both were by David Ogilvy: *Confessions of an Advertising Man* and *Ogilvy on Advertising*.

"Is this the Ogilvy book festival?" Steve asked.

"Sort of. It's the easiest reading you'll have. Not because it's simple, but because it's fun, it's a point of view. It's a guy whose spirit you can touch. And you hope it touches you." Zhao continued, "Just don't think about profit models. Enjoy yourself. Look at ads. Think about what they're supposed to do. And what they actually do. We'll talk about it next week.

"One other thing." Zhao grabbed a dog-eared paperback from his shelf and tossed it to Steve. "Try reading chapter one in *ABC of Reading* by Ezra Pound. These two guys, Ogilvy and Pound, are real characters. They've become very good friends to me. I hope you like them."

Steve stuffed the books in his pack and left.

Three days passed. It was Tuesday night, slightly after 8 o'clock. Steve's phone rang somewhat insistently. He didn't want to pick it up. He'd been finding the phone to be an increasingly irritating device, designed not just for communication but for intrusive interruption.

The answering machine finally clicked in. Steve was surprised to hear Zhao's voice. Zhao never called. Steve grabbed it.

"Sorry," he said, "I just got in from the other room."

"Watching wrestling again?" Zhao joked.

"No, just doing some work on my strategy for the building supply business."

Zhao turned sober. "I'm very sorry to interrupt you, Steve, and I apologize for making a big mistake last Saturday. I forgot to ask you to do something very important."

"No problem. What is it?"

"Remember when I asked you to have fun looking at ads?"

"Yes."

"I forgot to ask you to do one thing: Find three examples where two exactly identical products or services command very different price levels because of brand power."

"Oh, no problem," Steve said. He felt trapped into making a polite response, which was the opposite of how he really felt.

"Okay. See you Saturday."

"Good night." Steve put the receiver back.

"Damn," he thought. "How am I going to do this?" A mild panic began to filter into his mind as he thought about his workload for the week .

"Damn, damn, damn," was all his brain could produce. Tuesday was over. He had meetings till four tomorrow and Thursday. There was a dinner meeting scheduled with Cathy and several colleagues tomorrow night. And he'd promised his friend Suzy that they'd go to her sister's engagement party on Friday night. There was no way he could pull this off. No way.

His mind started scrambling in full damage-control mode. He'd have to think of something. Soon.

12
Brand Profit

January 11. Steve looked bleary-eyed.

"Up late?" Zhao inquired.

"Till 3:30 a.m."

Zhao pursed his lips, inwardly smiling but externally impassive.

"Did you read Ezra Pound?" Zhao asked.

Steve sighed. He'd forgotten about the reading assignment until that very morning—a semi-deliberate mental block, no doubt. Then he'd spent half an hour over his morning coffee trying to make his way through the first chapter of *ABC of Reading*. He'd barely begun to make sense of it. It was a jumble of observations about Chinese ideograms, Stravinsky, and the paintings in the Prado, mingled with snide remarks about people unknown to Steve whom Ezra Pound apparently disliked.

Now he wondered what to say. "I tried reading Pound," Steve said, "I really did. But frankly I have no idea what he's talking about."

Zhao nodded thoughtfully. He didn't appear surprised. "No, I don't suppose you do," he remarked, almost to himself. Then he turned to face Steve directly. "And yet, it's really not that difficult. You let the apparent subject matter—poetry—convince you that Pound is irrelevant. That's a mistake."

Steve protested, "But I just couldn't follow Pound, and I haven't heard of half the people he mentions . . ."

"I know, I know," Zhao replied impatiently, brushing Steve's objections aside with a hand. "But the points Pound is making are still clear. You at least absorbed the story of Agassiz and the fish, didn't you?"

Steve turned a little red. He'd completely forgotten that anecdote. His mind began to race: *Agassiz? Fish? Where was that story, anyway?*

"Never mind," said Zhao, almost soothingly. He seemed eager to forgive Steve. "Read it now. It starts on page 17."

Steve pulled the book out of his backpack and turned to the story:

> No man is equipped for modern thinking until he has understood the anecdote of Agassiz and the fish:
> "A post-graduate student equipped with honours and diplomas went to Agassiz to receive the final and finishing touches. The great man offered him a small fish and told him to describe it.

"Post-Graduate Student: 'That's only a sunfish.'

"Agassiz: 'I know that. Write a description of it.'

"After a few minutes, the student returned with the description of the Ichthus Heliodiplodokus, or whatever term is used to conceal the common sunfish from vulgar knowledge, family of Heliichtherinkus, etc., as found in textbooks of the subject.

"Agassiz again told the student to describe the fish.

"The student produced a four-page essay. Agassiz then told him to look at the fish. At the end of three weeks, the fish was in an advanced state of decomposition, but the student knew something about it."

Steve looked up. "So who was this Agassiz?"

"Who do you think?" Zhao asked.

"A fish expert?" Steve's tone was mildly sardonic.

"Obviously," Zhao replied. "More than that, he was the preeminent naturalist in nineteenth-century America—almost our equivalent to Darwin. But that's not the point of the story. What is?"

Steve thought. "I guess it's about the importance of observation—about getting beyond what you read in textbooks and learning instead from close, direct, unfiltered study of real things. The way the student in the story learned something meaningful about fish by actually *looking* at a fish rather than reciting scientific terminology. It's the difference between knowing something indirectly and knowing it directly."

Zhao pointed an index finger at Steve's chest. "Exactly!" he replied. "And how does that apply to profitability?"

"I guess the idea is that we can learn the most about how profits are created by studying profitable companies—by figuring out their business models and then thinking about how they might apply elsewhere."

"And how would you observe a business if you wanted to examine it the way the student in the story examined the fish?"

"Look at the P&L? Read the annual report?"

Zhao shook his head. "No, no!" he declared. "Those things are fine in their place, but they're more like the textbooks that the student in the story had already memorized. If you want to know a business, you've got to *look* at it first-hand like a biologist studying a specimen. You've got to visit their stores or their factories or their offices, try their products, test their services, cruise their websites.

"Most important, you've got to talk with their customers—or better yet, live with them. Get to know their needs and wants and problems by spending time with them, seeing what they do, what works for them and what doesn't, what annoys them and what makes their lives easy or productive or fun. Reading about focus groups and survey results is okay. But you'll learn more by meeting a real, live customer and spending an hour with him than you can learn from fifty research studies or analysts' reports."

"I see what you mean," Steve said. "So Pound is talking about learning things by approaching them in a scientific spirit—and that's what you're saying about business."

Zhao looked relieved. "Yes, that's a big part of it. Not all by any means—but a big part of it."

"Like what we're doing now with the building supply business."

"What's that?" Zhao wanted to know.

"We're doing in-depth interviews with several dozen customers and our top fifty dealers, trying to define what they *really* want and will pay for when it comes to filters and screens and insulating material and all the other things we sell."

"Are you learning anything?"

"Actually yes. Eye-opening stuff. It turns out that half the things we always assumed to be true were just that—assumptions. No one ever bothered to check before."

"That happens in a lot of businesses. And you're right—that's a key to what Ezra Pound is saying."

Steve laughed. "So now I understand *one page* of Pound's book, anyway!"

Zhao laughed. "That's a start! But what about your homework assignment—to come up with examples of pure Brand Profit," Zhao went on. "Did you find anything?"

"Only three items . . . one of them inconclusive."

"Tell me."

"The first was from *The Economist* magazine, 1994. It's absolutely delicious. It's about NUMMI, the Toyota-GM joint venture in Fremont, California. Same factory, same workers, same processes, two nameplates. The Toyota nameplate fetches pricing that is $300 per car higher than the GM nameplate."

"Pretty good. Do you know the rest of the story?"

Steve was crestfallen.

"Don't feel bad, you couldn't have found it. It's not public information. Not yet."

"What is it?"

"A retailer in Japan is planning to get into the used car and auto service business. Has huge equity with his customers, huge trust around his *own* brand name. Plans to recondition used cars and use his own name. Plans to take the Toyota nameplate right off."

"Wow!"

"Other examples?"

"Well, one that isn't from a literature search."

"Does anyone care about the origin?"

"I guess not. Anyway, my girlfriend and I were in Boston last week visiting friends. We went shopping Wednesday morning at the Star Market at the edge of Cambridge and Watertown. There were two soda vending machines side by side. President's Choice Cola for seventy-five cents and Coca-Cola for a buck."

"A fairly clean comparison."

"I'd say."

"But, Steve, they are not exactly the same product. The formulas are different, the ingredients are different, the tastes are different. Anything else?"

"Well, an inconclusive one."

"What is it?"

"There was an article in the *Wall Street Journal* about a guy in Texas who was upsetting Hollywood by putting fresh gossip and inside stories up onto his web site."

"So?"

"There was one story that caught my eye. One of the major studios was testing an upcoming animated film. They split-tested it. With one audience, they introduced it as their product and used their own logo. With the other audience, they stuck on the Disney logo. The exact same cartoon. The viewers liked the second one better. When this story came up on the web site, the studio denied it. But I wonder."

Zhao smiled. "The mind works in wondrous ways." He put his hand to his chin, rubbing it in contemplation. "Any others?"

Steve grimaced in frustration.

"Feelings of frustration are the greatest enemy of progress that I know," Zhao said. "Start a folder. Label it 'Brand Profit.' Put these examples in it. Build it. Call me in a year. Tell me how many you've gotten by that time. But I want specific facts and numbers, not speculation like the movie example—although you could start a separate file on that one."

"Okay."

"Here's another for you. The year was 1994. The context was the cutthroat PC business. In this world of selling boxes, some pretty careful research documented that a Compaq box—the exact same box as other PC makers produced—commanded a $200 price premium. Two hundred dollars.

"And one more for your folder. When I was reading *The Profit Zone*, I was struck by Nicolas Hayek's story on page 117. To measure the economic meaning of brand, he tested exactly the same watch in three markets. The only difference was the inscription. One said 'Made in Switzerland,' the second 'Made in the U.S.,' the third, 'Made in Japan.' He also priced them differently. Swiss: $107, U.S.: $100, Japanese: $93. In several markets, customers preferred the Swiss watch, even at a $14 premium. Fourteen dollars on $93 — a fifteen percent premium."

"Pretty incredible."

"Isn't it?"

"How does this happen?" Steve wondered.

"Ah, one of the great mysteries of business. The triumph of the irrational in a hyper-rational world. I can take a little of the mystery out, but by no means all of it."

"Do tell."

"It all started with a simple little graph from Ogilvy. That was my first clue. I'm doing this from memory, so it's only right within ten or fifteen percent, but you'll get the point. Ogilvy measured the impact on revenue and profit of sustained advertising investment, versus those companies who pulled back on their ad spend during a recession. Those who continued advertising during the recession increased revenues faster, and profits much faster, after the recession, compared to their rivals who cut back. What's going on here?"

Steve thought about it. "Cumulative impact?"

"Exactly. Pretty simple, isn't it?"

"So Brand Profit is partly a function of history."

"Yes, of cumulative investment in effective advertising to be precise. But when you say history, you're very close.

"This is close to a universal truth. Take any category of product. Beta-blockers, a heart medication to reduce blood pressure, for example. Heavily advertised, heavily promoted. You can measure how much. The category was created in 1976 with the introduction of Inderal, Jimmy Black's great discovery. By 1985, there were six entrants. Here's their share." Zhao sketched a series of columns on the next page of his pad.

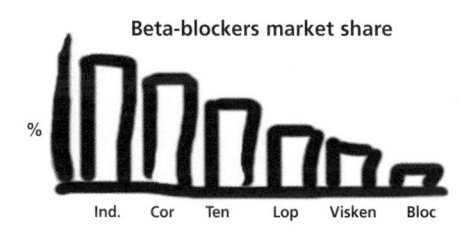

Beta-blockers market share

%

Ind.   Cor.   Ten   Lop   Visken   Bloc

"I measured their spending cumulatively, in constant dollars. The ratios were the same as the market share ratios."

"Cause or consequence?" Steve asked.

"That's exactly the problem. But then think about it. Do you believe spending drives share or share drives spending?"

"It should be the former, but we know that sometimes it's the latter."

"Right. You spend what you can afford. So I measured this for ten other pharmaceutical categories, then another ten outside pharmaceuticals. I found some fascinating stuff. With undifferentiated products, cumulative investment drives share. Ogilvy was right. The persistent spenders win out in the long run."

"Are there exceptions?"

"Fantastic ones."

"What do you mean?"

"There are at least a dozen examples of products that got two or three times as much share as they should have, given their level of spending."

"Kind of breaks the rule, doesn't it?"

"No, it reinforces it."

"Excuse me?" Steve was puzzled.

"For every apparent exception, there was a brilliant reason why. They found a more leveraged, more efficient way to invest their marketing dollars. They had a better message, or a non-standard, differentiated benefit, or a better channel position, or a better focus on the share-determining segment."

Steve was taking notes rapidly. "Share-determining segment? What's that?"

"The SDS is the most important segment in the market. That's the one where high share today translates into high share of the whole market tomorrow."

"Example, please?"

"Specialists in medicine are a great example. Cardiologists not only write a lot of prescriptions for heart medications, but they also influence what the general practitioners write. Another example is eighteen- to twenty-five-year-olds in tobacco. It's an odious example, I know, but it's very real. And there's still another example from the building supply field—the one you're immersed in right now."

Steve was ready. "Sure, architects," he said. Their decisions and preferences for materials and design styles filter down to the contractors and ultimately to the do-it-yourself repair and remodeling markets."

"Exactly. And in all of these categories, spending a dollar on the SDS is worth more than spending five dollars on the average customer."

"So there are efficient ways to build brand," Steve observed.

"Hyper-efficient."

"So price premium is not the whole story."

"Most of it, but not the whole story — not by any means."

"Who do you think has done the best job?" Steve asked. "That is, who has the highest price premium and the most efficient brand-building?"

"Great question. You tell me."

"I don't know."

"Of course you don't, but who are the candidates?"

"Can I think about it?"

"Of course you can, but tell me the candidates now."

Steve scratched his head and started throwing out names. "Coke. Marlboro. Budweiser. Swatch. McDonald's. Nike."

"You're looking in the right places. Now go measure."

"That's a lot of work."

"Tell me what you've found out in twelve months. Add it to your list of brand premiums. It'll make your understanding more complete. And give yourself lead time. The combination of curiosity and lead time can convert any chore into a delightful, exploratory puzzle. Puzzles solved have far more penetration and staying power than chores completed."

Steve relaxed. "Twelve months, huh?"

"You'll find that that's an amazingly short time to get control over something this valuable."

"I'll take your word for it."

Zhao smiled shrewdly. "I wouldn't do that if I were you. Ever."

13
Specialty Product Profit

January 18. When Steve arrived, Zhao remained silent for several moments, staring at his yellow pad, creating an oasis of quiet in a hurly-burly New York world. Steve was seduced into it in no time. It was hypnotic.

Finally, Zhao looked up. He nodded a greeting to Steve, then began speaking with no other preamble. "I first learned about Specialty Product Profit in 1978. I worked with a dyestuff company in North Carolina. They used to make gobs of money. Pharma-type profits.

"But by the late 1970s, that wonderful *feeling* of profitability started to go away. With that transition, there was a lot of confusion about how to think about products. That's what the boss asked me to work on.

"I could understand the confusion. I was thoroughly baffled myself. I spent a couple of months poring through data—of which they had a ton—and I still couldn't find the pattern. The needle was eluding me. I knew it was somewhere in that haystack, but I just couldn't find it.

"Then one Saturday afternoon, I was reading about the history of the industry, and I came across an incredible picture. It was a simple bar chart that counted the number of new product discoveries in dyestuff. It started in the late nineteenth century and rose dramatically in the early twentieth century. Then the number started to drop precipitously. The last decade shown was the 1950s, with at most a handful of discoveries.

"I then remembered how much money the company made off its youngest dyes. Gross margins of sixty percent in a business where overall gross margins were twenty-five percent.

"It was exhilarating. I raced through my other folders, and within a couple of hours everything fell into place. I oversimplified, of course, but you always do that when you're struggling to see the real picture hiding in the confusing excess of data that you're drowning in.

"Here's what I realized. The dyestuff business *had been* a specialty product business, just like the pharma business. Lots of little unique patented products that had huge margins. As long as there were plenty of new discoveries to be made, the system worked. The key question was what projects to work on, because some were far more valuable than others. But they were *all* profitable.

"As I worked through the endless reams of product data, I found that ten years ago, more than eighty percent of their revenues came from those relatively unique patented, high-profit specialty products. Less than twenty percent came from commodity products.

"I started racing to calculate the ratio today. It was just under twenty percent. This is the one picture I took to the CEO that week. We talked about it for three hours." Zhao's pen had been flying on the pad. He turned the picture around for Steve to see.

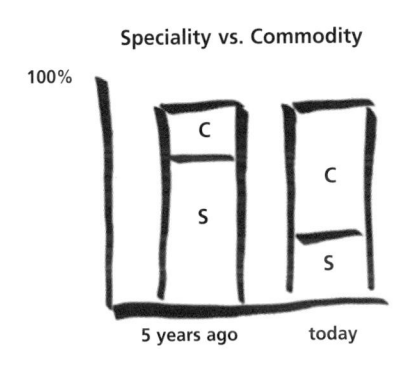

Speciality vs. Commodity

[Chart showing two bars. Left bar labeled "5 years ago" reaches 100%, with C on top and S below. Right bar labeled "today" is shorter, with C on top and S below.]

"What was the key point?" Steve asked.

"That the profit model had shifted from specialty product to cost and cycle management. It wasn't an easy meeting for him or for me."

"Why?"

"For him, because he was new on the job, and this insight made it clear that he would have to turn the company's culture upside down. From a mindset shaped by the generous profits of a specialty product business to a mindset that said, 'Dyestuff is a commodity, margins are in single digits, and if we don't get two steps ahead of the cost curve, we will quickly become a part of the industry's history rather than its future.'"

"And for you?"

"For me, because I thought I had discovered a great little profit model. Unfortunately, there was no way I could learn more about it in this company. As far as they were concerned, the specialty product era was over."

"Which means what?" Steve asked.

"What do you think?"

"I guess it means you have to find a new profit model."

"You're on the right track," Zhao acknowledged. "It's a kind of shape-shifting that every business has to do periodically — at least, if they hope to outlast a generation or two.

"But for now, let's get back to the specialty product model. As I say, I'd missed my first chance to study it. It was years before another chance came along."

"And where was that?"

"It was at another specialty chemicals company—in New Jersey. They were operating in a technology domain that had not yet experienced the technology depletion that occurred years ago in dyestuffs. Dyestuffs were like the Texas oil fields, where the oil is gradually running out. This company was more like Alaska, where the oil reserves still have two or three decades to go. For them, the specialty product model would be viable for a considerable while."

"What was their ratio?"

"When I started, it was seventy percent from specialty products and falling fast. They hadn't been managing their pipeline. You could project that the ratio would be about fifty-five percent within three years because of patent expirations and new substitutes being introduced.

"Ann Linen, the head of R&D, invited me to help with a major review of their portfolio of projects. I'll never forget the day, a cold, dark Friday in November. It was freezing outside. It was dark and freezing inside as well—an incredibly depressing day. We went through sixty-two projects, one by one. We started at 8 a.m. and went until 6:30 in the evening. People were poorly prepared. Most of the important customer questions and technical feasibility questions went unanswered or were poorly answered.

"At the end of the day, Ann asked me what I thought. I said, 'Ann, I wouldn't give a nickel for this portfolio. It's a disaster. What have people been doing here for the last five years?'

"Ann frowned. She knew I was right. This was her first year in this new position, and she could feel the clock ticking, the pressure building.

"Over the next four weeks, we met for several days to assess the damage. Ann agreed that it would take several more meetings at much higher levels of preparation to get the R&D portfolio under control.

"We attacked the portfolio at the two ends of the distribution, the most- and the least-valuable projects. The high-value projects were poorly structured and formulated. The least-valuable ones had been allowed to generate costs for far too long.

"I helped Ann draft a set of memos to the project leaders of this first batch of highest-value and lower-value projects. Ann asked very detailed questions. She cleared her calendar for a month to work through the problem projects.

"Within two months, she discontinued a dozen projects and upped the resources for the top ten. But this was only a first approximation. The top ten project leaders got more resources and more management mindshare. Things started to move more quickly, as Ann sent a clear message that top ten status would be reviewed in depth within sixty days. People became very alert and focused.

"These moves still left forty projects to fix. There was value in there somewhere, but there was no system in place to discover or even to begin guessing where the value really was.

"Inside a couple of months, we put a system together, and monthly portfolio reviews resumed. For every project, the same hard questions got asked every month. The level of preparation rose dramatically. The answers got better, more accurate, more realistic, more supported by data.

"Our first big breakthrough came in March, when a project leader gave a presentation to the portfolio review team that killed his own project. Three million dollars a year of spending got shut down.

"Ann responded brilliantly. She *promoted* the project leader and reassigned the talent on the project to important assignments on lead projects. The organization got the signal. In the next two months, ten more projects folded. We were down to a total of forty.

"However, there still wasn't enough value in the lead projects, and there still weren't enough projects that would pay off within the next three years. So we organized a major licensing, project-swapping, and joint development effort. Within four months, we swapped away seven projects that were more valuable in somebody else's hands, licensed in four projects with short-term potential, and entered into joint development agreements on three major projects that had high potential value and enormous risk.

"Our twelfth portfolio review meeting was a dramatic improvement over our first. We were down to thirty-five projects. The value of the portfolio was significantly higher, the risk was better covered, and the time structure of the portfolio was significantly improved—we were projecting returns in Year 3 rather than Year 10. You could project our specialty ratio falling to sixty percent, not fifty-five percent, because of the swaps we'd made. In three years, we'd be back to seventy percent, or even higher."

Zhao was silent. He sat in his chair with his shoulders drooping slightly. He looked as though he'd been reliving the conflict, the emotional roller-coaster, and the fatigue of this tough process. He had been. Steve could feel it.

"By the way, Steve," Zhao abruptly asked, "what's the difference between Specialty Product profit and Blockbuster profit?"

Steve was caught off guard. He thought back to the discussion of blockbusters.

"It seems to me that a blockbuster business requires a real all-out warrior like Marc Geron."

"Are you saying someone like Ann Linen couldn't handle it?"

Steve paused. "She sounds tough enough. But I don't think she needed to be a Marc Geron."

Zhao sat up. "Why not?"

"Because her business was different."

"How so?"

Steve was stopped again. He could feel the difference, but he couldn't articulate it. After a moment, Zhao chimed in.

"Your feeling is right, Steve. When you think of specialty products, think fine chemicals, think dyestuffs, think specialty papers, think specialty foods. Think *niche*. The key is finding a legitimate need or variation and addressing it.

"When you think blockbuster, think pharmaceuticals, think Hollywood movies, think best-selling books, think pop music. Either the development costs are extremely high, so you need big hits to pay for them, or the demand is highly influenceable, so you need a brilliant, intensive marketing campaign. Or both. Pills and movies are the former, books and music the latter."

"Actually, pills and movies are both, aren't they?" Steve interjected.

Zhao smiled. "Right again."

"Is there a reading assignment?" Steve finally asked.

Zhao's attention returned to the present. He knitted his brow.

"It's about time for *The Art of War*. It's long overdue, in fact. Read the Samuel B. Griffith translation."

"Will do. By the way," Steve added as he rose to his feet, "guess who just became the newest VP at NetCom?"

Zhao smiled. He saw that Steve was still upset about how NetCom had jumped on the Switchboard idea. "Your buddy Frank, of course," Zhao said.

"Exactly," Steve said, sounding a little bitter. "Another rat deserts the sinking ship."

"Don't speak too soon," Zhao cautioned.

"Wasn't it you who warned me how quickly a business can collapse once the foundation is cracked?"

Zhao nodded. "That's right. The challenge is telling the difference between cracks in the foundation and chips in the plaster. Are you sure about which description applies to Delmore?"

Steve looked grim. "Not yet. But it doesn't matter what I think. In time, we'll find out what the markets think."

14
Local Leadership Profit

January 25. "Hi, Steve, how are you?" asked Zhao, polite but reserved.

"Excellent," Steve replied. He, in fact, looked more cheerful than he had in several weeks.

"Good, let's begin." Steve slid into his chair.

"How many locations does Starbuck's have?" Zhao asked.

"I have no idea," Steve admitted.

"Then guess."

"How old are they?"

"They started their current business model back in 1987."

"Cafes?"

"Everything—cafes, office building locations, kiosks."

Steve started estimating.

"Estimate out loud for me," Zhao requested.

"Well, let's see. They're fourteen years into the business. Maybe an average of fifty new stores per year. Ten per year in the early years. A hundred per year about now. So maybe around fifteen hundred stores."

"Not a bad estimate. The number of stores in the U.S. at the end of the year 2000 was 3,000."

Steve smiled. "What, are you—a shareholder?"

"Yes, in fact, I am. But more important, I'm a student. Now, what was the *pattern* of store growth?"

"What do you mean?"

"Sprinkled across the country? Regional? City by city?"

Steve thought about it. "Regional," he guessed.

"Wrong." Zhao turned the yellow pad toward himself and started drawing.

"Fill the column"

[Bar chart titled "Number of stores" showing cumulative store openings by year for three cities:
- *Seattle: 89, 90, 91, 92, 93 (solid), 94 (dashed)*
- *Chicago: 91, 92, 93 (solid), 94 (dashed)*
- *Vancouver: 92, 93 (solid) (dashed top)]*

"This is data from their IPO prospectus. Each layer of each bar shows the year in which stores were opened. Look at Seattle, then Chicago, then Vancouver. If every city has an approximate number of possible locations and you think of that number as a column, they've certainly worked hard to fill the column in each city, not leaving very much daylight or oxygen for competitors.

"Now, let's fast-forward three years. The strategy continues. Now tell me, how do you think the profit works for Starbuck's as compared to, say, their leading competitor?"

Zhao ripped off the cover sheet and handed the yellow pad to Steve. Steve paused and thought a moment. Then he started talking and writing at the same time.

"Suppose they have forty locations and their competitor has ten. First, their purchasing costs will be significantly lower."

"*Cuanto?*"

"Maybe two percentage points."

"What else?"

"They'll have captured most of the better traffic locations."

"And how much is that worth?"

Steve rubbed his cheek. "Hmm. Maybe three percent of sales. The incremental margins here are quite high."

"Any other cost item?"

"Yes. Recruiting. Recruiting always has fixed costs. Advertising, for example. I imagine their costs are lower and their yield is better."

"*Cuanto?*"

"Don't know. Maybe a percent of sales."

"So far, you've built a six-percentage-point advantage. Is that it?"

"Well, with forty stores, they're everywhere. It's like having forty billboards. Hundreds of thousands of dollars of advertising at no incremental cost."

"So?"

"Another one percent of sales."

"What about their pricing?"

"I think it can be higher due to solid foot traffic and higher awareness."

"*Cuanto?*"

"Maybe two to three percent."

"All to the bottom line?"

"More or less."

"And the total is—?"

"Nine or ten percent. So their competitors could be breaking even while they're making ten percent on sales."

"What about a case of fifty-fifty?" Zhao asked.

"The relative position falls dramatically."

"How much?"

"Maybe five percent margins for both?"

"What's the impact of that lost five percent of margin?"

"I see two impacts. First, it reduces the potential growth rate."

"Why?"

"Lower profit. Lower multiple. Lower valuation. Less capital available to pay for growth."

"And the second impact?"

"Bad long-term economics."

"Why?"

"A viable competitor. A competitor who is encouraged to invest and play the game. The competitor who's breaking even can't afford to play or doesn't want to."

"Okay," Zhao nodded. "You have it. Now shift gears. How many stores does Wal-Mart have?"

Steve had read the number recently, but he'd forgotten it.

"Estimate."

"Five hundred?"

"Only ten per state?" Zhao shook his head.

"A thousand?"

"Keep going."

"Two thousand?"

"As of the year 2000, it was actually around three thousand. What do you think the growth pattern was?"

"City by city."

"Close. County by county. Here's how it worked." As he talked, Zhao quickly sketched a circle. Dots around the circumference. Then the dots filled in.

"Saturate the circle"

"Starbuck's filled the column within each city. Wal-Mart saturated the circle in a county. Exact same idea. How much difference did it make?"

Steve went through a logic path like the one he'd traced for Starbuck's. After a few moments, Zhao summed it up: "All told, about six percentage points extra to Wal-Mart's bottom line. Now, how disciplined do you suppose Walton was in sticking to this profit model?"

"Very."

"Simple, isn't it?" Zhao said.

"It really is," Steve marveled.

"Then why do so few people do it?"

"Another profit paradox? Another case of people refusing to see or act on the obvious?"

"Exactly." Zhao paused. "One more thing."

"What's that?"

"This strategy was like a natural phenomenon, a natural disaster for the competition. It was like a tsunami radiating out from northwest Arkansas, and you could actually measure its speed. The Wal-Mart wave was heading towards Hartford at a speed of seventy miles per year. The most profitable model with the highest growth rate, covering territory in concentric circles expanding at the rate of seventy miles per year . . . and all fueled by the extraordinary profitability of its earliest stores."

"So, from the point of view of Northeast discount chains like Ames or Bradlee's, it was like boulders against eggshells."

Zhao smiled. Steve had been reading *The Art of War*. "Precisely," he agreed.

"The margins of those other chains might be two or three percent?"

"Yes. And that was *before* Wal-Mart's entry depressed price levels."

". . . Driving them below break-even."

"Exactly. Now, how far would Wal-Mart have gotten without the local leadership that fueled its profitability?"

"They would have been a decade late," Steve ventured.

"No, they would *never* have gotten there. There wouldn't have been enough financial fuel to support the expansion."

Steve pondered the implications for companies like Ames—regional businesses that never made it out of their region because there just wasn't enough profit for them to do so. "So most companies in Local Leadership Profit businesses get stuck in the middle."

"Just about."

"Pretty boring."

"Pretty low-profit as well."

"This strikes me as pretty uncomplicated," Steve remarked.

"You think so."

Was this a question or a statement? Steve couldn't tell.

"Tell you what," Zhao continued. "There are two books to read. Read them. Then tell me how complex it is."

"It's a deal. What are they?"

"Sam Walton's *Made in America* and *Pour Your Heart Into It* by Howard Schultz of Starbuck's. Why every retailer doesn't read these books at least three times is a total mystery to me."

Steve's voice rose in protest. "But I read Walton already. Twice!"

"I know. Now read it for the third time, for a different purpose. To understand how local leadership happens, how it's built, how much it's worth."

Steve sighed. "Anything else?"

"No, you'll barely have the time to get through those two. But if you don't, we'll have wasted the last hour. And one last thought: Don't read them for pleasure, although they're fun reads, both of them; read them to learn. In fact, imagine—seriously imagine, for more than five minutes—that you are running a typical business model for a locational or Local Leadership Profit business. Tell me what changes you'd make based on analyzing the distilled knowledge in these two works."

"Okay."

"We're done. See you next week, same time, and bring your list of what changes you'd make to your locational business. One page only, please. Oh, and by the way—what's the latest with Delmore Supply?" Zhao asked.

Steve was halfway out the door, but he paused, tapped his nose with a forefinger, and smiled a cat-that-swallowed-the-canary smile. "Pyramid under construction," he remarked.

"Across the board?"

"In selected product lines. Air conditioning filters, insulation, screen doors. We expect to have products at three levels in each area. Special merchandising displays are being designed. Dealer training should start next month. By March, the whole thing should be in place. The marketing people are truly psyched. It's the first time in a decade that we've had a real plan for growth. If we play our cards right, sales of the high-end products should triple next year. And if that happens, profitability for the division should double—from around four percent to eight percent. Fingers crossed," he concluded, and matched gesture to words.

"Are you sure the whole team is on board with the Pyramid concept?" Zhao asked.

Steve looked a little puzzled. "Sure, I think so. Why?"

"Remember our conversation about gasoline. If you're going to do it, you've got to do it right. Otherwise you complicate the choices for consumers without offering any clear benefits."

Steve was relieved. "Oh, we're okay about that," he answered. "We're going to promote the hell out of our new high-end products. Green and gold packaging, seal of approval from the Eco Foundation, three hundred thousand giveaway booklets with energy-saving tips for consumers, the whole nine yards. They'll have plenty of reasons to pay extra for the good stuff, believe me." Steve glanced at his watch. "Yikes, gotta go—I'm meeting a friend for brunch uptown. So long."

Zhao closed the door behind Steve. He stood there a moment abstracted in thought. Then he returned to his desk, flipped up the screen on his laptop computer, and turned on the power. Within a few moments he had logged onto *delmoresupply.com*. As he scrolled through the online catalog of building supplies, his pen flew across a fresh yellow pad, jotting down product names, price points, specifications, sizes, and styles . . . *Do they really know what it means to build a Product Pyramid?* he was wondering. *And if they do, do they have the self-discipline to pull it off?*

15
Transaction Scale Profit

February 1. Steve was on the verge of annoyance. He and Zhao had been discussing Transaction Scale Profit for twenty minutes. The advantages had quickly become obvious. Steve could see that big transactions meant bigger profit, that cost per unit rose slower than revenue per unit the bigger the deal became. He could also see that this model applied to any brokerage-type business, to any transportation-type business—but... "But so what?" he finally blurted. "What can I *do* about it?"

Zhao regarded him intently. Should he answer or not? Finally, he reached a compromise. "How would you answer your own question?"

"There *isn't* an answer," Steve insisted. "There's a random distribution of projects. The flow of available business is what it is. You take what you can get... as much as you can get."

"That's what every salesman says about every customer," Zhao said, a bit dismissively. "'Got to get the revenue.' However unprofitable it might be. And it's true—until you change the rules, until you change your system. So that's the question: How can you change your system?"

"But you can't get to the big transactions just by wanting to."

"Right. So how *do* you get to them?"

"I don't know." Steve was frustrated. He thought about it. Nothing came. He doodled on his pad. He wrote down the business examples: real estate, investment banking, air travel. Then another occurred to him. "This works in advertising too, doesn't it?"

"Absolutely. Just think of an advertising campaign as a kind of big transaction, one that takes longer to execute."

"So if I owned an ad agency, who would I go after?" Steve wondered out loud. The silence returned. Another few minutes went by.

Finally, he answered his own question. "The big accounts."

"But *everybody* wants the big accounts," Zhao said, anticipating Steve's next objection.

"That's right," Steve said, falling into dejection once again.

More silence. Zhao's urge to speak was strong. He controlled it.

"But wait a minute," Steve finally continued. "I just said that everybody's trying to get all the business they can get, regardless of its profitability."

Zhao's focus on Steve intensified. Still he said nothing. Steve went on: "But maybe you have to take risks to bias yourself towards the big business. Turn small business away to concentrate on the big accounts."

"Yes, risk-taking is one element. What are the others?" Zhao asked.

"Skill. Persistence."

"What else?"

Steve thought some more. "Reference development."

"And—?"

"And, and, and…" Steve kept thinking. He was on the verge of giving up. He looked at Zhao, who was doodling on his telephone pad, drawing what looked like little pigs with flapping wings attached.

Steve remembered his friend Deborah. They'd been at college together. Afterward, she'd landed a job at a regional investment bank—a classic deal-chasing environment. While working there, she made a comment that always bugged him.

"Steve," she said, "I was part of the team that landed the Forrester Bank deal. We did a super job on that transaction, worked day and night for nearly three weeks. It was a fabulous team. I had a bunch of terrific ideas for what the team should do next. But as soon as the deal closed, all the principals—on both sides—headed off for vacation. Since I seemed to be a rising star, I got a plum assignment with Boston Edison. After a weekend of sleep, I became totally focused on the Boston Edison assignment, because we were under a tight deadline. You know what? To win, you've got to concentrate."

Concentrate. Right. But on what? Steve thought.

He slowly drifted back to the present. Zhao was still doodling. Now he was drawing bridges. Bridges over water, bridges over ravines, bridges between buildings, bridges over highways. Steve became fascinated.

Suddenly Zhao looked up. His expression said, *Don't ask.*

"Ready to continue, Steve?"

"There's the element of risk, skill, persistence, reference development, and …"

"And—?"

"And there's the open door syndrome."

"The open door syndrome?"

"Yes. You work for years to open the door to the kind of opportunity that matters—and then you don't walk through it."

"Fear of success?"

"I can't explain it. But it happens." He told Zhao about Deborah's summer experience. "I suspect that this isn't as much of an exception as one might think, " Steve concluded.

Zhao chortled, "An exception? I've seen it a hundred times. Your friend was pretty non-strategic, wasn't she?"

"Incredibly so. But the company she worked for was worse."

"Pretty amazing."

"Yes, is it ever."

"No, I don't mean that!" Zhao challenged.

"What then?"

"Pretty amazing how clearly we see it in *others*."

Steve caught his intonation. "You mean, we should ask how often have *we* behaved this way."

Zhao nodded. "Japanese managers have a saying. 'When you point a finger at someone, always remember that three fingers are pointing back at you.'"

"So you think I've done the same thing?"

"I have no idea. I just want you to think back over the last twelve months. How many open doors did you refuse to enter?"

"Hey, wait, that was *my* metaphor," Steve protested with a laugh.

"And a good one," said Zhao, and he gave a little bow.

Steve thought for a moment, and another. Several minutes went by. It was totally quiet once again, except for the ticking of Zhao's clock and the light tap-tap of Frances working the word processor just outside Zhao's office.

Finally Steve spoke. "At least two times that I can remember." It was like a confession.

"So forget about Deborah's story. Think about your own. Why did it happen?"

"The next thing came up. It was like Deborah's case. Acting like a rainbow trout."

"A rainbow trout?"

"Irresistibly drawn to the shining lure of the next thing that came up. Trout fall for the silver-glistening lure, and they get caught. We're the same. Psychologically, it's a fascinating moment, a zone of temporary economic insanity. We lose all sense of long-term self-interest, all sense of strategy, all sense of the really smart thing to do. It's like entering an electromagnetic field that disables your compass."

"I like the image of the lure." Zhao interjected. "It reminds me of the old line-in-the-sand story."

"What's that?"

"A Chinese general once said, 'I'll draw a line in the sand, and my enemy will be incapable of crossing it.'"

"How so? Because of the distraction?"

"That's part of it, but the underlying principle is much broader. It's about controlling the mind."

"Just as the lure exercises an almost absolute control over our behavior."

"Over our thinking." Zhao corrected. "The behavior follows."

"It's happened to me," Steve said ruefully.

"That's in the past," Zhao said with a wave. "The question is, 'How many times do you think it will happen to you in the *next* twelve months?'"

Steve smiled broadly. "You got me. It'll probably happen *at least* two or three times."

"Then that's where the profit is. Don't focus on Deborah, don't focus on the doors you walked by already. Focus on the next three. Better still, focus on the next *one*."

Steve was overcome. Utter simplicity. Utter undoability. He wanted to change the tone of the conversation. "How about a counter-example?" he asked.

"My friend Alice, the real-estate broker."

"Tell me about her."

"She struggled for years, surviving on the scraps of the business. She sold my wife and me each of our three houses. I liked Alice. She was honest and well-intentioned. But, like most of her colleagues, she covered a lot of mileage and made very little profit."

"What happened?"

"Today she sells only six or seven houses a year. However, they happen to be million-dollar houses. At six percent, that's four hundred thousand dollars in commission, of which she gets half. Not bad."

"How'd she figure it out?"

Zhao smiled. "I told her."

"About how to do it?"

"No, about where the profit really was and always would be. She figured out the rest."

"What did she do to get the big transactions?"

"She paid attention to the potential million-dollar buyers. She asked herself, 'How do these people want to be treated?' She didn't overdo it. She was unobtrusive. But she was always around. She gave them information. She followed their needs. She built her rolodex. She noticed the shoddy treatment plenty of other agents provided, and she offered an alternative. She wasn't as aggressive as her colleagues, which cost her some sales early on. But it won her many more sales later. Much larger sales."

"How long?" Steve asked.

Zhao got the intent of the question. "About seven years."

"A long time."

"Not really."

"Maybe we have different concepts of time," Steve said, thinking of *Einstein's Dreams*.

Zhao shrugged.

"It's a paradox," Steve added.

"How so?"

"You get to the big transactions through great relationships."

Zhao grabbed the yellow pad, thus helping Steve not to say another word.

The diagram he drew was a simple one, just four lines. Underneath it he added a simple equation: Big transactions = f (relationships).

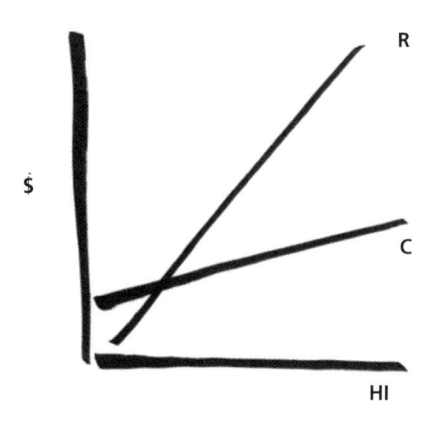

Transaction scale

Big transactions=f (relationships)

He tore off the sheet and handed it to Steve.

"We're done. See you next week."

"Any reading?"

"Not this week. Spend a little extra time reviewing or just thinking. You've earned it."

Steve nodded. "I might even catch a movie or game of darts. I haven't done those things much since you and I started working together . . . and since Delmore really hit the skids."

"I hear they're selling the telecom business."

Steve shrugged. "Might as well. The customer base is worth something, and so is the factory. And God knows we need the cash." He shook his head. "But where next year's cash is coming from is another question."

"You're not the only one working on it, you know."

"Sometimes I'm afraid I am."

16
Value Chain Position Profit

February 8. By the time Steve got to his office, Zhao was already waiting for him, apparently doodling on his yellow pad.

"Hi, Steve. Come on in, sit down. I have something to show you."

It turned out that Zhao wasn't doodling at all. Instead he had sketched a panoramic landscape with mountains, rivers, valleys, forests, and open plains. Amid the forests and cataracts a few signs of human existence could be seen—a bridge here, a road there, a cluster of little houses.

As Steve examined the drawing, Zhao spoke. "I often think about this line from Sun Tzu: 'He who occupies the mountain pass can easily battle a thousand.' Just as some moments in time are more critical than others, so too are some places more important than others."

Zhao began to point to different parts of the drawing as he continued: "Some places are much more critical than others. The high ground. The river ford. The mountain pass. The bridge. The isthmus. The channel— think of Gibraltar, Suez, the Bosphorus.

"What's true in geography is true in business. There are places on the landscape, places in the value chain, that are ten times more valuable than others in terms of profit, power, and control. These special places are the control points of the business landscape.

"When earthquakes, tremors, floods, or other natural disasters occur, the location of these special places changes, making some vulnerable and others blessed.

"Think about the examples of Value Chain Position Profit that you know—cases where there is an extremely lumpy distribution of power in the value chain, with enormous concentration of power and profitability in one place."

"Well, the obvious ones are Intel and Microsoft," Steve replied.

"Good. Profits in the PC box business are almost non-existent, but the two companies you name have been able to capture huge value as suppliers to the industry. Any others?"

Steve bit on his pencil and thought for a couple of minutes. "Nike?"

"Good one. All the power is concentrated in the hands of the marketer and designer. Any others?"

Steve thought some more. "Do these positions always pre-exist, or can they be created?"

"What do you think?"

"I think they can be."

"Do you have an example in mind?"

"How about what Ovitz did in the 1980s and early 1990s?"

"Not bad. Ovitz changed the basic business design of the business in a way that fundamentally redistributed power and profit in Hollywood. But can you think of other examples of Value Chain Position Profit?"

Steve thought hard, but further examples weren't coming to him.

"Think about retailing or publishing," Zhao suggested. "Would you rather be a supplier to Wal-Mart or Wal-Mart itself? Would you rather be Tom Clancy or Tom Clancy's publisher?"

"That's easy. I'd rather be Wal-Mart. Or, for that matter, Home Depot or Toys R Us. But in publishing, I'd rather be Tom Clancy or Stephen King."

They were quiet for a minute. Then Steve threw a question to Zhao. "Are there any examples of pre-existing control points?"

"Good question. That's your homework for the week."

"Okay," Steve said, and jotted it down. "Anything else?"

"Yes. Number one: pre-existing control points. Two: most radical shifts in control points. Three: new control points you think will arise in the next two years."

"Can I try doing the homework now?"

"Shoot."

"One: There are *no* pre-existing control points. They're conditional depending on the circumstances."

"Interesting. What kind of circumstances?"

"Relative value added, or rather the trajectory of relative value added."

"Example?"

"Microsoft and Intel versus the PC makers. Or Wal-Mart versus its suppliers."

"What other circumstances?"

"Creation of scarcity. Or seeing the bottleneck and capturing it."

"Any others?"

Steve thought for only a moment. "Connection to the customer."

"Meaning what?"

"Meaning a better connection than the other value chain players have." Steve was feeling almost cocky.

"How then does the profit happen?"

Again, Steve's pause for thought was very brief. "Predictability," he quickly answered.

"Predictability?" Zhao queried.

"Yes. The company that owns the control point sets the pace. Its business plan defines the future. The others react, always a step behind."

Zhao was startled. Steve's formulation was incomplete, but it was on target.

Steve continued. "Question two: most radical shifts. I can see three places where there's been a control shift from an integrated system to specialists who control the action—in computing, in athletic shoes, and in Hollywood.

"Finally, question three: new control points. That one I'll have to think about." Steve sat back, a smile on his face, looking rather satisfied with himself.

Zhao found himself feeling a little relieved that Steve had finally run out of gas. "Good," he said. "Think about it and give me three examples next week. Explain why. And how long you think they'll last."

"Any reading?"

"Yes. Read "The Computerless Computer Company." It's the best article in the *Harvard Business Review*, ever. It's about many things: how the rules change, how the control point shifts. Read it three times, one day apart. You won't want to, but just try it. Write out the key points after the first reading. Do it again on a separate sheet of paper after the second reading and again after the third. Then compare them. That's all.

"We're done for today. We'll take a week off for the Presidents Day holiday. My wife has been angling for a couple of days with me down in Hilton Head. I'll see you in two weeks."

17
Cycle Profit

February 22. The moment Steve walked through the office door, Zhao grabbed his yellow pad. "Which of Delmore's businesses are cyclical?" he asked.

"A lot of them," Steve replied. "Building supplies. Chemicals. Paper. Plastics. Even aircraft parts. It's one of the big problems we've been wrestling with. How the heck do we keep from going broke during the downturns? And then how do we gear up fast enough to take advantage of the upswings?"

"This is the mental picture most people have of a cyclical industry," Zhao declared. He drew two strokes and a wavy line.

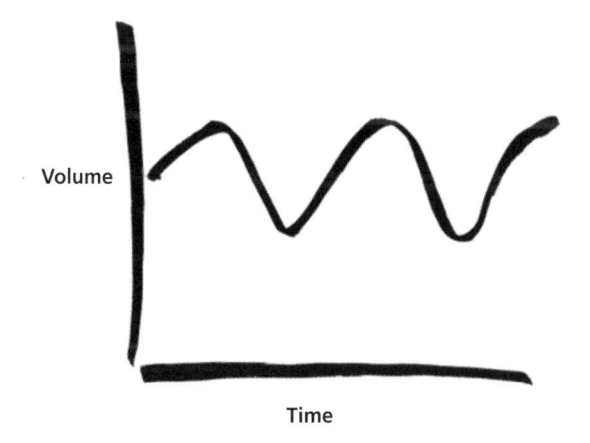

"Unfortunately, it's the wrong picture," Zhao continued. "It focuses on volume, and it obscures the relationship between the cycle and profit. Let's change that."

Zhao paused. Steve had learned how to enjoy Zhao's silences. *He uses silence the way a composer uses rests,* Steve reflected. *There's nothing random or accidental about the pause.*

"Let's start with this," Zhao resumed. "What happens to cost when utilization goes up?"

Steve was about to answer when Zhao cut him off. "No, just draw it," he said, tossing Steve the pad.

Steve flipped to a fresh page. He drew three strokes and added two labels.

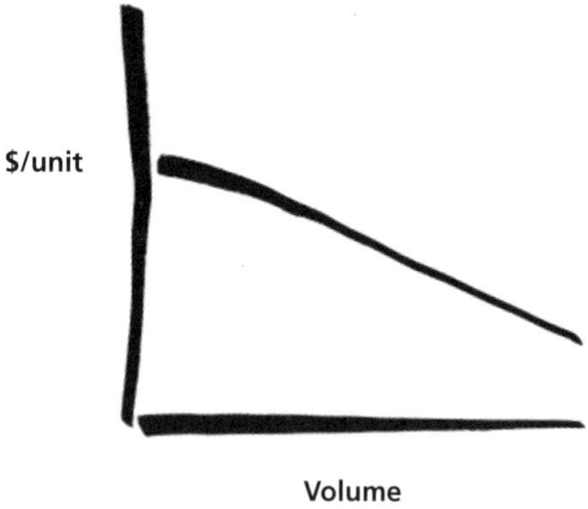
$/unit
Volume

"Good," Zhao agreed. "Now what happens to price?"
Steve drew again.

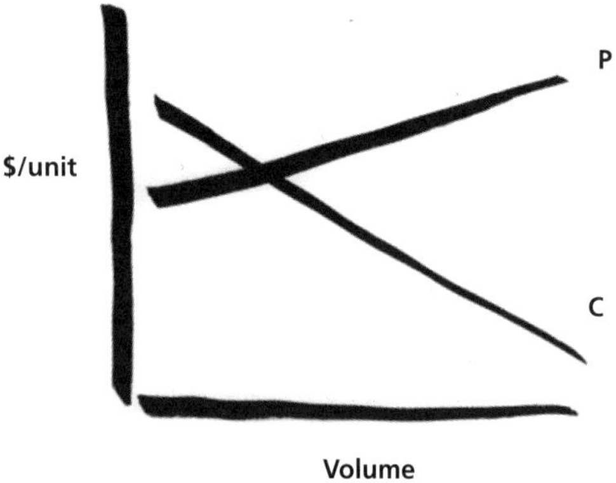
P
$/unit
C
Volume

"Good." Now Zhao took the pen and added four letters to Steve's drawing.

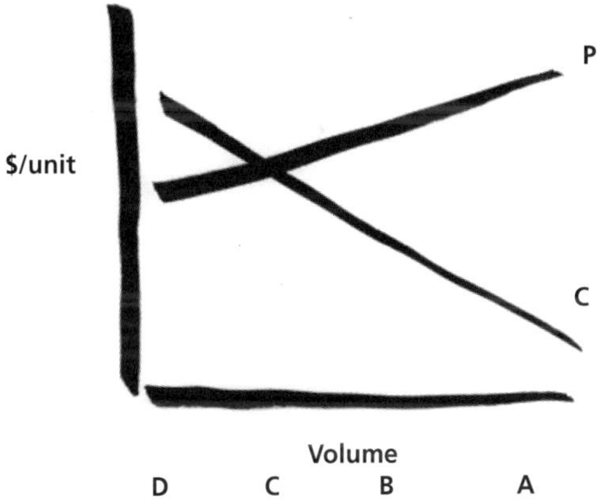

What happens at D?" Zhao asked.

"You lose money."

"At C?"

"Break even."

"At B?"

"Make money."

"At A?"

Steve chuckled. "Make an obscene amount of money."

"Okay. So how does profit versus utilization look?"

Steve took the pen, flipped the page, and drew again. Four strokes. Four letters.

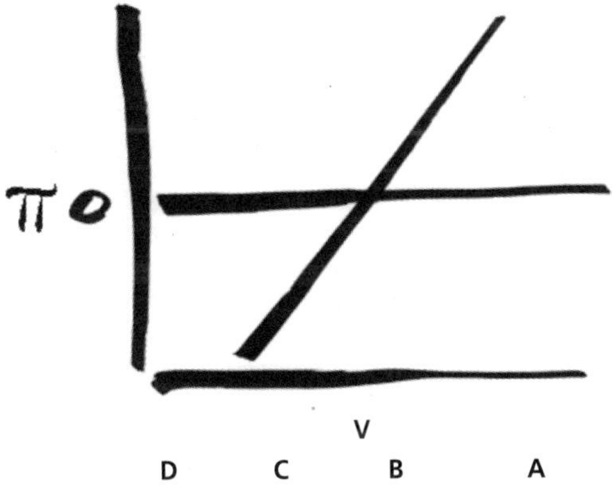

"Good. Now think about a great Cycle Profit company," Zhao said.

"Ummm... Toyota?"

"Good choice. How do they do it?"

Steve thought. He remembered a *Wall Street Journal* article on the company. "By driving down the breakeven point?"

"You bet. How?"

"They reduce costs, especially fixed costs."

"Exactly. Draw me the picture."

Steve thought about it, then added a dotted line to the drawing.

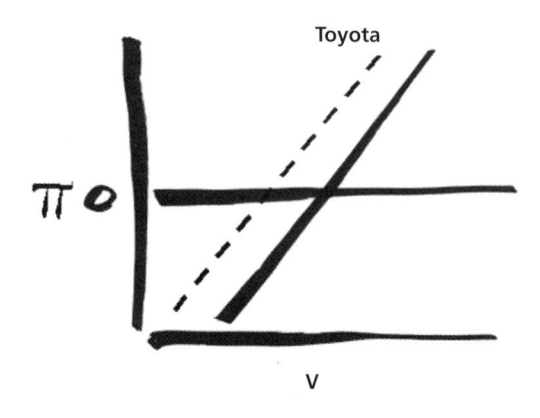

Toyota

π 0

V

"Exact again. And their aim?"

"When others lose money, they break even. When others break even, they make money. It keeps them permanently ahead."

"Good explanation. It helps explain the pile of cash that they've built up."

"How much?" Steve wondered.

"Guess."

"Ten billion?"

"More than that."

"Fifteen billion?"

"More. Over sixteen billion in late 2001, the last time I checked." Zhao shifted gears. "So that's Toyota. Who else manages Cycle Profit tremendously well?"

Steve frowned and stared at the table. "Don't know."

"Universal Chemicals," Zhao threw out. "I once worked with a guy named Scott there. Scott taught me that there's magic in pricing. You need data on capacity and on customer activity, along with tremendous confidence. Then you lead the price up, by a couple of quarters, and lag the price down. Here, Steve," he said, pushing the pad across. "Draw me a picture."

Steve drew.

Zhao shook his head. "Wrong."

Steve flipped the page and drew again.

"Wrong again." Zhao turned to a fresh page and drew a graph with a dark wavy line. "Market price," he said. Then he added a dotted line so close to the solid line that the two nearly touched. "That tiny, tiny lead and lag difference translates into enormous profit dollars—enormous. This is not about manufacturing, it's about arbitrage."

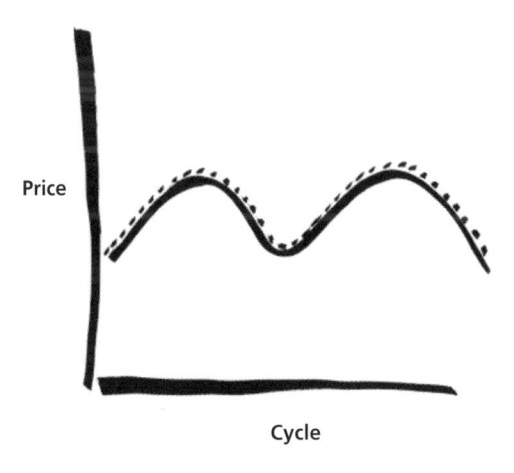

"Gee, is it that simple?" Steve wondered. He thought about his friend Jerry, an assistant VP at DelChem. Jerry was always complaining about being whipsawed by shifts in the marketplace. In the past five years, DelChem had enjoyed three boom years, with profits over thirty percent, and two bust years, with double-digit losses. It was anybody's guess what next year would look like. Two or three bust years in a row could help sink Delmore.

"That simple, and that hard," Zhao replied. "Scott retired from Universal Chemicals two years ago. They called him Mr. Money. There were a dozen great pricers in the company, but he was in a league of his own. Totally informed, totally fearless, totally brilliant. They gave him a solid gold watch. They should have given him a solid gold Cadillac for the hundreds of millions of profit that he helped create over the last twenty years—in the upcycles and the downcycles as well. But especially during the last five years."

"Why the last five?"

"Scott knew he was going to retire. And he knew that pricing would become both more critical and more difficult. He roamed around the company looking for good students. He found them, recruited them, and pulled strings all over the place to get them into the game. Not one of them is nearly as good as he is. But as Scott will tell you, collectively they are much, much better. His legacy is worth a billion dollars.

"You know, profit is funny. A few people are incredibly important: sellers, pricers, project managers, inventors. In fact, the more you think about profitability, the more you sense how dependent it is on a few key talents in an organization. The discoverers of molecules, like Jimmy Black. The brilliant project managers at places like MITRE, Merck, or Boeing, who keep impossibly complex projects hurtling forward unstoppably through time, like so many runaway freight trains. The three brilliant copywriters at an ad agency. The two genius designers buried in the bowels of Chrysler's engineering group. The six rainmakers who drive seventy percent of a law firm's new business creation.

"Profit works in highly definable pathways, and in many cases, it's a handful of players in a vast organization who are the true catalysts, the triggers that cause the right things to happen.

"Here's another way to think about it. Picture a ten-billion-dollar chemical company with twenty key talents—pricers and project pickers.

"Now picture the same company with the same ten billion dollars in revenues. But now, through restructuring, re-engineering, and just plain under-management of talent, most of the money-makers are gone. The before-and-after comparison can be a truly frightening picture."

Zhao grabbed the pad, drew a pyramid, and populated it with twenty tiny stars, "These represent key talents," he said. He labeled the pyramid "Before."

Before

"Buy the stock"

Underneath it, he drew another pyramid with most of the talents gone, and labeled it "After."

After   "Sell Short"

Steve took out his pen. Next to "Before," he wrote BUY THE STOCK. Next to "After," he wrote SELL SHORT. Zhao and Steve exchanged smiles.

Zhao couldn't resist asking, "Which picture is Delmore today?"

Steve thought for a second, reached into the pencil cup on Zhao's desk, and grabbed a red marker. He pointed to the "After" sketch. "This is the one," he said, "But don't forget, they have *me* working there." And with the red marker he drew an extra star in the middle of the pyramid.

"Let's hope that makes a difference," Zhao chuckled. "What about your building supplies pyramid? Is that still shaping up?"

"It's almost ready to roll out," Steve nodded. "At least, I think so."

"Any doubt in your mind?" Zhao gently pressed.

Steve hesitated. "I'm not sure I saw the last version of the marketing materials. But the ones I saw two weeks ago seemed a little—I don't know—"

"Off-target?"

"Maybe so. They sure pushed the high-end products aggressively. But the low-end, firewall stuff looked kind of cheap and crummy. I'm afraid they might be missing the boat there. Isn't it important to keep the low-price product really strong, so that competitors can't grab that market?"

"That's the idea, Steve."

"There's a lot of no-name building supply product ready to steal market share if we're not careful—store brand stuff manufactured for the big hardware store chains, for example."

"Hmm. Could be a miscalculation in the works."

"That's what I'm afraid of. Any suggestions?"

"Do you have the customer data to back up your points?"

"Probably."

"Then go in and argue your case. With Cathy's support, of course."

"I guess I'd better."

The lesson was over. Zhao had made his points for the day.

"Any reading assignment?" he asked.

"Sure. It's time to learn Warren Buffett. You may think you understand him from the quick-and-dirty explanations you get on TV or in *Money* magazine, but you probably don't. His own essays make great reading, but they're not easy to track down unless you happen to own shares in Berkshire Hathaway—they appear in the company's annual reports. So the best way to begin is with the best book about Buffett—*Of Permanent Value* by Andrew Kilpatrick. But don't stop there. Make the effort to get copies of the Berkshire annual reports and read Buffett's essays."

"That's a lot of reading."

"You bet it is." Zhao said gruffly, unapologetic. Then he softened. "But take two weeks. It'll be worth it."

"Okay. See you in two weeks."

The lesson was over.

18
After-Sale Profit

March 8. "That reading was absolutely fantastic," were Steve's words of greeting to Zhao.

"Good," Zhao said. Nothing more.

There was very little ceremony at the start of today's session. Instead, Zhao immediately began peppering Steve with questions.

"Is buyer price sensitivity a constant? Is price sensitivity the same for all purchase occasions?"

"No, I don't think so," was Steve's knee-jerk response. "But I guess I'm not sure."

"Does it vary a little or a lot?"

"At least a little."

"What about a handful of examples? Let's say a cup of coffee, a television, a plane trip, a car."

Now it was easy. "A cup of coffee—very low. That's the basis of Starbucks' whole business. People will pay up to two or three dollars for the stuff, even though the marginal cost is a dime.

"With a television, it's different," Steve continued. "People pay more attention to price. They'll even go from store to store, looking to save twenty or thirty dollars, for the satisfaction of having gotten the lowest price.

"With a plane ride, the sensitivity is much higher. They'll search hard for bargains. They'll make reservations months in advance."

"What's going on there?" Zhao asked.

"The ticket price is a big one, it's a scary number, and everybody knows that if you work hard at it you can get a big reward—you can save a hundred or two hundred dollars."

"So big ticket *and* high variability in the market."

"Yes."

"What about cars?"

"Cars are enormous. The biggest ticket of them all, except for houses. Big variability as well. Huge price sensitivity. Even the timid and the negotiation-averse will overcome their natural tendencies when they step into a car dealership. They'll start to haggle."

"Unless—?"

"Unless?"

"When will the car buyer agree to the asking price?"

Steve thought a moment. Then he remembered a wealthy friend buying a Ford Expedition at the height of that car's popularity. He had to wait two months for the model to be available. "They'll pay if it's the car they really want, *and* if they have to wait for it."

"So, what general principles are at work?"

Steve ticked them off. "Price sensitivity is highest when ticket price is high, variability is high, and there are lots of options."

"Conversely?"

"Price sensitivity is lowest when ticket price is low, variability is low, and there are few options."

Zhao gave a little bow. "Thank you. You've just described the basis of high profit in the After-Sale Profit model. There are lots of businesses where the action starts with a high-visibility, big-ticket sale. Computers, cars, copiers, industrial equipment.

"The purchase transaction occurs in the buyer's maximum price sensitivity zone. Buyers will go to the wall to get the lowest price. Their zeal, their energy, their enthusiasm to hunt for the bargain drives the price down and the profit out.

"But then a funny thing happens. The initial transaction creates a new situation, a need for follow-up stuff that did not exist before. You didn't need the service contract before you bought the elevator, or the PC, or the pickup truck. You didn't need the replacement part or the accessories.

"But now you do. A whole new mini-market has been created, brought into being by the initial sale.

"Now think about the characteristics of this mini-market. It's stuff you gotta have, and the ticket prices are one-tenth or one-hundredth as high as the initial transaction. Much better characteristics than the initial sale."

"Isn't this just another variation on the Installed Base model?" Steve wondered.

"Is it?" Zhao tossed the question back at him.

"Looks like it to me."

"There are similarities," Zhao agreed. "But who profits from the Installed Base model?"

"The makers of the product, of course."

"Right. And who profits from selling the auto insurance policy, or the PC software, or the service plan on the appliance?"

"Different people—the insurance company and the broker, the software maker, the appliance retailer."

"That's the point," Zhao nodded.

"So why don't the hardware sellers collect on the follow-up stuff?"

"Great question. For me, it is one of the enduring paradoxes of business. The big-ticket hardware folks invest the capital, take all the risks—which are huge—suffer the losses and the write-downs, and then let somebody else capture the business that has predictability, lower price sensitivity, higher margins, recurring revenue, and the opportunity to create an ongoing customer relationship, because the frequency of purchase is ten times greater than the frequency of the initial transaction.

"So I don't understand why the computer guys let others sell the follow-up memory, why the car guys let others sell the insurance and the extended warranty, and so on."

"I get it," Steve chimed in. "There's a fundamental flaw in *their* business design—call it incomplete scope. It opens up a huge profit opportunity and customer relationship opportunity for others."

"What should they be doing instead?" Zhao asked.

Steve paused and thought some more.

"They should be expanding their scope to include a full-court press on the after-sale stuff. They should also be customizing the after-sale stuff to the original sale product, so that the customer has a compelling reason to buy the after-sale items and services from them."

Zhao gave Steve a little thumbs-up gesture. "That's it."

Steve continued, "They should be working hard to convert the After-Sale Profit model into an Installed Base Profit model."

"And meanwhile?"

"Meanwhile, there are huge profit opportunities out there for the rest of us."

"How can that be?"

Steve paused again. "Psychology?" he ventured.

"Say more."

"All the sex and prestige in the business is associated with getting the most market share, selling the most units of the big-ticket stuff."

"And . . .?"

Steve stopped again. His mind raced through the different situations that he and Zhao had discussed. They kaleidoscoped on his memory screen like a montage of movie clips. He sensed that there was a common thread in there somewhere, then he finally caught it.

"It's a *completely* different business model!" he exclaimed. "You need different skills, different people, different systems, different databases. There's also less psychic satisfaction, less glamor, and less visibility compared to the glamor of the original equipment business. As in 'I sold ten auto insurance policies today.' Big deal! Or 'I sold ten elevator maintenance contracts today.' Big deal! You don't get great press notices or win trips to Hawaii for that."

"No, you don't. You just make a lot of profit."

"So you have to create a separate and very different organization and system to run that business and then figure out a way to meaningfully connect it back to the base organization."

"Sounds like a lot of trouble," Zhao observed.

"At least trouble enough to explain why it doesn't happen more often."

"Right," Zhao agreed. "Now you've given me two reasons why is doesn't happen more often, psychology and different business model. Are there any others?"

Steve was stumped. Maybe he'd just run out of mental energy.

Zhao waited patiently. When he saw that nothing would happen soon, he asked, "How many people in the base organization—car makers, computer makers, copier makers, and so on—are responsible for and incentivized on profit?"

Steve was back on track, his internal screen flashing through Delmore's businesses. He thought about the auto and aircraft parts divisions, the pharmaceutical chemicals division, and the machine tools division. "Very few—sometimes only a handful."

"Quite right. Now, suppose there were *hundreds* of people in the organization whose bonus was totally dependent on the profit number?"

"There would be incredible pressure to overcome the hurdles in building the After-Sale Profit model."

"And what of the players who aren't in the OEM part, but are focused on the after-sale stuff? What kind of organizations are they?"

"Well, a lot of them are entrepreneurs, private companies, and so on."

"And what is their understanding of and focus on profitability like?"

"Crystal clear and intense. So when profit passion collides with profit indifference, the outcome is foreordained. Like boulders against eggshells."

"More or less."

Steve was scribbling notes furiously, trying to capture the substance of the dialogue. As Zhao fell silent, Steve kept writing. A minute passed, then two minutes, then five. Steve filled a page with notes, flipped it over, then filled a second page. Suddenly it struck him that most of the notes were about his own observations. Many of them were ideas for divisions at Delmore, and some had nothing to do directly with today's lesson. The last words he'd written, all in capital letters, were these: *AIRCRAFT DIVISION – COCKPIT SEAL PROJECT – TAKE OVER AIRLINE SECURITY PROGRAMS? – CUSTOMER SOLUTION – DE FACTO STANDARD?*

The sensation he felt was one of turning a corner. But he said nothing about this. He merely tucked his notes away in his backpack for further consideration later. He glanced up. Zhao was quietly watching him, a slight smile playing across his lips.

"Any reading for the week?" Steve asked Zhao.

"Two books again." He waited for Steve's groan. There was none. Zhao went on. "The first is *Paradigms*. It's about how realities shift when minds change. The second is *Profit Patterns*. It applies almost the same idea to profit models. That's a fair amount of reading. Take two weeks to do it right."

Steve jotted down the titles. "Any other homework?"

"Certainly. Give me five great examples of After-Sale Profit businesses. And by the way, asking friends about it is okay. I don't care. Only you'll have to explain to them what it is you're asking for."

As he was leaving, Steve paused at the doorway and looked back at Zhao. "These business examples, if they're public, they may be pretty good investments, no?"

Zhao looked up at him, sideways. He was already leaning over a pad on his desk writing. *Bitten by the Buffett bug*! he thought. He paused, undecided between silence, a slight nod of the head, an enigmatic smile, or a response.

"Steve, I thought you'd never ask. Just be sure to check it out carefully before you decide to make a move."

"Of course, of course."

"I mean it."

Something in Zhao's tone got through to Steve.

"Remember," Zhao added, "there's a ton of money lost somewhere in the zone between great idea and brilliant application. It's the brilliant application that counts. And one more thing . . ."

"Yes?"

"If you're going to become an investor, talk to customers. It's as important for investors as it is for managers. It's something that is always done poorly."

"Why is that?"

"Two reasons. First, people ask the wrong questions. They go into conversations asking, 'What do I need to know?'"

"What *should* they be asking?"

"They should ask, 'What am I afraid to find out?' It's those things that tell us our business design is obsolete, or our investment idea is not as great as we thought. Listening to those things takes a lot more courage.

"The second reason is perception. We don't see things as *they* are, we see them as we are. Keep that in mind when you read *Paradigms*. Tell me next time whether it's true for you as well.

"See you in two weeks, Steve."

19
New Product Profit

March 22. Steve sat in his usual guest chair waiting for Zhao, who was uncharacteristically late. Steve was fidgeting, incessantly drumming his fingers on the desk.

Zhao wasn't late. He was standing behind a file cabinet on the other side of the hall, looking through the half-open doorway into his office. He saw that Steve was in the grip of a nervous force that tossed him about the way a storm bounces a rowboat on the surface of a lake.

Not a good way to begin a difficult lesson, he thought.

When Zhao glided into his office, Steve had gotten out of his chair and was standing by the window, looking out at the Statue of Liberty in the distance and running his right hand through his hair. Zhao reached out and laid a calming hand on Steve's shoulder. Startled, Steve jerked around, staring.

"Tell me about it," Zhao said.

"About wha..."

Steve stopped in mid-word. He realized he could hide nothing from Zhao. Instead, he grinned and tossed off a one-liner: "What are you, one of those Chinese doctors who can tell your whole medical history just by taking your pulse?"

Zhao quietly repeated, "Tell me about it."

Steve sighed. "It was the presentation I made yesterday. We were working with the aircraft parts people. They've been crashing a program for cockpit security seals to thwart terrorists and other intruders. We'd come up with an idea to turn the program into the core of a new business. We were proposing that Delmore create complete, unified security systems for the airlines—baggage holds, passenger compartments, airport checkpoints, cockpit controls, you name it. Cathy and I threw the idea together very fast, and I was leading the presentation.

"I thought I had it aced. But I blew it. The last two questions we got took me by surprise. I didn't know what to say. So I rambled. By the end of my answers, I think I completely lost them. Cathy jumped in to try to save me, but she hadn't spent enough time on the details to really have the right answers. Frankly, it was pathetic. The looks on their faces—!" He shook his head.

Zhao nodded sympathetically. "It happens. Have you had a chance to rethink the questions?"

"That's the most frustrating part. I was thinking about them on the subway ride down here, and it became clear to me what my answers should have been. As soon as I thought of them, they seemed ridiculously obvious."

Steve's voice was ragged, tinged with self-disgust.

Twenty years ago, Zhao would have succumbed to the contagion of Steve's distress. The next hour would have been completely wasted.

Zhao sat down across from Steve. He pulled several sheets of blank stationery from his desk drawer and handed them to Steve.

"Write down the last two questions you were asked yesterday."

It was a curious statement, weirdly uttered. Something halfway between a suggestion and a command.

Steve couldn't protest. He scratched out the two questions. Zhao looked at them.

"Now write out your subway answers. You have thirty minutes. I'll return just before the time is up."

Steve sat down and started writing quickly. Zhao took off his Swatch and laid it on the desk in front of Steve. Then he slid out of the room. It was 8:35 a.m.

At nine o'clock. Zhao walked in, smiling broadly. "Time's up," he said. He held a tray with two bagels, two cups of orange juice, and a pot of coffee.

Steve stopped writing. "This is pretty good," he said, pointing at his work. Three pages were filled with Steve's densely-packed scrawl.

"It often is when you think for eighteen hours before you start to write. Let me have the pages. I'll read what you wrote and send you an e-mail with my comments."

"Thanks. And you know what? I think I can use these answers to write a memo to send to the aircraft people tomorrow morning. Something like, 'We've done some additional research into the issues you raised, and here's what we discovered . . .' Maybe I can turn this thing around."

"Maybe you can," Zhao agreed. "Meanwhile, grab a bagel."

Steve was famished, and Zhao's exorcism had cleared his mind completely. He pulled the plate and the cup of juice toward himself, arranged them neatly before his chair, and waited. A magic moment, suspended.

Zhao bit into his own bagel, and only then did Steve follow.

Wiping a crumb from his chin, Zhao began, "Well, what other examples of After-Sale Profit did you find?"

Steve had almost forgotten about last week's assignment. He pulled a folded sheet out of his jacket pocket and spread it out, somewhat crumpled, in front of Zhao.

Zhao liked the look of the crumpled page. "Did you know that Bach wrapped his lunch with his music? It shows that the right attitude can take you pretty far."

There were five entries on the sheet. Zhao stared at them, knitting his brow in puzzlement at the last three. The first two were clear, even obvious. The last three were problematic. One of them was clearly wrong. Zhao was crestfallen. But he didn't show a trace of it.

This wasn't the moment to push. He folded the paper and put it in his shirt pocket. "Thank you for remembering to do the exercise during a busy week," he remarked.

Steve was surprised. He had never expected a "Thank You" for doing what he was supposed to do. But he liked the feeling.

"Our time is short," Zhao observed. "I'll give you a note on this list together with the e-mail I'll send you about your aircraft project.

"Today we have a tough one. New Product Profit. People always confuse it with Time Profit or with Specialty Product Profit. Here's the icon." Zhao drew three strokes: a vertical, a horizontal, and an "S".

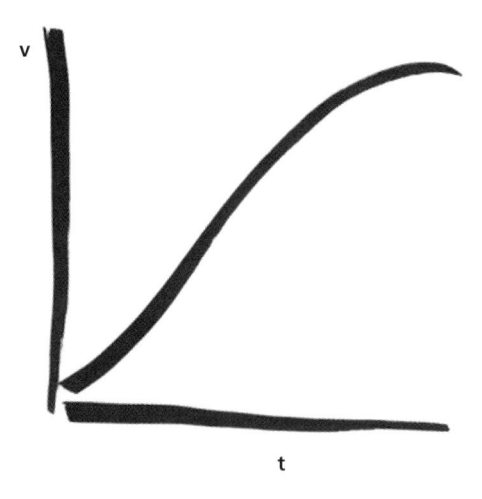

"The profit explosion happens at the bottom, during the gold rush days," Zhao explained. "Margins are fat and volume is skyrocketing. Multiply these two and you get a growing ocean of profitability. It's the opposite of a no-profit zone — a super-profit zone.

"New Product Profit is all about psychology. People get so caught up in the new product gold rush that they refuse to think forward three years, refuse to think clearly about what will happen on the other side of the parabola."

"The parabola? I thought we were talking about an S-curve."

"We are. But think about its first derivative."

"Its first derivative?" Steve felt lost.

"The S-curve tells you about volume. Now think about the curve that describes what happens to total profit in the industry. Draw it."

Steve was taken aback. His mind tightened. He felt for an instant as if he had been beamed back into the room where yesterday's presentation had taken place.

Zhao sensed the tightening immediately. He took the pen from Steve's hand and used it to gesture as he began one of his vintage stories.

"Never mind that right now. Listen instead. Thirty years ago, I worked with an electronics chemical company. They sent me to Singapore to interview their customers. There was a marketing manager, George Hawkins, who was my host on the trip. At a spectacular dinner one evening, George got a little tipsy, and launched into one of his favorite topics — the marketing curve."

"'The marketing curve?' That's a new one on me."

"It's a new one for anybody. George had totally misnamed it. But wild horses couldn't get him to change the name of his invention. It took him three strokes to draw it on a napkin."

Zhao took a pencil and made three quick strokes on his yellow pad. "But I won't use George's title. I'll call it what it really is." Zhao neatly printed a title over the three strokes: The Profit Parabola.

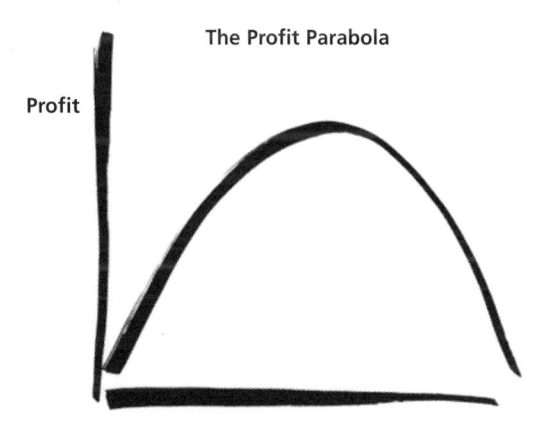

The Profit Parabola

Profit

"George maintained that this was a universal truth, and that people lost a lot of money because they didn't believe it and chose to work against it. His formulation was simple beyond measure: 'The total profit earned by all players in a market goes up, peaks, and comes down to zero.'

"He was right when he said that most people didn't believe it. I was one of them. I rejected the idea immediately. It was too pessimistic, too hopeless, too *dark*. I went into immediate denial. I didn't deal with it honestly for a decade.

"But I couldn't get it out of my mind either. It kept resurfacing. Especially when I began to develop a sense, a feel for some large-scale sequences."

"Such as?" Steve asked.

"Such as radios, TVs, VCRs, Walkmans. Such as desktops, laptops, servers. Such as sedans, minivans, sport utility vehicles. Such as faxes, fax-printers, fax-printer-copiers. The history of each one of these products seemed to suggest that George's curve was right."

As Zhao talked, Steve listened with absolute attention, but he was distracted by a thought triggered by the first series. Radios, TVs, VCRs, Walkmans . . . the series stirred a memory of a story he'd studied last October about the early days of color TV, the hundreds of competitors whose numbers quickly dwindled to ten. "May I?" he asked, pulling the yellow pad toward himself.

"Be my guest."

Steve took a pencil and drew three phrases near Zhao's diagram. On the left side of the parabola he wrote, "Gold Rush." On the top he printed, "Pike's Peak." On the right side, where the parabola's down slope met the horizontal axis, he printed, "No Profit Zone."

Zhao smiled. "You have it. What else?"

"The big problem," Steve said thoughtfully, "is on the lefthand side, the up slope, the gold rush. Once you're swept into that psychology, into the zone where even weak producers make money because customer demand is so strong, you can't think clearly enough about how to manage strategically. Besides, everyone in the company is so busy making product that there's zero time left over to see and manage the larger picture."

"Precisely."

"What was George's system for dealing with this?"

"Oh, I don't know if I can tell you all of it. George was extraordinarily crude and earthy—borderline obscene, in fact. Let's give him the benefit of the doubt and call him a determinist."

"But what did he say to do?"

"Well, George's rule number one was to admit reality, to admit to yourself that the parabola was real—that this was going to happen. He believed that this was by far the hardest step. It was as hard as getting a twenty-five-year-old to admit to himself that he would someday become old, arthritic, forgetful, bald, and, George would emphasize, impotent."

Steve squirmed uncomfortably.

"That's right," Zhao commented. "That was pure George. He was *always* trying to make people feel uncomfortable. He thought it was good for them."

Zhao continued, "Once you admitted that to yourself, you could get down to business and manage the parabola strategically, which meant two simple rules. Overinvest, by a factor of *three*, on the lefthand side of the parabola, and underinvest, again by a factor of three, on the righthand side.

"On the lefthand side, above all else, fight for mindshare. Be seen as the leader in the new category in the mind of the customer. Merchandise your product mercilessly. Be everywhere. Build plants and do subcontracting deals as fast as you can.

"And start measuring things that will give you clues that you're approaching Pike's Peak. Year-to-year and quarter-to-quarter growth rates. Year-to-year and quarter-to-quarter price changes. Indices of customer excitement and customer boredom."

"And the objective of that is . . . ?"

"The objective is to reverse the investment ratio about a year before hitting the peak. Not getting out of the market, mind you, just managing the business to maximize cash flow and to minimize the risk profile on the other side of the parabola.

"George would start building flexible plants, rather than dedicated ones, for late-stage capacity. He looked hard for opportunities to sell dedicated plants to the inevitable latecomers who still wanted to get into the game. By selling plants, he felt that he was acting like a model corporate citizen, preventing an unnecessary capacity addition, delaying by nine months to a year the inevitable capacity overshoot point in the cycle and helping to keep prices firmer than they otherwise would have been.

"Most important, George wanted to be in a great position on the day things started getting ugly. He could pull back on advertising, because everyone knew his product from his early grab-mindshare merchandising efforts. He could have less capacity than he really needed. He could serve the good customers—there always are some—and drop the bad customers. Most important, he'd be right there looking for the next wave, because he always wanted to be first and to be big on that one."

"So George kept his margins high while others' margins crumbled?"

"Exactly."

"George may have been crude, but he sounds very smart," Steve commented.

"Not necessarily. He just lived through this a couple of times the bad way, learned from it, and became the best New Product Profit man I know of. He's still at it, you know."

"I thought you said you worked with him thirty years ago."

Zhao laughed. "I did. He was twenty-six years old then. Now he's just the same, only thirty years smarter. He's totally dispassionate when it comes to managing the parabola. When everyone else is succumbing to market hysterics, George has ice water in his veins.

"George also spends a tremendous amount of time scouting the landscape, looking for early signals of the peak of the inflection.

"He also keeps wonderful records. He's very proud of what he does. The last two times, he even sent me a graph showing how he performed against the industry, sort of like a money manager calibrating himself against the S&P 500."

"This *feels* very different from Specialty Product Profit," Steve remarked.

"Doesn't it?"

"But it does *feel* like Time Profit," Steve added.

"Yes. But is it the same?"

"I don't know."

"Think about it. Take a break. Then let's get back together at 9:30, and you tell me what the differences are among these three first cousins: Time Profit, New Product Profit, and Specialty Product Profit."

At 9:30, Zhao was in his chair. Steve was still pacing at the window. But it wasn't a nervous, fidgeting, fear-stricken pacing. It was a high-energy march. Compared to ninety minutes ago, much of his confidence had returned.

Steve decided he would play the game differently. Without a word, he sat down at the desk, pulled the yellow pad toward him, turned it horizontally, took out a pen, uncapped it, poised it over the gleaming yellow surface, and forced Zhao to wait, to say something.

Zhao didn't take the bait.

Damn, Steve said to himself. But he didn't raise his eyes to meet Zhao's. He focused on the pad, concentrating, and sat poised for another full minute. Then he started scribbling furiously.

Zhao watched, trying to anticipate what Steve would draw next. Zhao found he could see the words in his mind a split second before Steve wrote them. It wasn't about predictability; it was about getting the structure right.

	Time Profit	New Product Profit	Specialty Product Profit
Cycle	24 months	60 months	120 months
Skill	Speed	Shift resources	Select
Metaphor	Race-car driving	Surfing	Seismography
Motto	"When you see #2 in the rear-view mirror, step on the gas."	"Get off the last wave first, catch the next wave first."	"Find the richest oil fields—the place where customer need, technical feasibility, and lack of competition intersect."
Examples	chips, consumer electronics, financial instruments	cars, copiers	specialty chemicals, pharmaceuticals

Steve capped his pen and looked sideways at Zhao's desk, but not at Zhao. Not a word was spoken.

"Done," Steve announced.

Steve wanted to smile but didn't. He inhaled deeply, got up, and faced Zhao.

Zhao extended his hand. They shook.

"See you in two weeks," Zhao said. "My daughters are home for Easter next weekend."

"Okay," Steve agreed. "But that reminds me—before I go, I wanted to leave something for you." He deposited a neatly printed list on Zhao's desk. "If I missed one, let me know. See you on the fifth."

The door closed behind Steve. Zhao couldn't see the smile on Steve's face. He picked up the list. It read:

> Fast arithmetic technique (Mt. Fuji)
> Re-read technique (Walton)
> Folder technique (Brands)
> Take-off-the-paradigm-filter technique (Paradigms)
> Front-end loading technique (Young)
> Re-read with questions and intent technique (Walton, Schultz)

Zhao chuckled. An idea struck him. With nimble fingers, he began folding the list, turning it first one way, then the other. In a few moments, he had created an exquisite origami eagle. Carefully, he perched the eagle on his bookcase. He would show off his origami technique to Steve next time.

20
Relative Market Share Profit

April 5. Steve was excited. "A lot has been happening at Delmore since last time," he began.

"I've seen a couple of things about it in the media," Zhao acknowledged.

"You probably saw the aircraft security systems announcement," Steve went on. "Wasn't that something? The piece in the *Wall Street Journal* was the most complete. It was the first time in years that Delmore Aeronautics has been out in front of the competition. I loved the comment from the Boeing guy—what was it again—?"

"'If Delmore can deliver on this ambitious program, there'll be no reason to consider any other source for airline security systems,'" Zhao recited.

"Right! You *did* see it!" Steve cried, plainly delighted. "Of course, the whole plan was developed hand-in-glove with Boeing. A classic Customer Solution approach."

"I thought so," Zhao remarked. "Of course, his 'if' is a big one."

"You mean, '*if* Delmore can deliver.' Yeah, that's important. But I'm not overly worried about it, to be honest. I think the key was developing the program and the process. The technology itself isn't all that overwhelming. And the aeronautics people are really pretty good—always have been. Their problem has been that they've operated in a reactive mode, focusing on making pieces of the plane at the lowest possible price. Now they need to think in terms of designing entire systems as partners for the manufacturers."

"A little like Johnson Controls," Zhao remarked.

"Yes, only in the aircraft business instead of the auto business. So now we're trying to follow Johnson's model. We see how Johnson shifted from making one-off parts to building entire assemblies—whole cockpit interiors, from dashboards to seat assemblies. Maybe Delmore can do the same in the aircraft business, starting with security systems."

"If you can become as profitable as Johnson Controls, more power to you."

"Yeah, that'd give a pretty good goosing to the stock price."

"What else is going on? You said a lot had been happening at Delmore."

"Well, the other news isn't quite as exciting. Just that Cathy asked me to head up a strategy program for the paper business."

"Not as glamorous as the aircraft business."

"That's for sure. No growth. Flat market. Commodity business. Old technology. Competing on price. It looks kinda hopeless." Steve laughed. "Maybe that's why I'm interested. If I can come up a big idea for the paper business, I'll really be a genius!"

Zhao smiled. "Easy there. One step at a time, Steve."

Steve grinned. "You really mean, 'One genius to a room,' don't you?"

"Exactly! And in *my* office—!" Zhao didn't bother finishing the sentence. Both men burst out laughing.

"So that's all my news," Steve concluded. "Now what about my next lesson? By my count we have four more profit models to talk about—right? What's on tap for today?"

"Relative Market Share profit."

"Relative Market Share?" Steve echoed. "That's a familiar phrase, isn't it?"

"It is," Zhao agreed. "But there's more to it than most people realize.

"You see, Steve," Zhao began, "the discovery of Relative Market Share was like Newton discovering gravity. It explained so many things. It predicted so many things." Zhao drew three strokes and two labels, then turned the picture to face Steve. "And all the new data that came in during the 1970s just reinforced it."

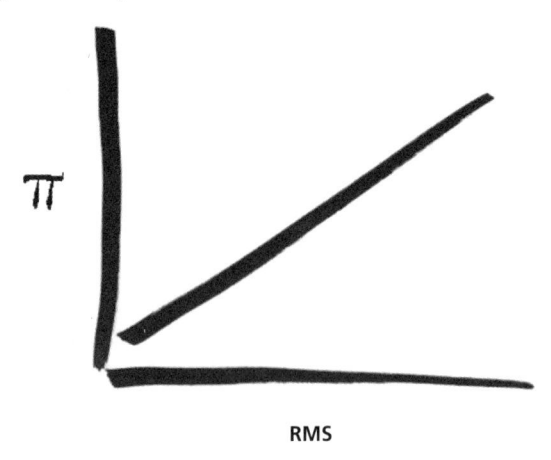

π

RMS

"Most important, RMS was prescriptive. It told you what you should do. Invest to win. Build a bigger lead. If you tried and failed, then cut your losses, or get out completely.

"It was discovered in the 1960s and fully formulated in the early '70s. It reached its zenith in practice in the early 1980s with Jack Welch, who was its most aggressive, most persistent, most unsparing, and most thoughtful practitioner.

"Bruce Henderson is the under-recognized innovator in the discipline—the Isaac Newton of strategy. But he wandered off into biology and Darwinism instead of completing what he started. That's why he was eclipsed by Michael Porter. Porter filled in the rest of the picture and gave managers methods they could use.

"But the whole intellectual underpinning of the thought system was Relative Market Share. Like gravity, it explained, it worked, you could measure it. You could make predictions based on it. No wonder it became the basis of classical strategy."

Zhao caught himself. He was doing all the talking. That was wrong. This was nearly the end of the course. He should let Steve do the talking.

"Why did RMS work?" asked Zhao.

Silence. Steve was thinking fast and furious.

Zhao spoke again. "What was the *most important* reason it worked?"

Still thinking furiously, Steve began, "Economies of scale in manufacturing. The biggest factor in understanding cost in the classic period."

"What else?"

"Well, related to it, but different, was purchasing advantage. The biggest player could pay the lowest price."

"And how important was that? How big was purchased material as a percent of total cost?"

Steve considered the question. "It varied from maybe thirty percent to as high as seventy percent. So it was a very big deal."

Zhao nodded. "What else?"

"The biggest player also had the advantage in marketing and advertising. They could afford to invest the most, and they had the lowest unit cost—that is, the lowest marketing cost or advertising cost per unit. A sort of economy of scale in marketing, not just in manufacturing."

"Was that all?"

Steve was warming up to the subject. "No. The biggest player also could have the lowest overhead cost per unit and the lowest R&D cost per unit, because they could spread these costs over greater volumes than any other competitor."

He fell silent. For the moment, he was done.

"So," Zhao said, "pretty simple arithmetic—the arithmetic of scale."
"Yes."
"Was that it?"
"That was most of it," Steve ventured.
"Anything else?"

Steve thought some more.

"Anything beyond the arithmetic?" Zhao suggested.

Steve thought back to some of the classic examples of RMS winners: GM, IBM, GE. "Well," he said, "in R&D, it was not just about spreading the cost over more units. It was also about attracting the best technical talent in the industry. They all wanted to work for the leader, the company with the best labs, the best equipment, the best budget. So it was a self-reinforcing upward spiral. Success drove more success."

"And this effect was just in R&D?"

"No, come to think of it. The market share leader position was also a powerful magnet for the best managerial talent. All the best players wanted to go to U.S. Steel, or to GM, or to IBM, or to Sears."

"And today?"

"Today they want to go where the stock price growth potential is the highest."

"Okay. Back to the classic age. You talked about scale economies in manufacturing, purchasing clout, lower per-unit manufacturing costs, lower per-unit costs for overhead and R&D. And you talked about being a magnet for the best talent in R&D and in manufacturing. Anything else?"

Steve frowned. What else could there be? Wasn't this enough?

The minutes ticked away.

"Hey, wait a second," Steve suddenly blurted. "They also had the biggest cash flow, so they could outspend rivals with ease and beat them in those arenas where being resource-rich mattered."

"And—?"

"And . . . " Steve suddenly remembered a story he heard in class about profit volatility. In the 1970s, GM's profit volatility was lowest, Ford's was moderate, and Chrysler's was enormous. In bad years, GM made a small profit, Ford broke even, and Chrysler lost a ton of money. "The leader had the least volatility!"

"Right. And if risk is about more than just profit volatility—?"

"The leader had the lowest risk by far. It could plan the market. It controlled the initiative. The others reacted. It was a great position to play from."

"And who has that kind of position today?"

"Well it depends. In certain industries, it's not the traditional market share leader, but the value chain leader—the player with the strongest economic position in the most important part of the value chain."

"Right. Any others?"

Steve thought, but only for a moment. "The owner of the de facto standard."

"Exactly. Today, those players exercise the kind of power that was exercised by the market share leaders of the classical age."

Steve was totally absorbed. He had never extended his thinking about market share this far before.

"So, RMS is still important, but it's a question of where and how," Steve said.

"Don't you think?" Zhao interjected.

"Yes, absolutely. So it *is* like Newton." Steve was dredging up faint memories from a college science class. "The classic laws of physics still work, but they don't work everywhere equally. At the frontiers, there are different types of forces and different rules and equations at work."

"Right."

"So the world is more complicated than we used to think?" It was a question more than a statement.

Zhao nodded. "I'm sorry," he said with a small, mischievous smile.

"And especially more complicated at the frontiers."

"Indeed."

"Is there any convenient, compact formulation of the new rules?"

"Good question, Steve. The answer is 'No, not yet.' We're in a transition period. That's why we have to learn so many profit models and understand the differences among them clearly enough to know how to apply them productively.

"You see, Newton's rule was simple—not that it didn't take a genius to discover it. Gravity's force was a function of mass over the distance squared. The classic rule of profit was equally simple. Profit was a function of RMS. The higher the RMS, the higher the profit. Today, profit can be a function of many things: time, location, offering, even local RMS.

"So I wish I could give you a unifying formula, but I can't. We sort of have to become like cardiologists, or neurologists, or physicists, or biochemists. We have to learn a lot of stuff, a lot of different facts and models, to interpret reality accurately and to manage it profitably."

"But then, it's the same in physics, isn't it?" Steve suggested. "Aren't they still struggling to create a unified theory of everything?"

"So I hear," Zhao acknowledged. He waited a minute, then went on. "More than models and equations, profitability is a way of thinking. Physics tells us about physical energy. Profitability tells us about financial energy. No profit means no energy, no ability to play in the future, no ability to build the future.

"Profitability is thinking differently, always asking: 'How does the high profit happen?'

"Ohno at Toyota always said, 'Ask "Why?" five times. By the fifth time, you'll start getting close to the real answer.'

"Profitability is the same. You have to ask 'How does it happen?' five times. By the fifth time, you'll start getting close to the answer."

Steve sighed. "It's exhausting."

"No, it's exhilarating if you treat it as a puzzle. If you treat it as a chore, you're right, it's exhausting and frustrating, and enervating. Ugh! Who needs it?"

"So, the idea is to play?"

"Yes, play. Play detective. Play archaeologist. Play cryptographer. Play scientist."

Steve's mood was pensive. He looked tired. The exhilaration of the last two weeks at Delmore seemed to have worn off during the past hour. He probably needed a few days off. The mental effort of absorbing yet more information had suddenly become too great, just the way a sponge eventually reaches the saturation point and can soak up no more liquid.

Zhao tried to buck Steve up. "But hey, now we've been through twenty of these models. We only have three more to go."

"Yes," Steve agreed, "but you said even these twenty-three won't cover every case."

"That's right. I was very honest with you about it. But again, you'll know the principles, the arithmetic, and the questions to apply in the cases that haven't been profiled yet."

"So what's left to go?"

"The next model is Experience Curve Profit. Do you know the experience curve?"

"Yes, a little."

"That's good. You know, it's funny. The experience curve is about one percent of the business school curriculum today. Back in the 1970s, it used to be sixty percent of strategy."

"Does it still work?"

"In the right circumstances, it's almost unbeatable," said Zhao. "See you next week."

Steve had one foot out the door when Zhao stopped him.

"Steve, I almost forgot." Zhao handed him a blue folder with maybe twenty pieces of paper. "Here are some numbers and explanations. The instruction sheet's on top. Play with them."

Steve's heart sank. "But I've already got a lot on my plate this week."

Zhao thought a moment. "Take two weeks. Come back on the nineteenth."

Steve acquiesced. He felt relieved, but only slightly.

Zhao could sense the overload effect. He was torn. He was tempted to take the folder back. He looked at Steve, trying to sense whether that would be the right thing to do.

It wasn't. Zhao let him go.

But he continued to worry about it for the next hour and a half.

21
Experience Curve Profit

April 19. Steve showed up precisely on time, bleary-eyed, rumpled, but with an attitude. He'd completed Zhao's exercise, and he thought—no, he was confident—that he had cracked the code.

He was about to collapse loudly into the chair, but he caught himself and descended gracefully. Zhao was looking straight at him, concealing his anticipation.

"Direct labor costs are coming down a perfect seventy-five percent slope," Steve began.

"Meaning?"

"With every doubling of cumulative manufacturing experience, costs are twenty-five percent lower."

Zhao watched and listened.

"Raw material costs are not as good, but close. They're coming down an eighty-five percent slope. It's more or less the same for energy."

"Meaning?"

"Costs fall fifteen percent with every doubling of cumulative experience."

"A well-run plant," Zhao commented.

"Yes, I would say so. Except . . . "

"Except—?"

"Overhead costs are rising up a 140 percent slope."

"Meaning?"

"With every doubling of cumulative experience, overhead costs are going up forty percent."

Zhao whistled.

"Yes, I've double-checked and triple-checked and quadruple-checked. With every doubling of experience, overhead costs are forty percent higher—completely out of control."

Zhao was ready to smile, but not yet. He said nothing. He waited.

"This is a $200 million denim plant," Steve went on. "Overhead is about fifteen percent of cost. It's now about $30 million. It should be no more than $22 million. The margins at the plant are only $10 million. Getting overhead costs to where they should be would nearly double the profit."

Now Zhao smiled.

"It took eighteen months," Zhao said. "But that's exactly what happened. The managers at the plant also found some ways to get material costs and energy costs down. In a flat market, revenue stayed at

$200 million, but profit rose to $24 million—a hell of a return in the textile business, especially operating in the U.S."

Steve smiled. He had cracked it, completely.

But a little voice nagged inside him. "Did I miss anything?" he asked.

Zhao's eyebrows arched. *Great question*, he thought, but he didn't say it. "What do you think?" he asked.

Steve felt that he was on a high plateau, but now it was time to raise his head and see if there was another mountain ahead.

"Yes," he said decisively. "I didn't see any evidence of a system being put in place for quarterly data-tracking, of incentive compensation tied to cost performance, or of time-structuring the projects so that there was a portfolio of short-term, medium-term, and long-term cost-reduction opportunities."

Zhao breathed in deeply. He closed his eyes, thinking back to 1978. "All those things were done," he acknowledged.

"And the outcome?"

"The business grew moderately. Five years later, the plant's revenue was $220 million. Despite steadily eroding prices, margins continued to improve. By 1983, they were up to fifteen percent. The plant made $33 million."

"Anything else?"

"Yes. Two competitors left the business. My client bought their plants at a ridiculously low price. Today, all three plants in the system are making twelve percent margins, despite terrible industry conditions. The continuity you described—what W. Edwards Deming would call constancy of purpose—was the key. But the initial breakthrough in insight and in attitude came from applying the experience curve idea."

"We don't run into it much today," Steve offered.

"You're right. It's seen as old-fashioned."

"But in a lot of businesses, it's a fantastic tool. It's their key to making money."

"Correct," said Zhao.

"So why isn't it used more often?"

"You already know the answer."

"Another profit paradox."

"Sadly, yes. I can't explain it, only report it. However, I should point out that the experience curve is potentially a very dangerous idea," Zhao continued.

"How so?"

"That's exactly what you're going to tell me . . . next week."

"All right, all right," Steve said. "But if you're going to make me work that hard, I have a question for you."

Zhao's eyebrows arched.

"There's one thing that's bothering me."

"Only one?" Zhao laughed.

"Well, for now," Steve smiled.

"What's that?"

"What's the difference between experience curve profit and relative market share profit? They're both about being the biggest, aren't they?"

Zhao was taken aback, even slightly annoyed. But he checked himself. *Would it really be better to have a student who didn't ask questions? Especially good ones. Remember, always remember, he told himself, no bad student, just bad teacher.*

"I'm glad you asked, Steve. Let's think about the differences for a minute. In fact, both *are* about being big, but the two models require you to manage different things.

"Let's imagine an equipment manufacturer for whom the cost of goods is seventy percent of revenues. There, it's all about using experience to bring down costs faster than competitors do. If you do that, you win.

"Now let's imagine a consumer products firm that specializes in luxury goods. Here the cost of goods is twenty percent. You can do great experience curve cost management on that twenty percent, but that won't be enough to win.

"If you're twice as large as your biggest competitor, you'll have a purchasing advantage. And you can spread your considerable overhead costs over more units sold. Ditto with advertising, sales, and marketing costs. All of which has a lot to do with scale, but nothing to do with experience.

"You also probably have a pricing advantage over smaller players. Again, nothing to do with experience."

"Okay," Steve agreed. "But it still seems to me that relative market share and experience overlap."

"They do — in the sense that the bigger firm has the advantage."

"But the reasons for the advantage are different," Steve went on.

Zhao perked up. "How so?"

"In one case, it's learning rate. In the other case, it's scale." Steve wasn't sure he had gotten it completely right. But he knew he was getting closer.

Zhao smiled and nodded. "Thank you. Brevity is the soul of wit."

Steve got up and was halfway out the door when Zhao stopped him.

"You didn't ask me about reading."

Steve was downcast. He was waist-deep in work at Delmore. He winced visibly and hoped Zhao would give him a reprieve.

Zhao knew this and felt for him, but he continued anyway.

"There's an article by Peter Drucker in *The Harvard Business Review* called "The Theory of Business." As far as I can tell, it's about the same phenomenon that Barker wrote about in *Paradigms*. Actually, it was best analyzed by Michel Foucault in *The Order of Things*. But it would take a year, not a week, to read that one. So I won't assign that one to you."

"Thanks for the favor," Steve said sardonically.

"I take it that things are hopping at Delmore." Zhao's inflection was flat, but Steve sensed that he was sympathetic—and a little curious. "What ever happened with Delmore Supply?"

"And the pyramid that wasn't?" Steve retorted.

"'The pyramid that wasn't?'" Zhao echoed.

"That's right," Steve said. "You warned me about it. The divisional people didn't really understand what a product pyramid entails. It was partly my fault. I probably made it sound like the concept was just to figure out a way to jack up the prices on a bunch of products and triple the product margins. So that's how they're handling their new product lines. I think it's a real problem."

"Can you tell so soon?"

"It's a little early," Steve agreed. "But sales of our basic products are down twenty percent this quarter, and we haven't raised enough on the high end to make up the difference. We haven't really got a firewall like basic Barbie. Instead, we have some low-cost stuff that we've made look cheap and crummy."

"It's not too late to fix," Zhao stated.

"No," Steve replied. "And I think we *will* fix it in the second half of the year. There's a new design for our basic products that should roll out in the fall. I think they'll be attractive and quite competitive. So we still have a shot at building a real pyramid. Anyway, we're going to give it a try." He brightened a little. "Meanwhile, we're on the upswing in the other divisions."

"For example?"

"The aircraft systems strategy has gotten a lot of attention. Three more manufacturers have come to us and said they want in on our planning. The government is encouraging us to pull together a consortium to develop uniform security standards for the industry. Could be an incredible breakthrough for Delmore."

"De facto standard?"

Steve nodded. "Looks like it."

"What's new on the paper manufacturing front?"

"Actually, that's why I look tired this morning," Steve answered.

"You're fishing for sympathy," Zhao said. "You *know* you won't find it here."

Steve rolled his eyes. But Zhao was adamant. "Steve, martyrdom is b-o-r-i-n-g."

Steve laughed. "Okay, okay," he yielded. "Anyway, I'm tired because I spent the last two days and nights with a team from Delmore Pulp & Paper at a giant printing plant down in Maryland, watching how they use our products. It's a hell of a lot more complicated and interesting than I ever realized."

"Really studying that sunfish, aren't you?" Zhao asked with a smile.

Steve was puzzled, then grinned. "Just like Agassiz ordered," he agreed. "And I think we can definitely expand what we offer our biggest customers—way beyond just delivering the product, I mean. There are dozens of related services we can provide to improve their economics. If we pull it off, we could absolutely become their supplier of choice." Steve stifled a yawn. "It's neat stuff. But it's more work being a business partner than just a traditional vendor—a *lot* more work."

Zhao nodded. "Under the circumstances, I hate to burden you further. But there is one more thing," Zhao said. Steve stiffened. *Another assignment?*

But almost instantaneously he relaxed. He recognized the tensing, the stiffening, as one of his old reactions—something he did because he didn't have the confidence to know he could win.

Zhao continued. "One of the ugliest moments in business is when the customer changes, the profit model changes, and so the business design has to change.

"It's horrible. You don't want to move mentally because you've been so successful. And yet you *must* move or you'll stagnate. Or go bankrupt. When the investor votes for the next generation, you don't want to be trapped in the last one.

"In fact, the more deeply you're enmeshed in yesterday's success system, the more impossible it is for you to imagine what tomorrow's success system will be."

Zhao pulled a book jacketed in lollipop-vivid colors from his shelf and handed it to Steve.

"*Value Migration?*" Steve asked.

"Yes. It's about the shift of market value from old business models to new ones. Read chapters two, five, and ten. In two weeks, tell me what it's really about and what the real problem is. Deal?"

Steve sighed and smiled. "Deal."

"See you next time."

22
Low-Cost Business Design Profit

May 3. Zhao greeted Steve with a broad smile. "Welcome," he said.

Steve took his usual seat. "You look happy," he observed.

"Why not?" Zhao countered. "Delmore, my favorite stock, is finally on the upswing—two and a half points this week."

Steve bowed a little. "How nice of you to notice. It's wonderful to be appreciated."

"Is the turnaround *all* your doing?" Zhao asked sarcastically. "I thought one or two other people might have had a hand in it."

"No, not really," Steve replied coolly. "I'm the only one studying profitability with David Zhao."

Zhao rolled his eyes. "Okay then, Jack Welch. If you're so smart, tell me how you managed with your assignment from last time. Did you figure out the danger in the experience curve?"

"I think so."

"Let's have it then."

"I think it goes something like this. I tried to imagine an organization completely and devoutly focused on experience curve cost management. Concentrating on every element of cost, graphing up the cost per unit over time, cost per unit versus cumulative experience, and so on.

"I can see them working very hard on every single detail. But I also see them operating totally inside a big cube that is limited by their own thinking and their own system. And I can see that they are completely focused.

"And focus is usually a great thing. Except . . . "

"Except—?"

"Except that it probably wipes out your peripheral vision completely. It's like wiping out your immune system."

"Hmmm. Focus and peripheral vision. And what's the relationship between the two?"

"I think that focus plus peripheral vision equals one hundred percent. The more you have of one, the less you have of the other."

Zhao and Steve were learning to speak shorthand together.

"Microscope meets radar screen," Zhao said.

"Exactly," Steve replied. "It's as if you had an instrument that had both capabilities, but it was governed by a function that allowed you to have more of one only at the expense of the other. Turn on a higher power of the microscope, and the edge of your radar screen loses function. Turn to the highest power of the microscope, maximum focus, and the edge of your radar screen goes dead completely.

"Conversely, put your radar screen on maximum, and your microscope becomes completely foggy, completely out of focus."

"So the experience curve danger is . . . ?"

"It's like having the microscope on maximum power. You lose your peripheral vision completely."

"And what happens at the edge of the radar screen?"

"Two things can happen, actually. The more traumatic one is when someone makes you irrelevant. Aluminum replaces steel in making beer and beverage cans. Plastic replaces aluminum when soda cans give way to bottles. And so on. The list is endless."

"Not so endless," Zhao demurred. "In fact, if we were continuing for a few more weeks, I'd ask you to make a list. You should probably make one in any event. But for now, go on," Zhao urged.

"The other, less traumatic instance, the one that leads to a slow and painful demise, is the invention of a completely new model that delivers the same thing at a twenty or thirty percent lower cost. Examples? Nucor. Southwest Air. Dell. Formosa Plastics. The incumbents are working meticulously and religiously to take cost out of the box, out of the current system, and someone comes along operating from outside the box and introduces the next system."

"Not bad. Any other examples?"

"Sure. Wal-Mart. Geico. Home Depot."

Zhao was satisfied. "Your conclusions?"

"You might need two organizations."

"Again?" Zhao chided. "That was your answer for After-Sale Profit."

"I stand by my story. You might need two organizations. The experience-curve demons and the blank-sheet-of-paper gang. Think of it as maximizing your current hand while simultaneously buying a big insurance policy on the future."

"What about market share?"

"The low-cost business design doesn't need huge market share to be hugely profitable. It is hugely profitable as long as it continues to be dramatically lower-cost."

"So market share doesn't matter any more?" Zhao challenged.

"Yes, it still matters, but in different places and in different ways. Newton's laws still work—except, of course, where they don't."

Zhao was happy. Steve had gotten it. But he had another question to ask. "Steve, what is *Value Migration* about?"

"It's all about how the rules of success change. About how you have to change your business design every five years. But . . ." he hesitated.

"But what?"

"Well, I see a puzzle here. A business design used to have a pretty long life—ten years, twenty years, even thirty years of economic life."

Zhao nodded. "That's right."

"Today, it's more likely to have a five- or six-year life."

"Yes."

"And there's so much friction inside organizations that it takes at least two or three years to change designs."

Zhao nodded slightly.

Steve spread his hands wide in a gesture of helplessness. "The equation doesn't work!"

Zhao was quiet for a moment, then prompted, "Unless—?"

Steve had almost expected that. "Unless . . ." he tapped his plastic pen against the yellow pad. "Unless . . ." he kept tapping. A light went on. "Unless they could see it coming. Unless they could anticipate the change and start preparing for it. Unless they could give themselves a two-year runway to get the new business design off the ground. Unless they could start sooner rather than moving faster."

"Or do both?" Zhao suggested.

"Or do both," Steve agreed.

"So," Zhao asked, "is this about predicting the future?"

"No, it's about . . . anticipation."

"And is that a skill people are good at?"

"Not really."

"Can it be learned?" Zhao tested.

Steve squinted, thinking. "I guess chess players learn it."

"Anyone else?"

"Linebackers in football. They can't predict what their opponent will do, but they can develop shorter reaction times and better instincts."

"Who else?"

Steve was stumped.

"Ever hear of Bill Russell?" Zhao said. "He was the center for the Boston Celtics in the 1950s and 1960s, when they won eight NBA championships. He studied the game and his opponents *ad nauseam*. He knew the patterns of the game better than anyone. Ever.

"There was a recent ad in which Russell said he always knew where the rebound would go *before* the opponent took his shot. Advertising hyperbole, of course. But not completely. Better than anyone, Russell knew where to be to get the rebound, depending on what the game situation was, who the shooter was, what team he played for."

"Anticipation," Steve remarked.

"Precisely. Russell was the best anticipator in basketball. In football, there was Lawrence Taylor, the great linebacker of the New York Giants. They used to say he had radar. In hockey, it was Wayne Gretzky. He explained his success by saying, 'You don't skate to where the puck is — you skate to where the puck will be.' And in baseball, it was centerfielder Joe DiMaggio. He almost never had to make a leaping or diving catch. He knew the opposing hitters so well he could usually be standing still, waiting for the ball before it came down."

"So can business people learn to anticipate?"

"What do *you* think?"

"It's tough, but it may be doable."

"It may be. There are two or three dozen patterns that repeat themselves. Know them, make your own list, and you'll find yourself surprised a lot less often. Remember *Profit Patterns*?"

"Sure."

"Read it again. It's an encyclopedia about how change happens. But think of that book as Volume One. You have to write Volume Two for yourself, depending on how your mind works and on what businesses you play in."

"Can you really learn to anticipate? Didn't Bill Russell do it by instinct?"

"It can be learned. But it's probably the hardest lesson of all." He paused. "Take a look at this as well." Zhao handed Steve a copy of *Sources of Power* by Gary Klein. "You don't have to read the whole thing. Just these pages." He gave Steve a slip of paper with the numbers 31-33, 39-40, 42, 148-151, 154-156, 169, 260, 289-290.

Steve arched his eyebrows. Zhao laughed. "No, I didn't go through it picking pages. I just looked in the index under 'Pattern recognition.'"

Steve stuck the book in his backpack. "Next week, then?"

"Two weeks."

Neither man said what they were both thinking. *One more session to go.*

23
Digital Profit

May 17. Steve's work with Zhao was almost over. Steve stopped before entering the lobby of 44 Wall Street. He looked southward to the Statue of Liberty and the gorgeous spring morning that spread out from Wall Street toward the open ocean beyond. He rode the elevator up with mixed emotions. If Zhao would only relent, he would love to continue through the summer. But Zhao had been adamant. Today's session would be the last.

Steve found Zhao sitting in his chair, staring out at the waters of the harbor. Steve put down his weekend bag—he'd be leaving for the Hamptons right after this morning's session—slipped into his seat and waited.

"Patterns?" Zhao finally asked, without shifting in his chair.

"I read them all again," Steve answered.

"And?"

"The book should have spent more time on the conventional ones, like deregulation, consolidation, fragmentation. They happen so often."

Zhao smiled. Steve couldn't see that, because Zhao was still looking out at the harbor. "Any others?"

"Sure. There's the manic-depressive cycle for an organization—ten years up, ten years down. And recession, and the irrational expansion that precedes it."

"Tell me more," Zhao encouraged him.

"Well, the memory of recession decays over time. And it decays fastest in Year 4 and Year 5 of the boom—when you need it most."

Zhao turned to Steve. "Does that surprise you?"

Steve chuckled. "Not really. Not any more. Business is mostly about paradox. You run into it every day. This is just another instance. Just like, 'The more obvious something is, the less often it's done.'"

"So," Zhao asked, "Have you started writing Volume Two?"

"I have."

"How many pages?"

"Just seven so far."

"Two weeks ago, you doubted you could learn to anticipate. Do you still feel that way?"

"Less so."

"How many patterns do you think the average manager needs to know?"

"I don't know . . . maybe forty or fifty."

"Is that a lot?"

"In a way. But in college I roomed with a second-string player on the football team for a semester. He had to learn more plays than that."

Zhao squinted. He hadn't thought of that, but it made him feel better. He'd been wondering whether a management team could master the complete set of patterns. Then again, given the rule of paradox, it wouldn't surprise him if 19-year-old college football players did more to study patterns and play-books than 40-year-old business managers did. They usually put more heart into their game, after all.

Steve interrupted Zhao's thoughts. "But the last pattern . . . that one bugged me."

"Which one — Conventional to Digital? Why?"

"It's different from all the others — a huge discontinuity."

Zhao was about to comment, but Steve was a step ahead of him. "So I did some research of my own. I read *Being Digital* and *How Digital Is Your Business?*"

"And—?"

"And I can't believe the profit difference that being digital makes — ten extra points to the bottom line. I even found a few examples not included in *How Digital Is Your Business?* Nokia. Oracle."

Zhao appeared curious. "How'd they do it?"

"You mean, what's the Digital Profit model?"

"Yes — if there is such a thing."

Steve paused. "I don't know whether there is such a thing," he finally answered. "But I do know that shifting from conventional to digital has a huge impact on profitability. Huge and mysterious."

"How so?"

"Well, it works along so many different dimensions. First of all, going digital enables a business to create tenfold improvements in productivity. Tenfold!"

Zhao was wide-eyed. "Really?"

"I couldn't believe it," Steve affirmed. "But here are some examples. Dell's inventory turns went from six a year to sixty. Cemex's response time on customer orders went from 180 minutes to twenty minutes. Oracle's customer interaction cost went from $350 to twenty bucks.

"But 10X productivity isn't all of it — not by a mile. Digital allows you to literally *reverse* your business processes, from push to pull and from guess to know."

"What do you mean?" Zhao asked. Steve was starting to get on a roll.

"In many cases — not all, but many — becoming digital lets a company's customers design the product or service they really want to buy. Think of

Dell's online configurator, or Herman Miller's z-axis design system, or Mattel's My Barbie. The seller creates a dynamic electronic menu, a "Choiceboard," that lets customers design their own products, picking the exact mix of features they want."

"That's nice. So what?"

"So—customers pay only for what they want and aren't forced to pay for anything they don't want."

Zhao grunted. "Sounds good for the customer, but not necessarily good for profitability."

"Hold on. Think about how most manufacturing works. You *guess* how much of each specific model your customers will want to buy. You manufacture those quantities and put them into the distribution channels. You hope the customers will buy them all.

"Of course, they never do. So you are forced to discount to move the merchandise. First twenty percent off, then forty percent off, then fifty percent off—or more. You're throwing the profit away."

"Hmm," Zhao replied. "So 10X productivity and Choiceboards drive up profit. But how much?"

"Wait a second, there's more. It turns out that customers want to do a lot more than design their own products. Give them half a chance and they'll shift their behavior from passive to active mode. They'll look up product info, prices, order status, and the answers to technical service questions. They'll schedule their own maintenance, download software, and so on. In fact, there are more than twenty different tasks like this that suppliers used to do that a digital business enables customers to do for themselves.

"I'll give you just one example. Cisco built a technical service database of frequently asked questions. Today, eighty-five percent of customer questions are answered by the customers themselves. Costs are down by eighty-five percent, while customer satisfaction scores are up by twenty-five percent. Put a few of these kinds of changes into your business and the profit impact starts to add up.

"There are other dimensions, too. Think about real-time info. Let's say I run a conventional business, you run a digital one. I get my information on sales, costs, customer moves, materials prices, market conditions, and so on within thirty days. You get the same info in twenty-four hours. Who sees the problems sooner? Who can take corrective action sooner? Who can redeploy resources sooner? Every one of these moves can have a big profit impact."

"*Cuanto?*" Zhao asked.

Steve shook his head. "I can't tell precisely from the outside. But look, every one of the digital businesses has profit margins ten points higher than competitors. Part of that is just plain good business design. Part of it is the Digital Profit effect. How much? It probably varies. My guess is that thirty to seventy percent of the difference is due to digital."

"My, my," Zhao murmured. "Sounds like economic magic."

"Not really," Steve protested.

Zhao's eyebrows went up. "Why not?"

"Because it can't redeem a crummy business design."

"You're right," Zhao agreed. "Without a fundamentally sound business design, the digital effect is worthless."

"So it's not economic magic—not quite. But very close." Steve sounded confident and excited.

Zhao was silent. *This is tremendous*, he thought. *I've never heard Steve so relaxed, so focused, so much in control.* Zhao was incredibly proud of Steve.

But he wondered whether that was all there was to it.

Steve paused. Zhao waited, pure patience.

Then a surprising thing happened. Steve started asking the questions.

"The key issue is this: What is the relationship between profitability and information?"

Zhao smiled, but only on the inside. *This might be wonderful*, he thought. He recalled a favorite line from Graham and Dodd, the great investment strategists: "You must think independently, and you must think correctly." Steve was getting close.

Zhao paused, as if thinking intensely. "The relationship?" he finally responded. "It's huge."

"How so?" Steve persisted.

"On a micro level or a macro level?" Zhao asked, as if playing for time. He wasn't.

Steve hadn't thought about micro. What *about* micro? But he didn't want to lose momentum. "Macro, of course."

The exchange had been quickening. It wasn't easy for Zhao to keep pace. He wondered whether he'd have been able to if he hadn't thought about these issues before.

"Well, at the macro level it's huge for the simple reason that profitability is often a function of *bad* information."

Steve sat up straight. He nodded furiously. "Right! Because of all the things that customers don't know. But the question is, *how much* of profitability is a function of bad information?"

Zhao paused, milking the moment for effect. He leaned closer to Steve and whispered conspiratorially, "*Most of it!*"

His words hung in the air, suspended, tense.

Then, as if on cue, both of them exploded in laughter simultaneously.

Steve felt himself flooded with warmth. He held Zhao's gaze. He wanted this to last a little longer. But, of course, it couldn't. He needed to bring it to closure.

"That's what I was afraid of," Steve said. "Nicholas Negroponte missed a really big idea in *Being Digital*."

"What's that?" asked Zhao.

"When he wrote about atoms and bits, he stopped one short."

"You mean—?"

"That's right: Atoms and bits, *and bits and profits*."

Zhao chuckled. "I like it," he commented. I really do. But here's one last assignment for you. It has two questions. First, I want you to list for me all the first cousins."

"First cousins?"

"You know, the profit models that are similar to each other, but not quite the same."

Steve pulled out his pen and started scribbling on the yellow pad. It was badly dog-eared by now, with just two pages remaining. After a few moments, he handed the list to Zhao.

> Installed base, de facto standard, after-sale
> Time profit, new product profit, specialty product
> Relative market share, local leadership
> Blockbuster, transaction scale
> Multi-component, profit multiplier
> Experience curve, specialization

Zhao examined the list and nodded. "That's it," he said approvingly. "If we were to continue, I'd ask you to describe the differences. In fact, I'll ask you to do it anyway, with a deadline. Remember: A project minus a deadline equals zero. So do it by tonight. Think of it as fun. A crossword puzzle.

"Now, last question: Was the sequence of lessons totally random?"

Steve was momentarily stumped. He looked at the list again. "You ended with the traditional, the oldest models—Cycle Profit, s-curve, RMS, and e-curve."

"Right."

"But you ended with a new one, one that subverted many of the traditional ones, like RMS and e-curve."

"Right."

"You ended on one that shows you can be hugely successful without being huge."

"Right."

"And you started with a new one—once again, a model where you could be hugely profitable without being huge, without having number one market share."

"Correct. Anything else?"

"You refused to place the first cousins together."

"Why?"

"Because if you had, I would have been sucked into focusing on the similarities rather than the differences."

"What else?"

"Isn't that enough?"

Zhao laughed a loud, almost painfully loud belly laugh that filled the room. It was clear that he was sad to see Steve go.

"It is enough. More than enough."

"But now I have one more for you, David."

Zhao smiled at the *David*. "One more question for me?"

"Actually, I have the question *and* the answer. The question is, 'Why do you like to assign *two* books on a given topic?' Oh, you didn't always assign them at the same time, but the pattern was clear. *Of Permanent Value* and Buffett's own essays . . . *Paradigms* and *Profit Patterns* . . . *Made in America* and *Pour Your Heart Into It* . . . the two books by David Ogilvy . . . *Profit Patterns* and *Sources of Power*."

"All right," Zhao agreed, "You've got me. What's your answer?"

"I think you were trying to drag me out of the 'I read the book' syndrome. You were trying to force me to focus on a topic and compare and contrast two points of view, or stories, or experiences, or data sets. To move me from saying 'I read the book' and ticking it off a list in the spirit of 'been there, done that' toward saying, 'What are the best ideas?' and 'Which of the great ideas have I applied to improve my business?'"

Zhao was very quiet. "Well said, Steve," he commented. After a pause, he remarked, "I received your e-mail yesterday. Congratulations are in order."

Steve nodded. "Thanks. But I don't think I want to accept the offer."

Zhao smiled. "Actually, I'm not too surprised. I didn't think that being a VP at Delmore Pulp & Paper would be your sort of job."

"No. The people are really nice—in fact, I like almost everyone at Delmore. And there's a lot that can be done with the business. But I'd rather help them get turned around, then move on to another assignment. There'll be time later to settle down in one industry." Steve grinned. "Right now I'm having too much fun playing the field."

"Are you sure you're not just reacting like a rainbow trout?"

Steve was surprised and pleased that Zhao had remembered his story about Deborah. "Being distracted by the lure of the next thing? No, I've thought about that. There are some doors we're not meant to walk through. I'm pretty sure this is one of those."

Zhao nodded in assent. "Do the Delmore people understand?"

"I think so. I know Cathy does. She says she'll support me whatever I decide. I suspect she'll be happy not to lose me for another year or two. And I think she knows that she needs to reward me appropriately. So I'm not worried about the financial side of it."

Zhao was pleased to hear it.

The two of them sat quietly for a moment. Finally, Zhao asked, "When's your friend picking you up?"

"In a few minutes. We want to beat the traffic to Long Island."

"Very wise."

Zhao got up from his chair, walked over to the window, crossed his arms, and stared at the Statue of Liberty. He was on the verge of making a comment about independent thought and about the Statue as a reminder. But he restrained himself.

He turned to Steve and held out his hand.

"Good luck to you, Steve. Thanks for sticking with it."

He was going to go on, sliding down a dangerously sentimental slope, but again he checked himself.

"And don't forget that you owe me a lot of money, and that I'm getting on in years."

Zhao laughed. They both did.

"Thank you," was all that Steve could think to say.

"You're welcome."

Steve turned and left the room. Zhao closed the door behind him and walked back to the window. He turned to look at the Statue once again, folded his arms, and kept studying it. *Maybe I'm the one who needs the reminder, not Steve.*

List of Readings

Asimov, Isaac. *Asimov on Astronomy*. Anchor Press, 1975.

Barker, Joel. *Paradigms*. Harper Business, 1993.

Cook, Paul M. "The Business of Innovation." *Harvard Business Review*, March-April, 1990.

Kilpatrick, Andrew. *Of Permanent Value*. McGraw-Hill, 2001.

Klein, Gary. *Sources of Power*. MIT Press, 1999.

Lightman, Alan. *Einstein's Dreams*. Warner Books, 1993.

Negroponte, Nicholas. *Being Digital*. Alfred A. Knopf, 1995.

Ogilvy, David. *Confessions of an Advertising Man*. Atheneum, 1963.

Ogilvy, David. *Ogilvy on Advertising*. Vintage Books, 1985.

Paulos, John Allen. *Innumeracy: Mathematical Illiteracy and Its Consequences*. Vintage Books, 1990.

Pound, Ezra, *ABC of Reading*. New Directions, 1934.

Rappaport, Andrew S., and Shmuel Halevi, "The Computerless Computer Company." *Harvard Business Review*, July-August, 1991.

Schultz, Howard, with Dori Jones Yang. *Pour Your Heart Into It*. Hyperion, 1997.

Singular, Stephen. *Power to Burn*. Birch Lane Press, 1996.

Slywotzky, Adrian. *Value Migration*. Harvard Business School Press, 1996.

Slywotzky, Adrian, and David J. Morrison with Bob Andelman. *The Profit Zone*. Times Business, 1997.

Slywotzky, Adrian, and David J. Morrison with Ted Moser, Kevin Mundt, and James Quella. *Profit Patterns*. Times Business, 1999.

Slywotzky, Adrian, and David J. Morrison with Karl Weber. *How Digital Is Your Business?* Crown Business, 2000.

Sun Tzu. *The Art of War*. Translated by Samuel B. Griffith. Oxford University Press, 1963.

Updegraff, Robert R. *The Power of the Obvious: Based on the Business Classic Obvious Adams*. Executive Press, 1972.

Walton, Sam, with John Huey. *Sam Walton: Made in America*. Bantam Books, 1993.

"What's in a Name?" *The Economist*, January 6, 1996.

Young, James Webb. *A Technique for Producing Ideas*. NTC Business Books, 1994.

About Adrian Slywotzky

Mr. Slywotzky is a Vice President and member of the Board of Directors of Mercer Management Consulting, Inc., a global strategy consulting firm that focuses on the development of strategies for growth in changing markets. He also contributes to the development of the firm's intellectual capital.

Since 1979, Mr. Slywotzky has consulted to companies in a broad cross-section of industries, including information services, financial services, consumer products, managed care, pharmaceuticals, computer hardware and software, chemicals, electronic materials, steel, broadcasting, and retailing. He has worked extensively at the CEO level for several major corporations on issues relating to new business development and creating new areas of value growth for the company. His focus has been on developing a strategic perspective on the customer and creating effective new business designs. Most of his work has been in the disciplines of marketing, new product development, new business design, sales strategy, licensing, acquisitions, and strategic alliances.

Mr. Slywotzky is the author of *The Art of Profitability* (a Mercer e-book, March 2002) and the co-author of *How Digital Is Your Business?* (Crown Business, 2000), *Profit Patterns: 30 Ways to Anticipate and Profit from Strategic Forces Reshaping Your Business* (Times Business/Random House, 1999), and *The Profit Zone: How Strategic Business Design Will Lead You to Tomorrow's Profits* (Times Business/Random House, 1998). *Business Week* magazine named the latter one of its Top 10 Business Books of 1998. In addition, Mr. Slywotzky is the author of *Value Migration: How to Think Several Moves Ahead of the Competition* (Harvard Business School Press, 1996).

As a frequent speaker on the changing face of business strategy and business design, he has been featured at The World Economic Forum at Davos and at numerous other major conferences.

Mr. Slywotzky holds degrees from Harvard College, Harvard Law School, and Harvard Business School.

About Mercer Management Consulting

As one of the world's premier corporate strategy firms, Mercer Management Consulting helps leading enterprises achieve sustained shareholder value growth through the development and implementation of innovative business designs. Mercer's proprietary business design techniques, combined with its specialized industry knowledge and global reach, enable companies to anticipate changes in customer priorities and the competitive environment, and then design their businesses to seize opportunities created by those changes. The firm serves clients from 22 offices in the Americas, Europe, and Asia.

Mercer Management Consulting

Beijing
Suite 1825B, Tower 2,
Bright China Chang An Building
7 Jianguomennei Avenue
Beijing 100005
86/ 10 6510 1758
86/ 10 6510 1759 fax

Boston
33 Hayden Avenue
Lexington, MA 02421
1/ 781 861 7580
1/ 781 862 3935 fax

Buenos Aires
Florida 234
Piso 4
C1005AAF Buenos Aires
54/ 11 4394 6488
54/ 11 4326 7445 fax

Chicago
10 South Wacker Drive
13th Floor
Chicago, IL 60606
1/ 312 902 7980
1/ 312 902 7989 fax

Cleveland
One Cleveland Center
1375 East Ninth Street,
Suite 2500
Cleveland, OH 44114
1/ 216 830 8100
1/ 216 830 8101 fax

Dallas
3500 Chase Tower
2200 Ross Avenue
Dallas, TX75201
1/ 214 758 1880
1/ 214 758 1881 fax

Frankfurt
Friedrichstr. 2-6
D-60323 Frankfurt
49/ 69 17 00 83 0
49/ 69 17 00 83 33 fax

Hong Kong
32nd Floor NatWest Tower
Times Square
One Matheson Street
Causeway Bay
Hong Kong
852/ 2506 0767
852/ 2506 4478 fax

Houston
1136 North Kirkwood
Houston, TX 77043
281 493 6400
281 754 4328 fax

Lisbon
Av. Praia da Vitória, 71-5.ºC
(Edifício Monumental)
1050 Lisboa
351/ 21 311 38 70
351/ 21 311 38 71 fax

London
1 Grosvenor Place
London SW1X 7HJ
44/ 20 7235 5444
44/ 20 7245 6933 fax

Madrid
Paseo de la Castellana,
nº 13 - 2º
28046 Madrid
34/ 91 531 79 00
34/ 91 531 79 09 fax

Mexico City
Paseo de Tamarindos 400-B
Piso 10, Bosques
de las Lomas
05120 Mexico, D.F.
52/ 5 081 9000
52/ 5 258 0186 fax

Montréal
600, boul. de Maisonneuve Ouest
14e étage
Montréal, Québec H3A 3J2
1/ 514 499 0461
1/ 514 499 0475 fax

Munich
Stefan-George-Ring 2
81929 München
49/ 89 939 49 0
49/ 89 930 38 49 fax

New York
1166 Ave. of the Americas
32nd Floor
New York, NY 10036
1/ 212 345 8000
1/ 212 345 8075 fax

Paris
28, avenue Victor Hugo
75783 Paris Cédex 16
33/ 1 45 02 30 00
33/ 1 45 02 30 01 fax

Pittsburgh
One PPG Place, 27th Floor
Pittsburgh, PA 15222
1/ 412 355 8840
1/ 412 355 8848 fax

San Francisco
Three Embarcadero Center
Suite 1670
San Francisco, CA 94111
1/ 415 743 7800
1/ 415 743 7950 fax

Seoul
5th Floor
Woori Investment
Bank Building
826-20, Yeoksam-dong,
Kangnam-gu
Seoul, 135-935
82/ 2 3466 3100
82/ 2 3466 3105 fax

Toronto
BCE Place
161 Bay Street, P.O. Box 501
Toronto, Ontario M5J 2S5
1/ 416 868 2200
1/ 416 868 2208 fax

Zürich
Tessinerplatz 5
8027 Zürich
41/ 1 208 77 77
41/ 1 208 70 00 fax

Internet
www.mercermc.com